YEATS AND POLITICS IN THE 1930s

MACMILLAN STUDIES IN ANGLO-IRISH LITERATURE

Nicholas Grene
BERNARD SHAW: A CRITICAL VIEW

Maeve Good
W. B. YEATS AND THE CREATION OF A TRAGIC UNIVERSE

John O'Riordan
A GUIDE TO O'CASEY'S PLAYS

Paul Scott Stanfield
YEATS AND POLITICS IN THE 1930s

Series Standing Order

If you would like to receive future titles in this series as they are published, you can make use of our standing order facility. To place a standing order please contact your bookseller or, in case of difficulty, write to us at the address below with your name and address and the name of the series. Please state with which title you wish to begin your standing order. (If you live outside the United Kingdom we may not have the rights for your area, in which case we will forward your order to the publisher concerned.)

Customer Services Department, Macmillan Distribution Ltd
Houndmills, Basingstoke, Hampshire, RG21 2XS, England.

Yeats and Politics in the 1930s

Paul Scott Stanfield

Assistant Professor of English
University of Nebraska, Lincoln

MACMILLAN
PRESS

First published 1988

Published by
THE MACMILLAN PRESS LTD
Houndmills, Basingstoke, Hampshire RG21 2XS
and London
Companies and representatives
throughout the world

Typeset by Wessex Typesetters
(Division of The Eastern Press Ltd)
Frome, Somerset

Printed in Hong Kong

British Library Cataloguing in Publication Data
Stanfield, Paul Scott
Yeats and politics in the 1930s. –
(Macmillan studies in Anglo-Irish literature
1. Yeats, W. B. – Political and social views
2. Politics in literature
I. Title
821'.8   PR5908.P6
ISBN 0–333–41756–9

To my wife, Barbara, and my daughter, Julia

Contents

Acknowledgements   viii

List of Abbreviations   ix

Introduction   1

1   Yeats and de Valera: the Old Poet in the New Ireland   8

2   The Blueshirt Episode and its Background   40

3   Yeats, Socialism and Tragedy   78

4   Yeats and Balzac   112

5   Yeats and Eugenics   145

Conclusion   184

Notes   189

Bibliography   217

Index   224

Acknowledgements

My thanks first of all to A. P. Watt Ltd, who authorised permission for me to quote from the published works of W. B. Yeats, and to Mr Michael B. Yeats, who granted me permission to examine the unpublished Yeats prose transcribed and edited by Professor Curtis Bradford, and now held in the Rare Book Room of Burling Library, Grinnell College, Grinnell, Iowa. In this connection, I should also like to thank the curator of the Rare Book Room, Anne Kintner, and express my debt to the careful and devoted scholarship of the late Curtis Bradford.

My thanks go also to Northwestern University for financial support over the years, and to the staff of the University Library. I should like particularly to thank the Special Collections department and its curator, Russell Malone, for the opportunity to examine Yeats's copy of *Nietzsche as Critic, Philosopher, Poet and Prophet*.

I wish also to thank the members of my dissertation committee, Professors Lawrence Evans and Herbert Tucker, and its director, Professor Donald Torchiana, for their time, energy and critical intelligence. My special thanks to Professor Torchiana, to whose *Yeats and Georgian Ireland* and to whose store of knowledge I am indebted in ways too deep for notes to acknowledge.

I wish also to thank Mr Desmond Kennedy, whose reading of the typescript kept me from committing several 'Americanisms' on matters of Irish history (Mr Kennedy is, of course, in no way responsible for whatever Americanisms remain).

Finally, I wish to thank my wife, Barbara, and my family (Paul, Asalee, Burns, Heather and Mac), for their encouragement, faith, and patience, without which . . . .

List of Abbreviations

The following abbreviations have been used in citing Yeats's works:

Auto.	*Autobiographies* (London: Macmillan, 1961; New York: Macmillan, 1961).
E.&I.	*Essays and Introductions* (London: Macmillan, 1961; New York: Macmillan, 1961).
Exp.	*Explorations* (London: Macmillan, 1962; New York: Macmillan, 1962).
'Genealogical Tree of Revolution'	'A Genealogical Tree of Revolution', in A. N. Jeffares, *W. B. Yeats: Man and Poet* (New Haven: Yale University Press, 1949) pp. 351–52.
Letters	*The Letters of W. B. Yeats*, ed. Allan Wade (London: Rupert Hart-Davis, 1954; New York: Macmillan, 1955; rept. New York: Octagon Books, 1980).
Letters on Poetry	*Letters on Poetry from W. B. Yeats to Dorothy Wellesley* (London and New York: Oxford University Press, 1940).
Memoirs	*Memoirs*, transcribed and ed. by Denis Donoghue (London: Macmillan, 1973; New York: Macmillan, 1973).
'Modern Ireland'	'Modern Ireland: An Address to American Audiences 1932–1933', ed. Curtis Bradford, *Massachusetts Review*, v (Winter 1964) 256–68.
Moore	*W. B. Yeats and T. Sturge Moore: Their Correspondence 1901–1937*, ed. Ursula Bridge (London: Routledge and Kegan Paul, 1953).
Mythologies	*Mythologies* (London: Macmillan, 1959; New York: Macmillan, 1959).
O.B.M.V.	*The Oxford Book of Modern Verse*, ed. W. B. Yeats (London and New York: Oxford University Press, 1936).

Senate Speeches   *The Senate Speeches of W. B. Yeats*, ed. Donald
                      Pearce (Bloomington: Indiana University
                      Press, 1960; London: Faber, 1960).

Uncol. Prose   *Uncollected Prose by W. B. Yeats*, eds John P.
                      Frayne and Colton Johnson, 2 vols (London:
                      Macmillan, 1976; New York: Columbia
                      University Press, 1976).

Var. Plays   *The Variorum Edition of the Plays of W. B.
                      Yeats*, ed. Russell K. Alspach assisted by
                      Catherine C. Alspach (London: Macmillan,
                      1966; New York: Macmillan, 1966).

Var. Poems   *The Variorum Edition of the Poems of W. B.
                      Yeats*, eds Peter Allt and Russell K. Alspach
                      (London: Macmillan, 1957; New York:
                      Macmillan, 1957).

Vision   *A Vision* (London: Macmillan, 1956; New
                      York: Macmillan, 1956).

Introduction

To study the closing decade of Yeats's career by examining the
political causes he embraced and the political questions he
addressed may seem to narrow unjustifiably the wide field over
which his interest ranged in those years: his fascination with
Indian religion and collaboration with Shri Purohit Swami, his
renewed interest in sexual love, his attempt to make his poems as
simple and profound as folk ballads. In that highly political
decade, however, even interests as near to Yeats as his work with
the Swami, his reawakened sexuality, and poetry itself often
either defined themselves by their contrast to politics, or created a
space for themselves by fending off politics.

For instance, Yeats's introduction to Bhagwān Shri Hamsa's *The
Holy Mountain* begins:

> 'I know nothing but the novels of Balzac, and the Aphorisms
> of Patanjali. I once knew other things, but I am an old man with
> a poor memory.' There must be some reason why I wanted to
> write that lying sentence, for it has been in my head for weeks.
> Is it that whenever I have been tempted to go to Japan, China,
> or India for my philosophy, Balzac has brought me back,
> reminded me of my preoccupation with national, social,
> personal problems, convinced me that I cannot escape from
> our *Comédie humaine*?[1]

Even while studying Hinduism in quest of answers to the
ultimate questions, Yeats felt a contrary urge towards the
immediate and, in the broadest sense of the word, the political.
Yeats wrote this seven- or eight-thousand word introduction, a
work which to all appearances required much study and much
consultation with the Swami, in the summer of 1933, the time of
his greatest interest in the possibility of an Irish fascist state: in his
letters of the time to Olivia Shakespear, he alternates news about
'my work for the swami' with news about General Eoin O'Duffy.[2]
Similarly, and for no easily detected reasons, Yeats devotes a

whole section of the *Holy Mountain* introduction to comparing Hegel's conception of history with Balzac's. The section's concluding sentence has quite audible political overtones: 'Hegel's Philosophy of History dominates the masses, though they have not heard his name, as Rousseau's philosophy did in the nineteenth and later eighteenth centuries, and has shed more blood.'[3] Yeats was later to argue in 'The Statues' that Greek art had 'put down / All Asiatic vague immensities':[4] in his own case, 'national, social, personal problems', symbolised by the solidity and complexity of the *Comédie humaine*, were if not a putting down of those immensities at least a weight that counter-balanced them. Sometimes, indeed, the two interests unexpectedly combine. In *Wheels and Butterflies* Yeats wonders if the doctrine of reincarnation would, in the event that it became influential in the West, in time create the basis of a state that would be the antithesis of the communist state.[5]

Sometimes Yeats's very impatience with the topic of politics serves to show how near to him it always was. For instance, it is natural enough for an older poet to give a younger one advice:

> Seek those images
> That constitute the wild,
> The lion and the virgin,
> The harlot and the child.[6]

Likewise it is natural enough for him to wish for love and youth to return:

> O that I were young again
> And held her in my arms![7]

In the thirties, however, political questions so pressed upon all else that even statements as natural as these could not be made until the topic of politics had been cleared away. So, the advice to the fellow-poet is prefaced with:

> I never bade you go
> To Moscow or to Rome.
> Renounce that drudgery,
> Call the Muses home.

So also, in the poem 'Politics', the fact that the wish for youth's return has nothing to do with politics becomes the remarkable thing about it:

> How can I, that girl standing there,
> My attention fix
> On Roman or on Russian
> Or on Spanish politics?

That Yeats dismissed politics in these two poems is somehow less striking – dismissing politics is, after all, on almost any occasion, the sanest thing to do – than that he evidently felt he needed to dismiss them before he could arrive at what he wanted to say. One could even go further, and say that in the two poems Yeats finds more satisfaction and significance in dismissing politics than he does in writing of the two subjects in favour of which he dismissed them. Both poems belong to an age obsessed with politics; both reveal that politics impinged upon Yeats's awareness as they did on everyone else's, that for him too the political significance of an event, situation, or work of art seemed to jut out uncomfortably.

Both poems reveal as well that this state of things sometimes irritated Yeats, but much more often he welcomed the occasions it provided him to attack all that he thought wrong-headed in various political orthodoxies (particularly those of militant Irish Catholic nationalism and of Marxism) and to articulate and defend his own political beliefs. Some of these occasions – the death of Lady Gregory, rereading Balzac, editing the *Oxford Book of Modern Verse*, writing introductions for *The Holy Mountain* or his own Cuchulain play *Fighting the Waves* – appear in retrospect unlikely ones to have provoked professions of political faith. Nevertheless, owing to the peculiar character of the thirties, they did. Each of the following chapters tries, by looking closely at the stances Yeats adopted on certain issues on certain occasions in the 1930s, to define one or another of his convictions.

The question of whether a poet's politics matter much remains. Naturally, they mattered to Yeats, who considered his political ideas inseparately part of his thought. In a 1919 essay, he wrote that when he was twenty-three or twenty-four a sentence had 'seemed to form in my head', commanding him, 'Hammer your thoughts into unity.'[8] Having at that time three apparently

unrelated interests, 'literature', 'philosophy' and 'nationality', by
sustained effort over many years he successfully harmonised the
three: 'Now all three are, I think, one, or rather all three are a
discrete expression of a single conviction.' In a sense Yeats had
three careers, as a poet, as a student of the supernatural and as an
Irish citizen. Early on we see him trying to reconcile the three into
one in the poem 'To Ireland in the Coming Times':

> Nor may I less be counted one
> With Davis, Mangan, Ferguson,
> Because, to him who ponders well,
> My rhymes more than their rhyming tell
> Of things discovered in the deep
> Where only body's laid asleep.[9]

Poet, patriot, mystic: these were the three callings that Yeats
claimed in 1919 to have hammered into unity, into a single
conviction. And though it is true enough that Yeats made his
religion and his politics suit his vocation, literature did not
unfailingly take precedence. His decision to support the Irish
nationalist cause changed his work in that it led him to write
drama, to make use of Irish legend, to rid his poetry of 'Shelley's
Italian light'[10] and his prose of 'that artificial, elaborate English so
many of us played with in the 'nineties . . .'.[11] Similarly, the
symbols of *A Vision*, inspired by his own work, in their turn
changed the nature of his later work by lending him that uncanny,
oracular self-confidence characteristic of the poems of the twenties.
Yeats's political beliefs, like his spiritual ones, were not auxiliary
poses to the main pose, but hard-won out of much thought,
experience and defeated hope, and in the end indissolubly part of
his imagination. By reason of his own effort to hammer his
thoughts into unity, any study of the poet's politics necessarily
becomes a study of the poet's whole thought.

   This unity has persuaded some writers that Yeats's politics are
best understood as aesthetics misapplied.[12] Perhaps hoping to
forestall any attack on Yeats's politics that would prepare for an
attack on and a dismissal of his poems, they present his politics as
not quite real politics, but (bad) poetry, hence not calling for
serious condemnation and not involving reassessment of the good
poetry, that confined to ink on paper. To argue this way is to
postulate that aesthetics and politics are wholly distinct spheres,

each uninterpretable in the other's terms. We ought to balk at that postulate for two reasons. First, it neuters art, as Cairns Craig has recently pointed out: if we assume that Yeats, Pound and Eliot 'were men who should not have raised their heads from the "cultural" sphere', if we must 'allow them their significance as artists by insisting that in politics they were myopic, that they were silly – and, therefore, excusable – citizens', then their art is 'neutralised by preserving its aesthetic value within the insulated world of "culture"' and 'we make ourselves impervious to its doing us any good as well as any harm'.[13]

Second, it goes against what Yeats believed. The power to do good or, perhaps more likely, harm – 'For if I triumph I must make men mad'[14] – Yeats thought inextricably bound up with his gift and his vocation, and his poetry is powerful, I would argue, partly because of its sense of its own power. Yeats did not readily distinguish sway over words from sway over matter. Consider this 1909 journal entry:

> By implication the philosophy of Irish faery lore declares that all power is from the body, all intelligence from the spirit. Western civilisation, religion, and magic alike insist on power and therefore body and these three doctrines – efficient rule, the Incarnation, and thaumaturgy. . . . The Incarnation involved modern science and modern efficiency and also modern lyric feeling which gives body to the most spiritual emotions. It produced a solidification of all things that grew from the individual will.[15]

The ease with which Yeats moves, via 'power' and 'body', from 'efficient rule' to 'modern lyric feeling' shows not only the unity of his thought but also his conviction that poetry did not occupy a sphere of innocence remote from actual power. Poetry, like Christianity, participated in the peculiar, uncheckable power created by the translation of the spiritual into the physical, the bodiless into a body. This conviction is discernible as early on as his first important essay, 'The Poetry of Sir Samuel Ferguson', published in 1886, in which Yeats declares his independence from his father's generation (through an attack on his father's friend, scholar Edward Dowden) and from English taste and poetic tradition (by arguing a then little-known Irish poet's superiority to Tennyson and Arnold). The essay ends with the young poet's naming of what he hopes will become his audience: 'those young men clustered here and there throughout our land, whom the emotion of Patriotism has lifted into that world of selfless passion in which heroic deeds are possible and heroic poetry credible'.[16] Just beneath the rhetoric we can see an aesthetic programme linked with a political one. Yeats seeks an audience for whom romance is real, in which a poetic ideal will find a body and gain the power to effect a political change. The 1916 rising is already implicit in this sentence written thirty years earlier.

The tendency to consider Yeats simply as a faculty, that of writing verse, and the whole rest of his thought as appendages to that faculty, probably would not have arisen at all were his thought more like what most of us think. Yeats's admirers may be moved by his invitation to the shade of W. T. Horton, in 'All Souls' Night', to inhale the odour of the poured wine, but are usually bored or embarrassed by his interest in tables that move by themselves. Similarly, they may be moved by his evocation of the 'bloody, arrogant power' that 'Rose out of the race, / Uttering, mastering it', in 'Blood and the Moon', and disgusted by his interest in a movement of shirted thugs. The simplest solution, and one which the unity he sought and achieved makes all the more plausible, is to say that he erred, was bound to err, when he acted on what ought only to have been written down. The essential statement of this view is Auden's famous elegy 'In Memory of W. B. Yeats', a poem so successful on its own terms that one overlooks the fact that its major premise is that Yeats was a crackpot. That he was a crackpot matters not at all, the poem argues, 'For poetry makes nothing happen.' What a poet thinks is of no consequence, for he makes no difference by what he writes, and so must be judged only on whether he has written well or ill. On that score, Auden graciously allows, Yeats passes with flying colours. From this assumption on the nature of poetry comes, perhaps, the idea that Yeats transgressed in confusing politics and aesthetics. Politics makes things happen. Poetry makes nothing happen. Ideas and attitudes may frolic as they will in poetry, where they can harm no one, but are a shame and a sin and a danger in the actual world, the one we have to live in. Yeats did not believe anything like this; relative to us, he is on the far side of an important divide. Not only did he choose to hold his spiritual beliefs, so far as he could, literally – once we do so, he wrote in 1931, 'All about us there seems to start up a precise inexplicable teeming life, and the earth becomes once more, not in rhetorical metaphor, but in reality, sacred'[17] – but he also believed poetry made things happen. Many times he repeated the story of how Thomas Davis's poetry had brought John O'Leary to the Irish nationalist cause, and he himself may have been attracted to the movement partly because there, as hardly anywhere else in modern life, poetry retained some of its ancient power. In 'The Man and the Echo' he wonders what his poetry made happen and failed to make happen. Among the things it made to happen, some (though not Yeats himself) have argued, was the Irish Free State itself.[18] Putting his convictions into poetry by no means sanitised them or made them ineffectual, so far as he believed. If anything, it made them likelier to make things happen. Modernity, Yeats knew, tended to isolate poetry in its own sphere, but he thought that no place for it. He desired that it again be as inseparable a part of communal life, as powerful, even as dangerous a part – 'When did the poets promise safety, King?' asks Seanchan[19] – as it had been in ancient Ireland and, he believed, in ancient Greece. Those who read and write poetry today are far from thinking any such revolution remotely possible, but we misunderstand Yeats if we forget he thought differently.

1

Yeats and de Valera: the Old Poet in the New Ireland

Irish writers of the late twenties and early thirties almost habitually thought their country a barren, constricted place. Older writers, in the way of older writers, felt keenly that something had changed for the worse. 'What is it all now but a bitther noise of cadgin' mercy from heaven, an' a sour handlin' o' life for a cushion'd seat in a corner?', complained a character in Sean O'Casey's *Purple Dust*, echoing the complaints in O'Casey's own autobiographies.[1] In Oliver St John Gogarty's loosely autobiographical works of the thirties, *As I Was Going Down Sackville Street* and *Going Native*, the writer's natural charm and grace are frequently tossed aside by eruptions about 'the havoc and destruction' brought to 'the comely life in Ireland' by 'the common man's malevolence'.[2] George Russell complained in a letter to Yeats of 'a nation run by louts'[3] and once, in the company of Frank O'Connor, stopped in the street to raise his fists and cry, 'I have to get out of this country before it drives me mad.'[4] The young writers, their imaginations formed in the terror and excitement of war, saw little in the routines of post-war Irish life save what was drab or painfully circumscribed. To Yeats, at least, it seemed that such novels as Francis Stuart's *The Coloured Dome*, Frank O'Connor's *The Saint and Mary Kate* and Liam O'Flaherty's *Mr Gilhooley* and *The Puritan* looked directly at 'the actual Ireland of their day' (as his own generation of writers had not, preferring the heroic past) and 'attacked everything that had made it possible . . .'.[5]

Yeats was not alone, then, when in his last years he began to find Ireland relatively arid and comfortless. Over the years, the love he had always felt for Ireland had often been flavoured by indignation or despair, but throughout the thirties the indignation turns especially savage, the despair especially bitter. From 1932 on, there is scarcely a Yeats poem or play on an Irish theme but betrays his dissatisfaction or unhappiness: 'Parnell's Funeral', 'The Curse of Cromwell', *Purgatory* and *The Death of Cuchulain* come immediately to mind, but even celebratory poems such as 'The O'Rahilly' and 'The Municipal Gallery Revisited' seem by their praise of the heroic past to accuse the decayed present. Recalling what Yeats had hoped for as a young man makes his later disappointment easier to understand. He had believed that an Ireland free of English domination might, by its unique spirituality – Christianity deepened by a pagan sense of the divinity of rock, stream and hill – and by art based on that spirituality, rejuvenate Europe. By 1932, however, the Irish writer was so hampered by the official censorship of the state and the unofficial censorship of various religious and political watchdog associations that it was 'impossible for him to live by distinctive Irish literature' (in the words of the circular Yeats sent to prospective members of the Irish Academy of Letters),[6] and Irish spirituality seemed confined to Jansenistical piety and commercialised pilgrimages. The younger Yeats had further hoped that the Irish, acting on the inborn sense of deference to the heroic and noble that seemed apparent in their legends, would find and follow a leader who was independent, well-born, 'cold' and 'lonely' in the Yeatsian sense of those words, a being apart, a Parnell, a Cuchulain. From 1932 until long after Yeats died, Ireland's dominant political figure was Eamon de Valera.

De Valera inspired little affection among Irish men of letters. O'Casey, for instance, found him lifeless:

> Sean couldn't see an excited De Valera rushing round a hurling field . . . he couldn't see De Valera abandoning himself to sweat and laughter in the dancing of a jig, nor could he see him swanking about in a sober green kilt and gaudy saffron shawl; or slanting an approving eye on any pretty girl that passed him; or standing, elbow on counter in a Dublin pub, about to lower a drink, with a Where it goes, lads.[7]

Gogarty wrote that 'De Valera and degeneration are synonymous',[8] and Russell cursed him 'as generations of Irishman to come will curse him – the man who destroyed our country!'.[9] The younger writers who had fought on de Valera's side during the civil war were not quick to champion him: O'Faolain's biography, for instance, seems lukewarm in its appreciation compared to O'Connor's biography of old enemy Michael Collins. Even Joyce, from as far away as Paris, sensed something stiff and oppressive in de Valera. 'Pardon the inquisition, causas es quostas? It is Da Valorem's Dominical Brayers', he wrote in *Finnegans Wake*, making de Valera one of the many elements compounding Shaun, Shem the Penman's brother and antagonist.[10]

One cannot compare de Valera to other Irish leaders, to Grattan or Parnell, Tone or Collins, O'Connell or Jim Larkin, without noticing how little he offered to a literary sensibility. He had no gift for oratory, his speaking style, O'Faolain suggested, having retained too much of the schoolteacher he had been before the Rising.[11] His one non-political passion was mathematics. He was a teetotaler. His Catholicism consisted in simple piety and observance rather than spiritual profundity, and in no way resembled the Catholicism of 'Julius the Second and the Medician Popes' once praised by Yeats.[12] Of humour and exuberance, as the already-quoted O'Casey passage suggests, he seemed to have been granted less than his full share, but neither did he cultivate the colder aristocratic virtues of a Parnell, possessing instead an egalitarian distaste for ceremony that led to his refusal to wear a silk hat at state functions.[13]

Most disturbing and least likeable, perhaps, was that his astonishing fixity of principle – proven once and forever by his stand against the treaty and for the Republic, which his opponents held responsible for precipitating the civil war – somehow co-existed with a sort of slipperiness and a 'capacity for something perilously near sharp dealing'.[14] Examples abound: the unclear semantic distinctions de Valera argued existed between Collins's and Griffith's treaty and his own Document No. 2, the oath he took yet did not take to enter the Dail in 1927, the indefinable 'special position' his 1937 constitution granted the Irish Catholic Church, the oddly qualified claim in the same document to the whole of 'the national territory'. The leading historian of this period has called de Valera 'the constitutional Houdini of his generation'.[15] However incomprehensible or infuriating his arguments or actions may have been to others, all apparent contradictions or difficulties seem to have been reconciled to his own satisfaction by his complete and unqualified self-identification with the mass of the people he led. His single famous utterance, made in the heat of the Dail debate over the treaty, turned on exactly this point:

I have been brought up among the Irish people, I was reared in a labourer's cottage here in Ireland. I have not lived solely among intellectuals. The first fifteen years of my life that formed my character were lived amongst the Irish people down in Limerick; therefore I know what I am talking about; and whenever I wanted to know what the Irish people wanted, I had only to examine my own heart and it told me straight off what the Irish people wanted.[16]

As his official biographers note, 'Few indeed are the leaders who could say this and not be laughed out of politics.'[17] De Valera's popularity with the voters, which lasted with scarcely an interval from 1932 to his withdrawal from electoral politics in 1959, makes his claim, great as it is, seem just. But if he was indeed Irishness itself, it was an Irishness of a new, modern kind: humourless, pragmatic, circumspect, indifferent to poetry, abstemious. Something of his spirit enters into the bloodless, unbending republican ideologues that began to populate Irish fiction and drama, the gunmen of *Juno and the Paycock*, Gallagher in O'Flaherty's *The Informer*, the IRA officer in Behan's *The Hostage*.

Yeats found more to admire in de Valera than did his writing contemporaries. Once, when de Valera's remark about looking into his heart to know what the Irish people wanted came under criticism in a conversation, Yeats responded, 'Where the devil else should he look?'[18] – better his heart than the newspapers, Yeats may have thought. The one time he personally met de Valera, he reported being impressed. Yeats objected, however, to de Valera's whole-hearted identification with the masses, to his assumption that what the masses willed was rightly and necessarily the nation's destiny. 'De Valera has described himself to somebody as an autocrat expressing the feeling of the masses. If we must have an autocrat let him express what Swift called "the bent & current" of a people not a momentary majority', Yeats noted in his journal in 1933.[19] It was Yeats's conviction that a nation's bent and current, its authentic destiny, was more likely to be expressed in the thoughts of a concerted few than be determined by totalling the yeas and nays of the mass. More particularly, the 'few' Yeats cared most about, the Anglo-Irish minority, hardly entered into de Valera's vision of Ireland. When an Irish leader boasts of having been reared in a labourer's cottage and of not having lived solely among intellectuals and their apparently corrupting influence, what becomes of the Ireland of great houses and the Abbey Theatre, of Lady Gregory and Yeats? Small as that Ireland was, it mattered immensely to Yeats, and had mattered immensely to Ireland, yet it was not the Ireland de Valera so much as glimpsed at when he looked into his heart.

Yeats once wrote that 'no man should be permitted to open his mouth in Parliament until he had sung or written his *Utopia*, for lacking that we could not know where he was taking us . . . .'.[20] De Valera sang his *Utopia* in a radio broadcast on St Patrick's Day, 1943:

> The Ireland which we have dreamed of would be the home of a people who valued material wealth only as the basis of a right living, of a people who were satisfied with frugal comfort and devoted their leisure to the things of the spirit; a land whose countryside would be bright with cosy homesteads, whose fields and villages would be joyous with the sounds of industry, with the romping of sturdy children, the contests of athletic youths, the laughter of comely maidens; whose firesides would be forums for the wisdom of old age. It would, in a word, be the home of a people living the life that God desires men should live.[21]

De Valera's is a strikingly utilitarian utopia: joy is inseparable from industry, comfort is qualified by frugality, firesides become forums, even leisure is put to the good purpose of maintaining ties with the Almighty, almost as if God would not approve of our importuning Him during working hours. The poet who wrote that 'only the wasteful virtues earn the sun' and thought the leisure of women of fashion as valuable as that of monks and scholars[22] would not have much sympathised with this practical utopia. Yet practical as it is, it also seems as remote from life as a tourist board brochure, and entirely overlooks the old Adam who was as likely to go on a rampage in Ireland as anywhere else. A national leader, Yeats believed, had to recognise that whatever his ideal for the national life was, it would have to confront and somehow master a fallen world in which man 'must earn his bread by the sweat of his face'[23] and a fallen humanity prey to every weakness. This double recognition Yeats lent to the Parnell of his poems, his type of the aristocratic leader. We see it in the two-line poem 'Parnell':

> Parnell came down the road, he said to a cheering man:
> 'Ireland shall get her freedom and you still break stone.'[24]

We see it also in the closing lines of 'Parnell's Funeral':

> Through Jonathan Swift's dark grove he passed, and there
> Plucked bitter wisdom that enriched his blood.[25]

The Anglo-Irish, in Yeats's eyes, offered Ireland a knowledge of the human need for a magnificence beyond utility coupled with an intellectual coldness able to clear away the vapours of wishful thinking. Alternately practical and sentimental in ways directly counter to this magnificence and this coldness, de Valera personified, for all Yeats's respect for him as an individual, the developments that had thwarted his youthful expectations. Yeats was bound to set himself in opposition.

Yeats first commented on de Valera in 1920. Both men were in New York in the spring of 1920, Yeats on a lecture tour, de Valera, then President of the as yet unrecognised Irish Republic, trying to raise funds and public support for the war with the English. Yeats desired Irish independence, but had doubts about de Valera:

> A living argument rather than a living man. All propaganda, no human life, but not bitter or hysterical or unjust. I judged him persistent, being both patient and energetic, but that he will fail through not having enough human life as to judge the human life in others. He will ask too much of everyone and will ask it without charm. He will be pushed aside by others.[26]

Yeats underestimated what at least some of de Valera's followers would consider too much to ask, but even this early on he saw in de Valera the fixity of principle upon which Irish unity would break two years later, the stone that would trouble the living stream. The break came when de Valera and the 'die-hard' republicans rejected the Anglo-Irish Treaty in 1922. Like the republicans, Yeats disliked the oath of allegiance to the British king that the treaty required of all members of the Dail, but his desire for an end to the chaos brought by the Black and Tan war led him to support the treaty and the Irish Free State it created.[27] De Valera and the republicans would allow no such compromise, refused even to abide by the results of a nationwide election that approved the treaty, and gradually led the country into the worse chaos of civil war. Yeats's 'Meditations in Time of Civil War' stand as evidence that his reaction to the war was much more than simple partisanship of the Free State against the republicans, but his public support went to the Free State. He accepted gladly a seat in the Free State Senate when it was offered, and became a dependable, though not unquestioning,[28] supporter of the Free State government of William T. Cosgrave. He particularly admired Kevin O'Higgins, the Minister of Home Affairs who was somewhat misleadingly called the 'Irish Mussolini' because he was the government's principal spokesman on the policy of putting down the republicans. As a Senator, Yeats ran the risk of having his house bombed by the republicans and supported the hard measures the Free State took to suppress the insurgents, which included seventy-seven executions.[29]

During his second three-year term (1925–8), however, Yeats's support for the Cosgrave government suffered several shocks. In 1925 the government disallowed divorce, thereby treading on the rights of the Anglo-Irish Protestant minority Yeats had hoped would be honoured and respected in the new nation. In 1927 Kevin O'Higgins, 'the finest intellect in Irish public life',[30] was assassinated. In 1928 a state censorship of literature was instituted. Given these shocks, it is remarkable that Yeats's opposition to de Valera, who had risen from the politically dead in 1927 by taking the oath and entering the Dail, not only remained firm but actually stiffened. In January 1932, just before the national election that was to turn out Cosgrave and bring in de Valera as head of state, Yeats published an article in the *Spectator* praising Cosgrave's government, perhaps in the hope of influencing voters, and suggesting what it was he disliked about de Valera and de Valera's party, Fianna Fail.

'Ireland, 1921–1931' begins with an account of how the traditional symbols of Ireland had changed in Yeats's eyes. The colour green and the Irish harp – though not, he insists, the shamrock – had 'ascended out of sentimentality, out of insincere rhetoric, out of mob emotion'[31] and come to symbolise an honest, responsible and honourable patriotism. Yeats attributed this change to the Cosgrave government, which had not been 'afraid to govern',[32] had been able to do what was right and necessary but unpopular – he notes the seventy-seven executions. The Cosgrave government had brought about economic prosperity (Yeats describes the impressively successful Shannon hydroelectric scheme) and a cultural flowering (he neglects to mention the institution of censorship).[33] Most importantly, the Cosgrave government had 'delivered us from obsession'.[34] That is, the Cosgrave government had freed itself and Ireland of the old nationalist dream of an undivided, Catholic, Celtic, Irish-speaking Christian Socialist Republic, the dream that in the earlier part of the century had, for Yeats, turned into 'sentimentality', 'insincere rhetoric' and 'mob emotion'. By giving up this obsession, the Cosgrave government had gained the freedom of mind it needed to govern well, gained strength from the Anglo-Irish tradition that had seemed alien to the nationalists. The Cosgrave government was perhaps not quite so enlightened on this point as Yeats made it out to be, but he chose to emphasise, on the eve of what all knew would be a closely-contested election, what he took to be the essential difference between the contending parties. It was the intransigent devotion of de Valera and his followers to the old nationalist ideal that had inspired them to take up arms in the civil war, and that ideal was the ideological core of their new party. Fianna Fail's avowed goals were:

1. Securing the political independence of a united Ireland as a Republic.
2. The restoration of the Irish language, and the development of a native Irish culture.
3. The development of a social system in which, as far as possible, equal opportunity will be afforded to every Irish citizen to live a noble and useful Christian life.
4. The distribution of the land of Ireland so as to get the greatest number possible of Irish families rooted in the soil of Ireland.
5. The making of Ireland an economic unit, as with a proper balance between agriculture and other essential industries.[35]

This programme translates into flat, modern political prose what Yeats called the nationalist 'obsession'. Beneath its aspirations

Yeats may have seen a self-willed blindness to the realities of partition, of the Irish language, of Ireland's economic ties with England. This squinting at facts to make them conform with nationalist hopes perhaps deserves to be called 'insincere rhetoric'. Also, since for Fianna Fail 'Christian' practically meant 'Catholic'[36] and 'native Irish' practically meant 'Celtic', and since the breaking up of the large farms and old social privileges would inevitably hurt more Protestants than Catholics, it is possible to see a veiled sectarianism in the programme, a stance quite opposite to what Yeats considered that of Cosgrave's party on this difficult subject.

In 'Ireland, 1921–1931', Yeats discounts the possibility that Fianna Fail will actually stick to their programme: 'If the Republicans come into power we shall have a few anxious months while they discover where they have asked the impossible, and then they in their turn will govern.'[37] After his election, de Valera immediately set himself to dismantling the treaty, and there were indeed some anxious months, especially once de Valera decided to withhold the land annuities the Free State had been paying to England, a decision which provoked an economic 'war' which badly depressed Irish agriculture, particularly the cattle industry. No admission that the impossible had been asked followed, however, and antagonisms left over from the civil war began to revive. Yet the new government represented not only a reversal of the outcome of that war, but also a change in the kind of men who governed, a change bringing with it another, equally charged set of antagonisms. Arthur Clery called it 'a change from government by Clongowes men to Christian Brothers men',[38] a shift resembling that accomplished in American political life by the election of Andrew Jackson. De Valera 'based his policy on the needs of the urban poor and the twenty-five acre farmer', one biographer has written,[39] and another has noted that 'the real secret of de Valera's power is to be found in the support of the "small men". . . . Class distinctions almost disappeared and British titles came to count for nothing.'[40] De Valera's preference for the soft hat over the silk hat thus acquired a political significance, and one could declare oneself by one's choice of headgear.[41] Gogarty tells how he persuaded Yeats to attend an uninteresting function by presenting it as an opportunity to protest the 'loutish ways of the bog' by wearing a silk hat.[42]

There is, to be sure, something ludicrous in this sort of class bias: 'Silk hats save Ireland!' is Gogarty's comment on this incident. But the ascendancy of the 'new men' may have been of some moment to Yeats since it coincided with the death, on 22 May 1932, of Lady Gregory, who had long embodied for Yeats all that was best and irreplaceable in the social class the new men considered dispensable. The kind of life Yeats had chosen to celebrate in much of his poetry seemed on the point of vanishing. 'All the nobility of earth', a visitor to Coole, looking at the family portraits, had told Yeats; 'How much of my own verse has not been but the repetition of those words,' he wrote to Olivia Shakespear.[43] Lady Gregory's death was a watershed for Yeats. He wrote no poetry for a long while afterwards: sixteen months after her death he wrote to Sturge Moore, 'For a year now I have written little but prose, trying for new foundations.'[44] In the preface to the volume which collected the few poems he had written in the two years following her death, Yeats wondered if the closing of Coole Park, 'where I had escaped from politics, from all that Dublin talked of', had 'shut me out from my theme; or did the subconscious drama that was my imaginative life end with its owner?'[45] This search for a new imaginative foundation included speculation over what direction Ireland would take in the near future, and this question preoccupied him during his last lecture tour of America in October and November of 1932.

'Modern Ireland', a lecture Yeats delivered on this final tour, begins with the claim that Ireland, like Germany, Russia and Italy, has entered into a period of 'fanaticism' and 'intensity'. 'I have tried to explore, for the sake of my own peace of mind, the origin of what seems to me most unique and strange in our Irish excitement.'[46] Its origin, Yeats decided, was in the conflict between two opposed forces in Irish history. The first force came to being at the close of the seventeenth century when 'the victorious Protestant governing class quarrelled with England about the wool trade', electing Ireland as its first allegiance. Berkeley enunciated its philosophy, Swift was its 'de Valera', its 'first turbulent self-assertion'. The second force came into being at the close of the eighteenth century, when the Irish peasantry 'began under the influence of the French Revolution to assert their will and in the process discovered constitutional agitation and democratic Catholicism'. Yeats is obviously thinking of Daniel O'Connell. An event at the close of the nineteenth century, the fall and death of Parnell, signalled the beginning of the period Yeats goes on to analyse in detail. Although the analysis proceeds

chronologically, it is less a straightforward history of the period
than an account of the conflict between the two forces, which still
fight each other 'in our blood', as Yeats says in the lecture's
conclusion.[47] In the first half of the essay Yeats presents in turn
Parnell, Lady Gregory and John O'Leary, and through their
portraits sketches the virtues of the old Protestant governing
class. They possessed self-sufficiency, found the strength they
needed in themselves: Yeats tells how young men praised Parnell's
'pride' and 'loneliness',[48] how Lady Gregory in her last year 'kept
an unmoved face amid great pain',[49] how young men filled with
'hatred of democratic compromise' were drawn to John O'Leary,
who seemed to stand above the shifting tides of popular opinion.[50]
To this self-sufficiency the other force in Irish history opposed
self-surrender, even self-sacrifice. Powers outside the individual
mind – the will of the masses, the doctrine of the church, 'Ireland'
itself – overruled the individual mind, and the highest form of
self-expression became self-negation, the sacrifice of the self to
some impersonal end. So Yeats characterises the cult of the
'mystic victim' that motivated Patrick Pearse in 1916, the hunger
strikers of the Civil War and the protagonists of modern Irish
novels such as Stuart's *The Coloured Dome* and O'Flaherty's
The Puritan.[51] The eighteenth-century force possessed also a
'magnificence' that went beyond the tangible and useful, a special
extravagance. Yeats describes the strange phenomena in the night
sky that attended Parnell's burial and the Christmas dinner scene
in Joyce's *Portrait* in which Mr Casey finally collapses in mourning
for his 'dead king'. Lady Gregory 'sought in the depths of her
mind what Aristotle calls "magnificence, greatness of soul"'.[52]
O'Leary, too, had this 'magnificence', which 'whether in life or
literature, comes, I think, from excess, from that something over
and above utility, which wrings the heart'.[53] To this magnificence
the nineteenth-century force in Irish history opposed the practical
middle class virtues: 'men were born to pray and save'. The
lecture presents this meanness of modern Ireland only obliquely,
by dwelling on the 'violence' of the satire of Irish life in Synge,
O'Casey, O'Flaherty, O'Connor and particularly Joyce, who as a
young man seemed to Yeats 'possessed with an extreme irritation,
mounting to almost ungovernable rage against all that [he] saw
and heard, even against the mere bodies and faces that passed
him in the street'.[54] Yeats did not venture any guesses on how the
conflicts in modern Ireland might resolve themselves, concluding

his lecture instead with references to the spoilt priest in Shaw's *John Bull's Other Island* who maintains that since in his religion there is but one place of 'horror and torment', Hell, our earth must then be Hell, and to the boy in a 'strange Eastern tale' who 'ran screaming from an abbot who had cut off his fingers, then standing and looking back, suddenly attained Nirvana'.[55] The very obscurity of this conclusion somehow suggests that Yeats believed a crisis in the conflict imminent.

De Valera is mentioned by name only once in the lecture, by way of explaining the position Swift held in the Protestant Ireland of the early eighteenth century, but he might well have embodied one side of the conflict as Parnell, Lady Gregory and O'Leary had embodied the other. De Valera and his party perceived themselves as the heirs of the 'mystic victims' of 1916, and counted in their numbers many of the hunger strikers alluded to by Yeats. They were in all respects the twentieth-century bearers of the tradition of 'democratic Catholicism' inaugurated by O'Connell, and it is plain that Yeats regarded them so from an interview he granted to the *New York Times Magazine* in November 1932. De Valera and his followers did not, as had the nineteenth-century nationalists, let a nationalist emotion rule their wills, but they did let a nationalist logic rule their wills: 'That period of the sentimental patriotic plays of Dion Boucicault has passed, the "broth of a boy" has passed,' said Yeats, 'and intellect of some form or other is taking the reins of government. It is not without symbolic importance that at its head is an ex-professor of Mathematics. . . . Emotion is now responding to logical statements instead of to slogans, though the statements are often as false as the slogans were.'[56] Tearful devotion to Cathleen ni Houlihan had turned to hard-eyed devotion to the abstract ideal of the Republic, but whether the will is led by slogans or by logic the self-sufficiency of Parnell, Lady Gregory and O'Leary is lost. Yeats also mentioned that, though 'a Cosgrave man', he supported de Valera in his economic 'war' with England, then Ireland's most controversial political issue, and in his aim 'to make Ireland economically independent of the rest of the world', but he feared what this ardent pursuit of economic prosperity might cost Ireland: 'Ireland will become a country of small manufacturers and farmers. How far it will be a country of intellect it is difficult to predict, though I believe that the intellectual tradition is strong enough to persist. The danger is that Ireland will choose prosaic prosperity in preference to other things. We may become self-supporting and yet no man can give his son anything that I would call an education.' That 'something over and above utility, which wrings the heart', be it a silk hat or literature itself, seemed in danger of disappearing from Irish life as de Valera came to power.

Both at this time and later, certainly, Yeats found something to admire in de Valera's inflexibility of purpose, his single-mindedness on the question of the Republic. When, in the introduction to the 'Modern Ireland' lecture, Yeats compared the 'intensity' of Ireland to that of Germany, Russia and Italy, he implicitly compared de Valera to Hitler, Stalin and Mussolini, and he explicitly made the same comparison in a 1933 letter to Olivia Shakespear.[57] To Yeats, the comparison would not have seemed necessarily insulting, for he admired strong leaders, particularly those who placed themselves above the democratic process. The decision of de Valera and the republicans not to abide by the national election that approved the treaty made an impression on Yeats,[58] and might have struck him as a gesture worthy of Coriolanus had he been more in sympathy with the republicans' aims. Devotion to an abstract ideal lent de Valera's party a keenness that Cosgrave's government had lacked. Yeats recorded privately that he found the new government 'sincere because logical', and in that respect 'very unlike the old government party in the Senate, who left upon the mind an impression of something warm, damp & soiled, middle-class democracy at its worst'.[59] But while Yeats respected the intensity of Fianna Fail's commitment to their vision of Ireland, he did not share that vision. Having spent the months following Lady Gregory's death hammering out a countering vision of his own, Yeats returned from the United States prepared to pit his vision against de Valera's; so began his last effort at personal participation in Irish politics.

While Yeats was in America, opposition to de Valera's policy towards England increased to the point where a new party, the National Centre Party, began to organise itself to oppose that policy. In January 1933 de Valera tested his support by dissolving the Dail and calling for an election, held on the 24th, which he won by a slightly larger margin than he had the election of ten months before. Yeats arrived back in Ireland on the 28th, his old appetite for controversy and political combat suddenly renewed, and by 2 February was writing to Olivia Shakespear in the following vein:

Here I am, I suppose, about to be involved in a four years' conflict with the ignorant. (An Irish government need not go to the country for five years.) While I was away free articles were sent to country newspapers from Dublin – from some Jesuit, anti-Catholic friends declare – attacking the Irish Academy of Letters. . . . If I were a young man I would welcome four years of conflict, for it creates unity among the educated classes, and force De Valera's Ministers, in all probability, to repudiate the ignorance that has in part put them into power.[60]

The letter ends here; that is, there is no qualifying 'but I am *not* a young man' sentence to temper the combativeness of the last sentence. The passage presents the conflict described in the lecture 'Modern Ireland' in balder, more politically provocative terms: Irish art versus Irish Catholicism, the educated minority versus the ignorant majority, all subsumed for the moment in W. B. Yeats versus the de Valera government. By March Yeats was 'in conflict with certain people in the government about the Abbey'. He met de Valera for the first time and was impressed by him, but failed to make him repudiate the ignorance that had in part put him into power: 'I had never met him before and was impressed by his simplicity and honesty though we differed throughout.'[61] The government's annual subsidy to the Abbey was reduced by a quarter, from £1000 to £750, and de Valera nominated for the position of government representative on the Abbey board of directors a man who Yeats believed 'would have brought us under complete clerical domination'.[62] While Yeats was defending the Abbey, an extraparliamentary and in some respects Fascist opposition to de Valera emerged in the form of an organisation officially known as the Army Comrades Association, unofficially the Blueshirts, among whose leaders were many of the Cosgrave ministers Yeats had known while in the Senate. By April Yeats had involved himself in this organisation, and by mid-summer he was enthusiastic over it: 'De Valera has forced political thought to face the most fundamental issues. A Fascist opposition is forming behind the scenes to be ready should some tragic situation develop. I find myself constantly urging the despotic rule of the educated classes as the only end to our troubles.'[63] We will discuss this episode in more detail in the following chapter. Here it will be enough to say that de Valera proved to be 'no von Papen', in the words of Conor Cruise O'Brien,[64] that he effectively

quashed the Blueshirts by the end of 1933 and emerged from the
struggle stronger than ever.

Yeats's hope for a return in his lifetime of the public virtues of
Parnell, Lady Gregory and John O'Leary had collapsed, and its
collapse left him feeling bitter and extraordinarily alone. The
poems he wrote in late 1933 and early 1934 and the commentaries
upon those poems he published with them in the volume *The
King of the Great Clock Tower* spill over with that bitterness and that
loneliness. The volume includes the marching songs he wrote for
the Blueshirts, here titled 'Three Songs to the Same Tune' and
altered so 'that no party might sing them'.[65] The songs here and
there retain the patriotic fervour proper to their genre, but in each
an ominous, troubling note occurs. The first describes a hanging,
the second ends by warning the marchers of the consequences of
failure ('Fail, and that history turns into rubbish'[66]), the third and
most ominous ends with a vision of leaderless Ireland toppled by
a levelling wind, and an old man desiring death:

> Where are the captains that govern mankind?
> What happens a tree that has nothing within it?
> O marching wind, O a blast of the wind,
> Marching, marching along.
> March, march, lift up the song:
> *'Who'd care to dig 'em,' said the old, old man,*
> *'Those six feet marked in chalk?*
> *'Much I talk, more I walk;*
> *'Time I were buried,' said the old, old man.*[67]

Yeats's 'Commentary on the Three Songs' does not mention the
songs at all until its last sentence, dwelling instead on the low
condition into which Irish art had fallen since the inauguration of
the Free State. Yeats blamed that low condition on the ignorance
of the larger part of the Irish public, and on the helplessness of
Ireland's leaders given the fact that 'the mob reigned'. 'If that
reign is not broken,' Yeats warned, 'our public life will move from
violence to violence, or from violence to apathy; our Parliament
disgrace and debauch those that enter it; our men of letters live
like outlaws in their own country.'[68] Any government or party
seeking to break that reign would require 'force, marching men'
and would promise 'not this or that measure but a discipline, a
way of life . . .'. Yeats concludes: 'There is no such government

or party today; should either appear I offer it these trivial songs and what remains to me of life.'[69] A writer searching to express Yeats's peculiar, alienated participant attitude to Irish public life at this time might easily hit upon the metaphor, 'writing marching songs for a party that did not exist'. That events had led Yeats to do exactly that shows how very alone in his convictions he was. The bitterness he felt over the turn Ireland had taken became the main figure of the short poem included in the postscript to the 'Commentary on the Three Songs' and later titled 'Church and State'. In the first stanza, the old poet imagines church and state regaining their old authority:

> O but heart's wine shall run pure,
> Mind's bread grow sweet.

The second stanza, however, faces the truth that in modern, democratic Ireland the authority of church and state has become the authority of the mob itself:

> That were a cowardly song,
> Wander in dreams no more;
> What if the Church and the State
> Are the mob that howls at the door!
> Wine shall run thick to the end,
> Bread taste sour.[70]

Yeats wrote in the preface to *The King of the Great Clock Tower* that the poem 'Parnell's Funeral', in this volume titled 'A Parnellite at Parnell's Funeral', came from a decision 'to force myself to write' after the long fallow period following Lady Gregory's death, and that in it he 'rhymed passages from a lecture I had given in America. . .'.[71] Neither this description, which makes the poem sound like an exercise in versification, nor the lecture 'Modern Ireland', plain though its anxiety over a subsidence in Irish greatness was, would prepare a reader for the unqualified scorn contained in what then stood as the final stanza of the poem. In this stanza, Yeats the bardic Majority of One damns the mass-mind of his nation and all that it wishes to believe of itself, and denies even that it can justly call itself human:

> Come, fix upon me that accusing eye.
> I thirst for accusation. All that was sung,
> All that was said in Ireland is a lie
> Bred out of the contagion of the throng,
> Saving the rhyme rats hear before they die.
> Leave nothing but the nothings that belong
> To this bare soul, let all men judge that can
> Whether it be an animal or a man.[72]

The 'Commentary' on this poem describes as 'Four Bells' the events that at the closes of the sixteenth, seventeenth, eighteenth and nineteenth centuries signalled a change in the governing dispensation of Irish history. With the addition of the flight of the Earls after the Elizabethan wars and the substitution of the Battle of the Boyne for the quarrel over the wool trade, the events are the same as those cited in 'Modern Ireland'. Although the 'Commentary' devotes much more space to historical Ireland than to twentieth-century Ireland, its theme also is the same as that of 'Modern Ireland', the conflict between the Ireland of O'Connell and that of Parnell:

> As we discussed and argued, the national character changed, O'Connell, the great comedian, left the scene and the tragedian Parnell took his place. When we talked of his pride; of his apparent impassivity when his hands were full of blood because he had torn them with his nails, the proceeding epoch with its democratic bonhomie seemed to grin through a horse collar. He was the symbol that made apparent or made possible that epoch's contrary: contrary, not negation, not refutation; the spring vegetables may be over, they have not been refuted.[73]

Although it is O'Connell's epoch that this passage refers to as the spring vegetables that would inevitably return, the force of the figure applies more readily to the apparently dead, but really only sleeping virtues of Parnell, which Yeats believed must eventually waken and flourish again, delayed though the wakening seemed to be. The likening of Parnell to spring vegetables, the claim that the celestial events at his funeral might 'symbolise an accepted sacrifice',[74] and the attempt in the above passage to endow him with self-inflicted (hence *antithetical*) stigmata all serve to unite the Irish poems in this volume with the play *The King of the Great Clock*

Tower, which, as does its revised version *A Full Moon in March*, draws heavily on myths of slain gods and regeneration.[75] From this time on Yeats grew more certain that the reckless, self-sufficient aristocratic mind would regain supremacy in Ireland, and that certainty lies in the background of many late poems, such as 'The Gyres', 'Hound Voice' and 'Under Ben Bulben'. He did not expect to live to see it, however, and the possibility of such a reversal actually occurring grew more remote. In 1934 no Irish party or politician represented what Parnell had represented; Yeats was the only 'Parnellite' left. He placed at the end of the 'Commentary' a poem which he later made the second part of 'Parnell's Funeral', and which specifies the ways in which independent Ireland's leaders (de Valera, Cosgrave and the Blueshirts' Eoin O'Duffy) had failed to live up to Parnell's example. The hardest words are reserved for de Valera:

> Had de Valera eaten Parnell's heart
> No loose-lipped demagogue had won the day,
> No civil rancour torn the land apart.[76]

The strength and sharpness of the disgust Yeats felt towards Ireland by 1934 derived less from the disappointment caused by a particular political defeat than from a sense that this was his final defeat, that the virtues represented by Lady Gregory and Coole would not rise again in his lifetime. The defence of those virtues was, after all, not a cause he had taken up only in the 1930s, nor was the conflict in the nation's imagination between Catholic Ireland and Protestant Ireland something he concerned himself with only on his last American tour. That conflict had determined the shape of his whole public career, and since 1904 his chief political goal had been to win a place for the virtues of the old governing class in the public life of Ireland. Yeats owed the black state he fell into in 1934 not only to the collapse of a campaign he had taken up in 1932, but also to the final collapse of a hope he had held and an effort he had maintained for some thirty years. A brief history of that hope and that effort will help explain why Yeats took the events of 1932–4 as hard as he did.

The conflict between nationalist and unionist, the single greatest Irish political issue during most of Yeats's lifetime, gathered

together several different conflicts under the question of who
would govern Ireland. There was a religious conflict: with some
notable exceptions, unionists were Protestants, nationalists
Catholic. There was a racial conflict: unionists were predominantly
the descendants of invaders from the neighbouring island,
nationalists predominantly of Gaelic stock. There was a class
conflict: most unionists (outside of industrialised Ulster) were of
the upper class or the higher bourgeoisie, landholders or
professionals, usually well-educated, while nationalists, having
only in the recent past escaped from the disabilities imposed by
the penal laws, were often irregularly or self-educated and
belonged to the working class, the peasantry or the lower
bourgeoisie. Owing to this complicated situation, a unionist who
chose to take the uncharitable view could despise nationalists not
only for their politics, but also for being members of a slavish
race, adherents of a superstitious religion and boorish, levelling
bog-trotters. Similarly, a nationalist who chose to take the
uncharitable view could despise unionists for being members of
an alien race, heretics and remnants of a decayed aristocracy or
rentier leeches.

By birth – by race, religion and class – Yeats belonged to
unionist Ireland. As a child he had 'thought I would like to die
fighting the Fenians'.[77] When as a young man he decided that
only an independent Ireland could lead Europe out of the 'autumn
of the body' and into artistic and spiritual renewal, and committed
himself to the nationalist cause, he felt that commitment included
allegiance to a religion, a race and a social class not his own, and
often in his early work he tries to live up to those allegiances.
Yeats's interest in Catholic authority and ritual, evident in the
Robartes-Aherne stories and in his evocations of Rosicrucianism,
thus has not only a *fin de siècle* side but also an Irish side, evident
in his making the hero of his unfinished autobiographical novel
the Catholic son of a Protestant landowner, and in early poems as
unremarkable as 'The Ballad of Father O'Gilligan' and as moving
as 'Red Hanrahan's Song about Ireland'. Similarly, *The Celtic
Twilight*, *The Wanderings of Oisin* and Yeats's untiring promotion of
Lady Gregory's and Standish O'Grady's retellings of the heroic
myths testify to his desire to bring before modern Ireland its
Gaelic heritage, a desire born not of an antiquarian but of a
political impulse, the wish to shape Irish imagination in preparation
for Irish independence. Nor did he stop short at the necessity of

abandoning his own class. 'In a battle like Ireland's, which is one
of poverty against wealth, we must prove our sincerity by making
ourselves unpopular to wealth. We must accept the baptism of
the gutter. Have not all the leaders done that?'[78] Yeats knew and
accepted – not entirely gladly, to judge from the phrase 'baptism
of the gutter', but still accepted – that the Irish struggle was in
part a class struggle. When the Irish National Theatre came into
being, Yeats virtually identified its goals with those of Gaelic and
Catholic Ireland, and saw himself as one of those who, like
Emmet, Tone, Davis and Parnell, had forsaken the interests of his
own class for the greater good of the whole nation.

> All Irish writers have to choose whether they will write as the
> upper classes have done, not to express but to exploit this
> country; or join the intellectual movement which has raised the
> cry that was heard in Russia in the 'seventies, the cry, 'To the
> people'.
>   Moses was little good to his people until he had killed an
> Egyptian; and for the most part a writer or public man of the
> upper classes is useless to this country till he has done
> something that separates him from his class.[79]

Although Yeats, unlike Moses, was Egyptian by birth as well as
by upbringing, a good deal of his early work consists of the killing
of Egyptians. In one instance, *Cathleen ni Houlihan*, the metaphor
almost becomes literal.

Yeats's commitment to Catholic Ireland began to chafe in 1903–
4. Yeats passed through one personal crisis after another in these
years, chief among them the marriage of Maud Gonne (to a
militant Irish nationalist) and the breaking up of the Order of the
Golden Dawn. He passed through a public crisis as well, the
controversy over Synge's *Shadow of the Glen*. At the centre of the
controversy lay the question of whether a theatre that claimed to
be nationalist, as did the Abbey, ought to show the Irish,
especially the country Irish, as anything other than brave, chaste
and high-minded (as they had been shown, for instance, in the
poetry of Thomas Davis and the Young Irelanders at mid-century).
In this controversy, and in the nearly identical one over *The
Playboy of the Western World* three years later, Yeats argued
eloquently that the Irish cause was best served by great art, and
that art which limited itself to sentimentality and flattery, even for

patriotic reasons, could never be great. In his anger, Yeats sometimes connected the philistinism of the nationalist movement to class ('the old bourgeois dislike of power and reality'[80]) and even to religion ('The half-educated mind is never sincere in the arts, and one finds in Irish chapels, above all in Irish convents, the religious art that it understands'[81]), perhaps indicating in these kicks two of the places where his commitment to orthodox nationalism had started to rub.

But the great problem, the problem which Yeats addressed with all the energy and eloquence he could muster, was that centuries of persecution, humiliation and frustration had worked to form and make sacred in Catholic Ireland's imagination an ideal as fixed as it was outdated of who the Irish people were and what the Irish nation was. Though Yeats had for a time subscribed to this ideal, it began to seem to him too unreal to be embodied in any honest art, and too fixed to permit the Irish renaissance he envisioned. 'All the past had been turned into melodrama with Ireland for blameless hero and poet; novelist and historian had but one object, that we should hiss the villain, and only a minority doubted that the greater the talent the greater the hiss.'[82] Yeats admitted that the ideal was strong because in part it was true – 'It was all the harder to substitute for that melodrama a nobler form of art, because there really had been, however different in their form, villain and victim . . .' – but this truth had become to nationalists what 'opinions' were to certain women, who, Yeats wrote, 'give all to an opinion as if it were a terrible stone doll'.[83]

Yeats partly (and, medically speaking, inaccurately) blamed the nationalist ideal for Synge's early death,[84] and in a long essay on Synge published in 1910, a year after the playwright's death, Yeats described in detail both the ideal and what he saw as its consequences:

Even if what one defends be true, an attitude of defence, a continual apology, whatever the cause, makes the mind barren because it kills intellectual innocence. . . . A zealous Irishman, especially if he lives much out of Ireland, spends his time in a never-ending argument about Oliver Cromwell, the Danes, the penal laws, the Rebellion of 1798, the famine, the Irish peasant, and ends by substituting a traditional casuistry for a country; and if he be a Catholic, yet another casuistry, that has professors, schoolmasters, letter writing priests and the authors of manuals to make the meshes fine, comes between him and English literature. . . . His hesitations and arguments may be right, the Catholic philosophy may be more profound than Milton's morality or Shelley's vehement vision; but none the less do we lose life by losing that recklessness Castiglione thought necessary even in good manners, and offend our Lady Truth. . . .[85]

That 'we lose life' in hugging our stone-doll truths – and Yeats, an Irishman who in these years lived much out of Ireland, may be thinking of his own experience in the first part of the passage – was the main theme of Yeats's contributions to the Synge controversies. Adapting a phrase of Blake, 'Kings and Parliaments seem to me something other than human life',[86] he argued that art's freedom from various necessities, such as the middle class necessity of getting on, the necessity of adhering to a religious orthodoxy, the patriotic necessity of conducting a 'continual apology' for Ireland, was what made art's engagement with life complete and so made it peculiarly valuable. Art 'delights in the soul expressing itself according to its own laws and arranging the world about it in its own pattern. . . . But the average man is average because he has not attained to freedom. Habit, routine, fear of public opinion, fear of punishment here or hereafter, a myriad of things that are "something other than human life" . . . work their will upon his soul and trundle his body here and there.'[87] In Ireland the patriotic necessity, with its certainty as to heroes and villains and its incitement to hate, threatened especially to interpose between the audience and art – that is, life:

> In a country like Ireland, where personifications have taken the place of life, men have more hate than love, for the unhuman is nearly the same as the inhuman, but literature, which is part of that charity which is the forgiveness of sins, will make us understand men no matter how little they conform to our expectations. We will . . . have a little distrust for everything that can be called good or bad in itself with a very confident heart. Could we understand it so well, we will say, if it were not something other than human life?[88]

The hope expressed in this 1904 passage, that Irish literature would in time temper or humanise Irish nationalism, did not

come to pass. Eighteen years later, when Ireland was engaged in
civil war, Yeats was still trying to make the same point, in almost
the same words, in 'The Stare's Nest by my Window':

> We had fed the heart on fantasies,
> The heart's grown brutal from the fare;
> More substance in our enmities
> Than in our love. . . .[89]

If we now recall Yeats's already-quoted 1920 judgment of de
Valera –'All propaganda, no human life, but not bitter or hysterical
or unjust . . . he will fail through not having enough human life
to judge the human life in others' – we can see that Yeats saw de
Valera as the inheritor of the political tradition that Yeats had first
participated in, then come to see as destructive: destructive of art
and intellect in the early years of the century, by the twenties
destructive of actual property and lives. And even though Yeats is
noting that de Valera is *not* bitter or hysterical or unjust, the
quickness with which those words occur to him suggests what he
thought the emotional consequences of too fixed an adherence to
the nationalist ideal normally were. Recall that Yeats wrote in one
poem of his 'blind bitter land', in another that politics had made
Constance Markiewicz's mind 'a bitter, an abstract thing', and in
yet another described a portrait of Arthur Griffith, leader of
Synge's attackers, as 'staring in hysterical pride'. Also relevant,
though international rather than Irish, are the 'hysterical women'
who out of political conviction cry down art in 'Lapis Lazuli'.

That latent inhumanity of the nationalist ideal, the lethal blend
of sentimentality and bloody intransigence that led Yeats to note,
'The soul of Ireland is become a vapour and her body a stone',[90]
permanently altered Yeats's commitment to the nationalist cause.
In a 1931 prefatory note to *Plays and Controversies*, he wrote, '. . . I
doubt the value of the embittered controversy that was to fill my
life for years, but certainly they [the pieces collected in the
volume] rang down the curtain so far as I was concerned on what
was once called "The Celtic Movement". An "Irish movement"
took its place.'[91] 'Celtic' excludes not only the Norman and the
English, but also, by extension, the Protestant and upper class;
'Irish' does not. From 1904 Yeats began increasingly to see in
Protestant nationalists, that minority of the minority, the leavening
of 'human life' that he thought Catholic nationalism badly needed.

Less hampered by such constraints as economic necessity, religious duty, poor education and the need to apologise for past defeats than Catholic nationalists often were, these men and women seemed to have in their daily lives the liberty to engage life that Yeats desired for Irish art, and could devote their lives, as Yeats wished to devote his art, to Ireland without surrendering that liberty. From this time on, most of Yeats's public career was the effort to revise the nationalist tradition that it might include the people it was inclined to view as its natural antagonists.

An early and unusually transparent example of how Yeats wished to revise the nationalist tradition is a never-published 1904 essay on Robert Emmet, leader of a doomed but romantic insurrection in Dublin in 1803, a Protestant doctor's son and a revered figure in the nationalist tradition.[92] Throughout the essay Yeats insists on Emmet's manners and magnanimity, on the largeness of mind that marked Emmet as a fellow of O'Leary and Lady Gregory, and contrasts Emmet's behaviour with that of the nationalists of Yeats's day, whose single-mindedness had betrayed them into shrillness, name-calling and the habit of attributing any form of opposition to base motives. If Emmet's manners and the world that fostered those manners should prove irrecoverable, Yeats concludes, nothing good will come of the nationalist movement. The indignation and abuse that surely would have followed any claim that fine manners and social grace had anything to do with Irish independence may have kept Yeats from publishing this essay, but his point was not all that far-fetched. Castiglione had persuaded Yeats that the *sprezzatura* indispensable to fine manners was indispensable as well to art and heroism. Where manners and art are mocked, what chance for genuine heroism?

A straight line runs, gathering intensity, from the Emmet essay to the 1907 essay 'Poetry and Tradition', which argues that Irish art and Ireland herself will thrive only by the re-emergence of the O'Leary school of nationalism and upholds aristocrats, countrymen and artists against the 'others' who 'cannot understand you if you say, "All the most valuable things are useless"' and who 'prefer the stalk to the flower, and believe that painting and poetry exists that there may be instruction, and love that there may be children, and theatres that busy men may rest. . .'.[93] These others are plainly the 'new class' to which, the essay claims, the leadership of the nationalist movement has passed, and which the essay's conclusion upbraids for its 'ignorance' and 'superstitious piety' and for having undermined Ireland's 'great moment'.[94] In the long passage from 'J. M. Synge and the Ireland of his Time' (written in 1910, published as a book by Cuala Press in 1911) quoted above, Yeats was continuing on this theme. The qualities he there claims the nationalist ideal kills, 'intellectual innocence' and 'recklessness', are qualities he associated with the aristocratic temperament.[95] During the 1913 controversy over Sir Hugh Lane's proposed Dublin Municipal Gallery, Yeats's anger at the dominance of Dublin's Catholic middle class, at its disregard of art and its ability to thwart Lane's aristocratic generosity, arrived at its peak in 'September 1913', with its damning juxtaposition of those who pray and save against three (Protestant) patriots who 'weighed so lightly what they gave'. The Easter Rising forced Yeats to qualify the attack made in this poem, but even in the palinode 'Easter 1916' the image of the stone indicates that Yeats thought the nationalist ideal still sterile though newly ardent, still 'something other than human life'. De Valera, as one of the two leaders of the rising to escape execution, became its political inheritor, and Yeats's 1920 judgment of him as lacking 'human life' is a blunter version of the more complex emotions of 'Easter 1916'. Throughout the 1920s Yeats continued his efforts to revise the nationalist tradition away from both middle class utilitarianism and from dry, self-immolating hatred by writing and speaking of the virtues of the other Ireland: its 'magnificence', its self-sufficiency of soul that drove all hatred hence. Yeats supported the Cosgrave government, as we have seen, because it had created an atmosphere in which such a revision seemed possible. What he feared of de Valera and Fianna Fail – by some potent amalgamation, both the heirs of the 1916 martyrs and the party of small businessmen – was that they would think any such revision out of the question. Hence Yeats's desire to see the de Valera government toppled, and his despair when it withstood both ordinary parliamentary opposition and the threat of the Blueshirts.

Yeats's contention with de Valera continued after the collapse of the Blueshirts. Anxiety over what the new government had in store for Irish writers may have prompted him to revive his dormant project of an Irish Academy of Letters. The letter sent out to prospective members over Yeats's and George Bernard Shaw's names struck a note of alarm and insisted on the need for united effort to oppose the censorship, but the Academy, once formed, failed to accomplish much on this score. During the first ten years of de Valera's government, seven of the Academy's nineteen founder members – St John Ervine, Liam O'Flaherty, Austin Clarke, Gogarty, O'Connor, O'Faolain and Shaw himself – had at least one of their works banned in Ireland,[96] and in 1937 de Valera drafted the censorship into Ireland's new constitution, a step which would make the lifting of the censorship, were anyone eventually to attempt it, much more difficult. De Valera also brought pressure to bear on the Abbey. After reducing the theatre's subsidy and taking advantage of the Abbey's policy of letting the government appoint one member of the theatre's board of directors by nominating the man Yeats thought 'would have brought us under complete clerical domination', and after the Abbey had fought off this unnamed individual, de Valera got them to accept Dr Richard Hayes, a decision Yeats had reason to regret when Dr Hayes vetoed the production of Yeats's *The Herne's Egg* on the grounds that the seven soldiers who rape the priestess Attracta symbolise (he believed) the seven sacraments, and that the play was for this reason blasphemous.[97] 'De Valera had won the argument and no one realized it,' writes Abbey historian Peter Kavanagh in summing up this episode.[98]

De Valera was less successful on another occasion. In the spring of 1934, some American citizens of Irish origin protested to de Valera that since the Abbey was a recognised state body, the state should stop the Abbey from performing in the United States plays which insulted Ireland, specifically *In the Shadow of the Glen*, *The Playboy of the Western World* and *The Plough and the Stars*. De Valera brought the matter up in the Dail:

I am aware that the Abbey Theatre Company intends to travel to America this year and I have informed the directors of the theatre that it is my opinion if they produce certain plays that are on the list for production in America, if they produce these plays then it is clear that they will damage the good name of Ireland and they will cause shame and resentment to the Irish exiles.[99]

According to Hone, Yeats 'stated publicly that he would prefer to forgo the subsidy rather than permit such interference',[100] and the threat of censorship of the American repertoire evaporated. When *The Sunday Times*, in an article that autumn on the departure of the Abbey players for America, mentioned this threat and Yeats's response, Yeats even took the trouble of writing to the editor and denying the whole thing: the government had asked only that the Abbey make clear that the government had no part in the selection of the plays, and the Abbey had gladly obliged. Since de Valera's speech in the Dail plainly asks not that a misunderstanding be corrected, but that the plays not be performed, Bernard Krimm has argued that the letter to *The Sunday Times* was meant to preserve appearances, and that Yeats must have dissuaded de Valera from his earlier stance.[101]

The episode is interesting for two reasons. First, it is a final skirmish in the long, terrible struggle documented in Yeats's *The Irish Dramatic Movement*, with the crucial difference that the section of opinion against which Yeats had then fought now had the ear of, or was identical with, the civil power of Ireland. That the Irish government was willing to accuse Ireland's dramatic masterpieces of insulting Ireland must have been discouraging enough, but perhaps more discouraging was de Valera's insistence that he had not even seen the offending plays, that 'he had never set foot in the Abbey Theatre', and that he was acting solely at the behest of the Irish exiles.[102] In condemning works with which he was unacquainted, de Valera manifested the very hypocrisy or helplessness that Yeats cried against in the 'Commentary on the Three Songs', written in the same month the problem arose. Whenever he went before a Minister as a representative of the Abbey or the Academy to defend the interests of Irish art, Yeats wrote, he 'came away with the conviction that the Minister felt exactly as I did but was helpless: the mob reigned'. If the masses were going to dictate to the leaders what sorts of art would be permitted, how long would Irish art survive Irish democracy? What democratic leader, compelled to placate public opinion if he would remain in power, would risk his popularity for a collection of pictures or plays, whatever their merit? If the class that had produced Hugh Lane and Lady Gregory disappeared, who would be educated enough to discern merit, wealthy enough to subsidise art, and independent enough to override public opinion? As far as Yeats could tell, no one. Rather, Irish political life would 'disgrace and debauch those who enter it', Irish artists 'live like outlaws in their own country'.[103]

Another Yeats publication of 1934, *Wheels and Butterflies*, carries on the campaign, though it is not directed at de Valera himself so much as at the egalitarian preference for the average over the extraordinary that characterised de Valera's political programme and political instincts. The 'Butterflies' of the title are the four plays collected in the volume, each dedicated to a particular friend; the 'Wheels' are the introductory essays to the plays, all addressed to the young intellectuals of Dublin, the 'Garrets and Cellars', as Yeats calls them. Yeats had been told that the Garrets and Cellars were 'without exception Catholic, Communist, or both!'[104] – making them, with allowance for youth's heat, perfect exemplars of de Valeran Ireland, which seemed disturbingly theocratic to some, disturbingly socialist to others, and both to Yeats. Countering the Garrets' and Cellars' desire to found the state on the common man, Yeats argues that the state must found itself instead on its extraordinary men, who must be placed by privilege above the reach of democratic majorities or economic egalitarianism. In the first essay, 'Introduction to *The Words Upon the Windowpane*', he argues that what Swift called 'the universal bent or current of a people', or 'what we even more vaguely call national spirit', did not naturally express itself through what most men thought and believed, but through the numerically much smaller group of 'such men as had won or inherited general consent'.[105] That small section of the Protestant governing class that, like Swift, had chosen to protect Ireland against English interests was just such a group, the essay suggests. Swift would never, Yeats continues, have mistaken the average man as either the foundation of the state or the object of its solicitude: 'I doubt if a mind so contemptuous of average men thought, as Vico did, that it [the bent and current] found expression also through all individual lives, or asked more for those lives than protection from the most obvious evils.'[106]

In the second essay, the 'Introduction' preceding *Fighting the Waves*, Yeats regrets that in Ireland 'we have come to think of self-sacrifice, when worthy of public honour, as the act of some man when he is least himself, most completely the crowd'. The heroic act is not a merging with the mass, but a lonely attempt at self-expression, 'an act done because a man is himself. . .'.[107] Commonality had displaced distinction as the criterion in judging

men and the social good. If science dared to return to its ancient
wisdom and prove the reality of the immaterial and the immortality
of the soul, this displacement might be reversed, and Ireland
might rediscover that 'States are justified, not by multiplying, or,
as it would seem, comforting those that are inherently miserable,
but because sustained by . . . those born out of themselves, the
best born of the best'.[108]

He returned to this idea in the third essay, 'Introduction to *The
Resurrection*'. Even if the idea 'that nothing exists but a stream of
souls', that 'every soul is unique' were not proven by science,
'Such belief may arise from Communism by antithesis, declaring
at last even to the common ear that all things have value according
to the clarity of their expression of themselves, and not as
functions of changing economic conditions, or as a preparation
for some Utopia.'[109] Possibly the idea of reincarnation would take
hold and eliminate class envy, and 'Perhaps we shall learn to
accept even innumerable lives with humility.'[110] The whole of
Wheels and Butterflies goes to show how extraordinarily alone Yeats
was in a nation that had decided, in the full extension of the
metaphor, to do without the top hat, and how willing he still was
to propagandise on behalf of his beliefs.

That willingness, though in the years after 1934 it co-existed
with the aloofness from partisan politics that dictated the poems
'A Model for the Laureate', 'Those Images' and the valedictory
'Politics', may have included a willingness to join forces with de
Valera. In Will Rothenstein's memoirs, he records that Yeats
'respected' de Valera, and Frank O'Connor believed that Yeats
would have accepted a position in de Valera's government had
one been offered.[111] That Yeats submitted his angry poem on the
Casement diaries to the *Irish Press*, Fianna Fail's party organ, may
mean that he wished to bring about a rapprochement. He was
usually interested in gaining what influence he could, and since
de Valera had recently shown considerable political independence
by declaring the IRA an illegal association and by resisting a
Catholic campaign to have Ireland intervene on Franco's behalf in
Spain, Yeats may have decided that de Valera was capable of
withstanding democratic pressure and governing well. However,
though 'Roger Casement' was much admired, no rapprochement
came about, and in any case Yeats retained his aversion to what
de Valera represented. In the poem 'The Statesman's Holiday',
included in *On the Boiler*, de Valera's name occurs in a list of

leaders who have conspicuously failed to use their authority rightly.[112] If T. R. Henn is correct, and the besieging forces in Yeats's last-completed poem, 'The Black Tower', are de Valera and his followers, that poem too shows that whatever attempts at a rapprochement may have been made, Yeats considered his interests and those of what Henn called 'the new order' irreconcilable.[113]

> Those banners come to bribe or threaten
> Or whisper that a man's a fool
> Who, when his own right king's forgotten,
> Cares what king sets up his rule.
> If he died long ago
> Why do you dread us so?[114]

The last two quoted lines may be another whispered seduction from the enemy, or they may be the reply of the besieged, for just as Yeats's aloofness from partisan politics co-existed with a desire to gain what influence he could, so his despair over modern Ireland co-existed with a wildly aggressive hopefulness. Coole, 'where a great Irish social order climaxed and passed away',[115] may have been about to be destroyed, and O'Connell Street may have in its aspect as in its name signalled Ireland's descent into middle-class domination, but the final defeat of all he cherished freed Yeats, with his cyclical view of history, to imagine its perhaps slow, perhaps sudden, but certainly inevitable return. His often-quoted description of O'Connell Street veers in exactly this direction:

> When I stand upon O'Connell bridge in the half-light and notice that discordant architecture, all those electric signs, where modern heterogeneity has taken physical form, a vague hatred comes up out of my own dark and I am certain that wherever in Europe there are minds strong enough to lead others the same vague hatred rises; in four or five or in less generations this hatred will have issued in violence and imposed some kind of rule of kindred.[116]

All Yeats's late discussions of the future have this same sense of a compensating vision, the same certainty that the vision will come to pass. Even Yeats's sketch of the Irish future in *On the Boiler*, mainly concerned with practical recommendations, takes as its premise some catastrophic reversal and the disappearance of the tendency to take the fostering of the average man, or average child, as the state's main end:

> I assume that some tragic crisis shall so alter Europe and all opinion that the Irish government will teach the great majority of its schoolchildren nothing but ploughing, harrowing, sowing, curry-combing, bicycle-cleaning, drill-driving, parcel-making, bale-pushing, tin-can-soldering, door-knob-polishing, threshold-whitening, coat-cleaning, trouser-patching, and playing upon the squiffer, all things that serve human dignity, unless it indeed decide that these things are better taught at home, in which case it can leave the poor children at peace.[117]

Yeats's final volume of poems, though dark in mood and often bitter about modern degeneration, similarly has its compensating vision in the form of the horsemen who appear in several of the poems.[118] Yeats once wrote in a letter that he was 'a forerunner of that horde that will some day come down the mountains',[119] and the horde he was likely thinking of was that ancient race of mounted warriors described to him by Mary Battle, and whose bones were lying dormant on Ben Bulben and Knocknarea. These are the bones that are shaking (quickened by the rising wind?) in the refrain of 'The Black Tower':

> *There in the tomb stand the dead upright,*
> *But winds come up from the shore:*
> *They shake when the winds roar,*
> *Old bones upon the mountain shake.*[120]

These are the 'fierce horsemen' who ride from mountain to mountain in the burden of 'Three Songs to the One Burden'. They are the answer, in the second of the 'Three Marching Songs', to the question, *'What marches down the mountain pass?'* although the poem's answer is *'No, no, my son, not yet. . .'*. They are the 'pale, long-visaged company' whose complexion and form prove them superhuman, and by whom the (Irish) reader is invited to swear, in 'Under Ben Bulben'. And Yeats's epitaph, whatever else it may mean, may be the forerunner of the horde's greeting and farewell to the horsemen who will one day descend from Ben Bulben, ride past Drumcliff churchyard and thunder across Ireland to impose rule of kindred upon Dublin and, no doubt, Leinster House itself.

2
The Blueshirt Episode and its Background

It is well known that Yeats was associated for a time with the Blueshirts, an Irish political movement which was at least superficially fascist, and which Yeats believed was fundamentally fascist. There are good reasons for not considering this episode especially significant. First, it was contemporaneous with other extravagant episodes – the Steinach operation, the collaboration with Shri Purohit Swami, the sponsorship of Margot Ruddock – the meaning of which seems to lie in their very extravagance, in their keeping with Yeats's wish, expressed in a poem of the time, to avoid 'all that makes a wise old man' that he might seem a 'foolish, passionate man'.[1] Second, the episode lasted less than a year, and Yeats ended by publicly dissociating himself from the movement. Third, the Blueshirts themselves enjoyed only a 'brief period of vigour', according to one of their founders,[2] their main accomplishment being their 'adding colour to the drabness of life in the 1930s', as historian John Murphy has wittily noted.[3] Since, however, Yeats was perhaps the greatest poet of his time, and fascism perhaps the most potent political force between the wars, so potent as to loom in our arguments and nightmares down to the present day, the episode is bound to interest us and provoke us to speculation. What did Yeats think fascism was? What attracted him to the Blueshirts? Why did he fall away from them?

In the summer of 1933, when Yeats's enthusiasm for the Blueshirts had reached its highest point, he promised to write some marching songs for them. Events moved so quickly that by the following year, when the songs were published by the Cuala Press in *The King of the Great Clock Tower*, Yeats wrote of his involvement in the past tense: 'Because a friend belonging to a political party wherewith I had once some loose associations, told me that it had, or was about to have, or might be persuaded to have, some such aim as mine, I wrote these songs.' It had turned out that the party neither 'would nor could' have such an aim.[4]

Yeats had expressed that aim plainly and succinctly some months earlier in the note that had accompanied the songs when published in the *Spectator*: 'In politics I have but one passion and one thought, rancour against all who, except under the most dire necessity, disturb public order, a conviction that public order cannot long persist without the rule of educated and able men.'[5] Before we do anything else, we must make clear what Yeats meant by that combination of acquired and inherent qualities, education and ability.

By education Yeats did not mean the attainment of literacy, or any other kind of conventional schooling, and he by no means meant the strict religious training which prevailed in Ireland, and which he held in particular disesteem.[6] He meant instead what he at various times called 'memories and habits of thought', 'inherited culture' or 'tradition' – a sense of the past wed to a sense of place. Folk tales and folk wisdom provided this kind of education, scholarly or artistic training and toil gave a semblance of it, but it took the form best suited for future governors in the intellectual training that accompanied an aristocratic upbringing. The 'gifts that govern men' were best learned on 'a spot where on the founders lived and died', where 'none has reigned that lacked a name and fame', where 'wings have memory of wings', among 'Beloved books that famous hands have bound, / Old marble heads, old pictures everywhere' and 'Thoughts long knitted into a single thought', to quote from three of Yeats's poems about Coole.[7] The words chosen – 'founders', 'memory', 'old', 'long knitted' – indicate that the greatest value of this kind of education is the continuity it forms with the past.

The newly powerful urban middle class of Ireland, 'who had risen above the traditions of the countryman, without acquiring those of cultivated life or even educating themselves',[8] had lost or wished to appear to have lost this continuity with its past, and accordingly its culture was a hastily concocted thing, an aping of the ephemera of materialist, sentimental England.[9] It was out of ignorance, Yeats thought, that this class mounted its opposition to Synge's plays,[10] and this assumption led him to ask that class to defer to the judgment of the leisured class in matters of art. 'The more an age is busy with temporary things, the more must it look for leadership in matters of art to men and women whose business or whose leisure has made the great writers of the world their habitual company,' he wrote in 1904, and in 1906, become

more combative, he wrote that if in the present century 'a man
has fine taste he has either been born to leisure and opportunity
or has in him an energy that is genius'.[11] By 1909, the fall from
power of the cultured and the rise to power of the uncultured
seemed to Yeats potentially disastrous not only for Irish art, but
for Ireland the nation. In two journal entries of that year he
blamed the nationalist movement's fall into impotent hatred on
inadequate education:

> All empty souls tend to extreme opinion. It is only in those who
> have built up a rich world of memories and habits of thought
> that extreme opinions affront the sense of probability.
> Propositions, for instance, which set all the truth upon one side
> can only enter rich minds to dislocate and strain, if they can
> enter at all, and sooner or later the mind expels them by
> instinct.[12]

> Ireland has grown sterile, because power has passed to men
> who lack the training which requires a certain amount of wealth
> to ensure continuity from generation to generation, and to free
> the mind in part from other tasks. . . . For without culture or
> holiness, which are always the gift of a very few, a man may
> renounce wealth or any other external thing, but he cannot
> renounce hatred, envy, jealousy, revenge.[13]

Again, the words – 'memories', 'continuity', in an unquoted
sentence of the second passage 'inherited culture' – indicate that
the education Yeats desired in Ireland's governors was that which
became peculiarly possible when government was a family
tradition. Years later Yeats discovered Burke, who had 'restored
to political thought its sense of history' and had proved 'the State
was a tree, no mechanism to be pulled in pieces and put up
again, but an oak tree that had grown through centuries',[14] and
asked that Burke be made part of every young Irish person's
education. As Yeats was to show in a famous poem written about
the time of his discovery of Burke, the image of the tree embodies
the unfathomable interdependence and unity of past, present and
future. No nation could manage well without some sense of that
interdependence and unity, Yeats thought, and no other section
of the people had acquired that sense, learned that lesson, so
thoroughly as had the landed aristocracy.

The particular ability Yeats desired of Irish governors he also thought of as ordinarily, though not exclusively, an aristocratic gift. Its nature is pointed to in a passage of Swift that struck Yeats with especial force when he came across it in 1930:

> . . . I should think that the Saying, *Vox Populi, Vox Dei*, ought to be understood of the Universal Bent and Current of a People; not the *bare Majority* of a few Representatives; which is often procured by *little Arts*, and great Industry and Applications; wherein those, who engage in the Pursuits of Malice and Revenge, are much more sedulous than those who would prevent them.[15]

Certain men, Yeats thought, possessed the ability to judge and act quickly and rightly without becoming bogged in doubt and without having to consult an authority external to themselves. This ability was the mark of an aristocrat. Just as Yeats came to value aristocratic education in seeing its regard for art, so he came to value aristocratic judgment in the person of Sir Hugh Lane, a nephew of Lady Gregory. Yeats said of Lane in a 1906 interview: 'He has a miraculous instinct for a picture. . . . The selection of picture is just as much a matter of individual power, of individual creative impulse as the teaching of painting.'[16] As Lane seemed able to judge artistic merit more quickly and more accurately than a scholar or expert, and had no need to consult a Berenson as an American tycoon would, so John Shawe-Taylor, another of Lady Gregory's nephews, seemed to know instinctively the nation's mind on the question of land reform without consulting an opinion poll, and seemingly before the nation itself knew what it wanted. Yeats wrote of him in 1911:

> He had made his swift calculation, probably he could not have told the reason for it: a decision had arisen out of his instinct. . . . He had, as men of his type have often, given an expression to the hidden popular desires; and the expression of the hidden is the daring of the mind. When he had spoken, so many others spoke that the thing was taken out of the mouths of the leaders; it was as though some power deeper than our daily thought had spoken, and men recognised that common instinct, that common sense which is genius.[17]

'Impetuous men' Yeats called Lane and Shawe-Taylor in 'Coole Park, 1929',[18] conveying by that adjective the 'energy of swift decision' and 'power of sudden action, as if their whole body were their brain',[19] that both men possessed. 'In Memory of Major Robert Gregory' praises its subject for this same quick, apparently effortless mastery of whatever he turned his hand to. Yeats believed it wiser to found the state on the few individuals who possessed this instinct and ability, 'who through the possession of hereditary wealth, or great personal gifts, have come to identify their lives with the life of the State',[20] than to found it on what Swift called 'the bare Majority of a few Representatives', and so argued in his 'Introduction' to his play about Swift, *The Words Upon the Windowpane*, in the passages we discussed in the last chapter. 'The will of the State,' Yeats declared, 'must always, whether interpreted by Burke or Marx, find expression through some governing class or company of men identified with that "bent and current" . . . .'.[21] Yeats desired of that class or company that they be trained for the exercise of power as part of a long-held family tradition, and be able, simply by consulting their own minds, to decide quickly and rightly what would best serve the nation's good.

That Yeats believed that in Ireland the ideal governing class would be that small part of the Anglo-Irish aristocracy typified by Lady Gregory's family has raised the suspicion that he was simply a reactionary snob. Was Yeats dazzled by the superficial glory of a class that was, in fact, wasteful, parasitical, based upon injustice? For all Yeats's immense admiration for such external shows as Georgian fronts, handsome bindings and fine manners, his respect for aristocracy and his belief in the aristocratic temperament's ability to govern were more deeply founded than that. What particularly marked that temperament was the freedom it enjoyed. This included freedom from economic necessity – we have already seen Yeats refer to the 'certain amount of wealth' necessary to provide education and 'to free the mind in part from other tasks'. It included also freedom from various everyday fears – fear of drawing upon oneself the judgment of one's neighbours or the denunciation of the priest, fear of losing business, fear of betraying one's origins, fear of unpopularity, the whole cumulative burden of small insecurities that created the hesitancy, defensiveness and perpetual embarrassment of the middle class temperament. As we saw in the previous chapter, Yeats decided as early as 1904 that the average man was average 'because he has not attained to freedom',[22] and blamed the decay of the nationalist movement on its leadership having passed to 'small shopkeepers, to clerks, to that very class who had seemed to John O'Leary so ready to bend to the power of others, . . . who because of their poverty, their ignorance, their superstitious piety, are much subject to all kinds of fear'.[23] The aristocratic temperament did not suffer under the necessities that made the ordinary temperament bend to needs from outside itself. Its education, for that reason, need not narrow horizons, as Yeats thought much Irish Catholic education did, or attempt to kick over the traces of its origins as middle-class self-improvement did, or rest on the assumption that 'the Past is criminal', to use Yeats's phrase about popular Marxism. For the same reason, it did not feel compelled to defer to outside authority in reaching a judgment; its own judgment sufficed. This freedom was not, however, license to run riot (though Yeats was ready to admire certain graceful species of running riot), but the mind's opportunity to choose and obey its own discipline. Yeats wrote of this freedom and this choice in 'An Irish Airman Foresees his Death':

> Nor law, nor duty bade me fight,
> Nor public men, nor cheering crowds,
> A lonely impulse of delight
> Drove to this tumult in the clouds. . . .[24]

Writing of Lady Gregory, Yeats said that 'a choice constantly renewed in solitude', not 'duty as the word is generally understood', had shaped her life.[25] He wrote elsewhere that 'ecstasy' was 'some fulfilment of the soul in itself, some slow or sudden expansion of it like an overflowing well',[26] and all these strands – freedom, choice, the soul's fulfilment and rushing water – joint together in the opening stanza of 'Ancestral Houses':

> Surely among a rich man's flowering lawns,
> Amid the rustle of his planted hills,
> Life overflows without ambitious pains;
> And rains down life until the basin spills,
> And mounts more dizzy high the more it rains
> As though to choose whatever shape it wills
> And never stoop to a mechanical
> Or servile shape, at others' beck and call.[27]

Although the second stanza owns that at our moment in history 'some marvelous empty sea-shell', not a fountain, best 'shadows the inherited glory of the rich', the introductory 'surely' retains its force: if such freedom is at all possible in this life, in this and only in this sphere is it possible.

Aristocratic education and ability mattered in government, but what peculiarly mattered was aristocratic independence, which made full use of education and ability possible. Swift's age believed, Yeats claimed, that the governing company of men who were a nation's 'bent and current' must 'be placed by wealth above fear and toil, though Swift thought every properly conducted State must limit the amount of wealth the individual could possess'.[28] Fear and necessity – any imposed, rather than chosen, obligation – would but misdirect the current as certainly as it would clog the fountain. It was 'the independence from class and family' interests that Shawe-Taylor had found at Coole that enabled him to act as he did to solve the land question, Yeats wrote in 'The Stirring of the Bones'.[29] Campaigning for Major Bryan Cooper in 1923, Yeats said that Ireland needed 'men of intellect, men not subservient to anyone; men free, and peculiarly free, as Major Cooper was, from all differences on industry and labour'.[30] In a democracy, on the other hand, leaders were constantly prey to fear and necessity: the necessity of winning and retaining the approval of a 'bare majority', the fear of losing it. To Yeats, this did not seem a safeguard of liberty or justice. At its worst, it encouraged outright lying and manipulation by unscrupulous power-seekers who lacked (as he wrote in 1903 apropos of certain Irish nationalists) 'the sincerity and precision of those Russian revolutionists that Kropotkin and Stepniak tell us of, men who would never use an argument to convince others which would not convince themselves, who would not make a mob drunk with a passion they could not share . . .'.[31] At best, it encouraged hypocrisy like that of Gladstone, who 'was in his private life, what he could not be in his public, a tolerant man of the world', who was 'charmed' by 'a well-known courtesan' introduced to him by Yeats's acquaintance Wilfrid Blunt, yet abandoned Parnell during the O'Shea divorce case for fear of alienating the less-tolerant voters. So were they all who abandoned Parnell, 'all tolerant men of the world', but 'all were caught in that public insincerity which was about to bring such discredit upon democracy. All over the world men are turning to Dictators,

Communist or Fascist. Who can keep company with the Goddess Astrea if both his eyes are upon the brindled cat?'[32] Or, to phrase the question unmetaphorically, how can one be both just and popular? 'Try to be popular and you think another man's thought, sink into that slow, slothful, inanimate, semi-hypocritical thinking Dante symbolised by hood and cloaks of lead,' Yeats wrote near the end of his life.[33]

In his career as a public man he had occasionally so sunk himself, and for that reason felt keenly how self-defeating it was. Of his withdrawal from his nationalist activities of the nineties, he wrote in 1907:

> All the while I worked with this idea [of re-establishing 'the old, confident, joyous world' of ancient Ireland], founding societies that became quickly or slowly everything I despised, one part of me looked on, mischievous and mocking, and the other part spoke words which were more and more unreal, as the attitude of mind became more and more strained and difficult.[34]

As a Senator, too, Yeats felt he had sometimes, wishing to persuade, paid lip service to 'abstractions' he did not really believe: 'I spoke in the Irish Senate on the Catholic refusal of divorce and assumed that all lovers who ignored priest or registrar were immoral; upon education, and assumed that everybody who could not read the newspaper was a poor degraded creature . . .'.[35] The men in Irish life Yeats most admired were those who ignored the shifts of public opinion and founded their persuasiveness and authority instead on their 'solitude', their self-possession, on the discipline they had set themselves and lived by: Parnell as Yeats imagined him, John O'Leary, who 'alone had personality, a point of view not made for the crowd's sake, but for self-expression',[36] and Kevin O'Higgins, who was not dissuaded from the course of government he thought right even by the threat, eventually fulfilled, of assassination.[37]

'Everyday I notice some new analogy between the long-established life of the well-born and the artist's life,' Yeats wrote in his journal in 1909,[38] and the most important of these analogies concerned freedom. A work succeeds when it chooses its own shape, obeys its own discipline. Yeats sometimes suggests this analogy by writing of art in the same terms he used in writing of aristocratic temperament: 'This moment [when a country's "character expresses itself through some group of painters, writers, or musicians"] is impossible until public opinion is ready to welcome in the mind of the artist a power, little affected by external things, being self-contained, self-created, self-sufficing, the seed of character.'[39] This recalls not only the opening stanza of 'Ancestral Houses', but more particularly the Yeatsian version of the aristocratic temperament in the ninth stanza of 'A Prayer for My Daughter'. Sometimes, Yeats writes as if artistic creation and aristocratic life are not just analogous, but variations in different spheres on the one phenomenon: 'In life courtesy and self-possession, and in the arts style, are the sensible impressions of the free mind, for both arise out of a deliberate shaping of all things. . . .'[40] Yet Yeats did not confine to discussion of art and politics this distinction between the will that freely chooses its own shape and the will that out of necessity takes on an imposed shape. This distinction also had a spiritual aspect. 'I am always, in all I do,' he wrote in 1930, 'driven to a moment which is the realisation of myself as unique and free, or to a moment which is the surrender to God of all that I am.'[41] This distinction, with the element of externality and internality emphasised, is the distinction between 'antithetical' and 'primary' in *A Vision*. 'Antithetical', Yeats writes when first defining the terms, has to do with 'our inner world of desire and imagination', 'primary' with 'that which is external to the mind', with 'outward things and events'.[42] When the soul forms itself, welling up out of the inner world of desire and imagination into a fountain that chooses what shape it wills, it is participating in the 'antithetical'. When an external force constrains it to obey a necessity not its own, it participates in the 'primary'. So, aristocratic government, in which leaders govern mainly by consulting their own minds, has an 'antithetical' character; democratic government, in which leaders recognise and submit to the authority of a majority, a 'primary' character. Yeats makes no such argument himself, but we may infer some such train of ideas from the two short sentences Yeats titled 'The Two Conditions': '*Primary* means democratic. *Antithetical* means aristocratic'.[43]

Yeats takes up the political aspect of *A Vision*'s central dichotomy again later in the book when describing the differences between 'primary' and 'antithetical' historical eras:

A *primary* dispensation looking beyond itself towards a

transcendent power is dogmatic, levelling, unifying, feminine, humane, peace its means and end; an *antithetical* dispensation obeys imminent power, is expressive, hierarchical, multiple, masculine, harsh, surgical.[44]

'Dogmatic' suggests the religious or moral genius, 'expressive' the artistic. 'Levelling' and 'unifying' point to conformity, enforced mediocrity, the founding of the state on the average citizen. 'Hierarchical' and 'multiple' point to the opposite, the varied efforts of unique souls harmonised through social subordination, the founding of the state on those extraordinary citizens who live by the severest self-imposed disciplines. The last three pairs of terms indicate where Yeats's aristocratic-'antithetical' bias, given the times in which he lived, begins to resemble fascism. Perhaps most telling is the counterposition of 'peace its means and end' with 'surgical'. Yeats did not always insist on this last part of the distinction. For instance, in the second and third stanzas of 'I See Phantoms of Hatred and of the Heart's Fullness and of the Coming Emptiness', Yeats gives a different version of the social dimension of the two terms. In the second stanza, following an old legend, he attributes the French Revolution to secret provocation of the people by the vindictive Knights Templar. The mob, whipped to frenzy by an agent outside themselves, are dogmatic, levelling, wind-driven, feminine perhaps in a Mme DeFarge way, but not humane or peaceful. In the third stanza, Yeats gives a contrasting, 'antithetical' vision:

Their legs long, delicate and slender, aquamarine their eyes,
Magical unicorns bear ladies upon their backs.
The ladies close their musing eyes. No prophecies,
Remembered out of Babylonian almanacs,
Have closed the ladies' eyes,

– that is, nothing immenser than themselves, the primary 'Babylonian mathematical starlight' of *A Vision* –

their minds are but a pool
Where even longing drowns under its own excess;
Nothing but stillness can remain when hearts are full
Of their own sweetness, bodies of their loveliness.[45]

'Self-delighting reverie' Yeats calls it in the next stanza, and its delight, its self-sufficiency, and the image of the pool all mark it as a scene of some ultimate 'antithetical' good. The immediate future, however, will be the time of the 'indifferent multitude' – numbing conformity. Increasingly from the early twenties on, Yeats believed that the world of self-delighting reverie would not be recovered but by violence. This is discernible already in 'Ancestral Houses', which remembers that the house was built by 'some violent bitter man, some powerful man', and asks if the gardens, lawns, chambers and galleries 'But take our greatness with our violence?'.[46] In 1930, musing in his diary over the possibility of a 'kindred' of those 'who preserve tradition' emerging to transform Europe, he asks, 'Can such a kindred once formed escape war? Will it not be war that must prove its strength?'[47] By 1937, when the revised *A Vision* appeared, the 'antithetical' had fully taken on its harsher, severer aspect.

The series of Irish controversies described in the first chapter created in Yeats a dislike of those who manipulated or bowed before public opinion, of those unwilling or unable to think for themselves, that made him distrust democracy, just as his opportunity to observe life at Coole awakened him to the possible advantages of aristocratic government. The opposition we have been describing here between the aristocratic and the democratic, the formed-from-within and the formed-from-without, the 'antithetical' and the 'primary', largely coincides with the opposition described in the previous chapter, that between what were to Yeats the two traditions of Irish patriotism, the Gaelic and Catholic tradition inherited by de Valera and the Anglo-Irish tradition Yeats wished to uphold. They do not coincide perfectly, of course. Yeats assigned Lady Gregory to a 'primary' phase in *A Vision*, and often used the poor, road-wandering countryman as an example of perfect freedom.[48] In the main, however, it was in Protestant Anglo-Ireland that Yeats saw the 'antithetical' life of freedom and full expression of the soul, in Gaelic and Catholic Ireland that he saw the 'primary' life of necessity, fate, the surrender of the soul to a power outside itself.

The 'magnificence' and self-sufficiency that Yeats spoke of in his 1932 lecture 'Modern Ireland' and associated with Parnell,

Lady Gregory and John O'Leary are 'antithetical' virtues, based on freedom from the view that turns utility to necessity and on something born within that spreads outward: Lady Gregory 'sought in the depths of her mind and expressed habitually in all she did and said virtue which Aristotle calls "magnificence, greatness of soul".'[49] By contrast, the urban, Catholic middle-class was hemmed in by necessities brought to bear from outside, such as that of getting a livelihood (labouring for others), that of maintaining propriety (living up to the expectations of others), or that of obeying the church (shaping the soul to please an external and infinitely removed other). Unable to judge for themselves, members of this class relied on 'the newspaper and the pulpit' for their opinions.[50] Even Irish Catholic patriotism struck Yeats as dictated by necessity and characterised by self-surrender, seen at its worst in the eternal necessity of lamenting the past and affixing blame, seen at its noblest in example after example of self-sacrifice and martyrdom. Catholic patriotism seemed acceptance of a fate, submission to a divine yoke laid on one at birth, while the Protestant patriot chose to be so. Suspended between English and Irish loyalties,

> Bound neither to Cause nor to State,
> Neither to slaves that were spat on,
> Nor to the tyrants that spat,

the Protestant patriot 'Gave, though free to refuse'.[51] Great and honourable things came of the 'primary' cast of mind: philanthropy, sanctity, martyrdom. The best government, however, came from men of an 'antithetical' cast of mind, as were, Yeats believed, the men who ruled Ireland in the century before the Act of Union in 1800, that fatal act of submission to a power external to themselves. Yeats did not recommend that the Catholics be once again oppressed, or even, though he may have thought on it, that the Anglo-Irish be again granted the largest share of civil power. He did believe that Ireland's new Gaelic and Catholic governors had to acquire the independence and self-sufficient 'loneliness' of the old Anglo-Irish governors before the nation would prosper materially or spiritually. In 1932 he saw and approved of a transformation of that kind in the Free State Ministers, yet also saw and feared that the transformation might not take: 'The eighteenth-century governing class is still with us, though it [is] now Catholic and sometimes can speak Gaelic, and the second period [that marked by "constitutional agitation and democratic Catholicism"] still fights against it in our blood . . .'.[52]

Yeats also saw the political dimension of the antithetical-primary opposition in the difference between two great Irish historical actors, Daniel O'Connell and Charles Parnell. The 'too-compromised and compromising' O'Connell[53] found his strength without, in the massive popular support he won for himself thanks to (as Yeats thought) sentimentality and insincere rhetoric, not to mention 'invective' and 'unscrupulousness'.[54] 'In his very genius itself,' Yeats said in 1914, 'there was demoralisation, the appeal – as of a tumbler at a fair – to the commonest ear, a grin through a horse-collar.'[55] Parnell found his strength within. Whenever he writes of Parnell, Yeats dwells on his pride, 'loneliness' and self-control. Though head of a popular movement, he refused to make the popular gesture and seemed less a politician than a monarch ruling by virtue of his 'proud, masterful, and practical' nature.[56] Yeats mentioned in his autobiography that Parnell 'had admitted no man to his counsel; that when some member of his party found himself in the same hotel by chance, that member would think to stay there a presumption, and move to some other lodging . . .'.[57] Twice Yeats cited the lament of Joyce's Mr Casey: 'My dead king.'[58] Three times he told the story of how Parnell, having responded with apparent impassivity to an accuser, was discovered to have torn his palms with his nails,[59] and these self-inflicted stigmata gave Parnell the proportions of an 'antithetical' Christ in Yeats's imagination: in *A Vision* Yeats wrote that the man of Phase 10, Parnell's phase, 'may end ambition by the command of multitudes, for he is like that god of Norse mythology who hung from the cliff's side for three days, a sacrifice to himself'.[60] Leadership ought to come, as it did in Parnell's case, from something intuitively known within the self, not from submission to or manipulation of a power without, a 'machine' in Yeatsian phrase, be it logic, a newspaper or matter itself as imagined by 'mechanist' philosophers.[61] Yeats wrote in his 1930 diary:

What idea of the state, what substitute for that toga'd race that ruled the world, will serve our immediate purpose in Ireland? . . .

When I try to make a practical rule I come once more to a

truism – serve nothing from the heart that is not its own evidence, what Blake called 'naked beauty display'd', recognise that the rest is machinery and should [be] used as such. The great men of the eighteenth century were that beauty; Parnell had something of it, O'Leary something, but what have O'Connell and all his seed, breed, and generation but a roaring machine?[62]

Trying to express the difference between these two leaders as concisely as he could, Yeats named O'Connell the 'comedian', Parnell, the 'tragedian'. Yeats first made this distinction in a 1909 journal entry,[63] and returned to it in *The Trembling of the Veil* in 1922: 'I had seen Ireland in my own time turn from the bragging rhetoric and gregarious humour of O'Connell's generation and school, and offer herself to the proud and solitary Parnell as to her anti-self, buskin following hard upon sock. . . .'[64] He used the figure again when writing his 1934 commentary on 'Parnell's Funeral': 'As we discussed and argued, the national character changed, O'Connell the great comedian, left the scene and the tragedian Parnell took his place.'[65] Yeats's figure is more economical than clear, but it is certainly suggestive. Does it mean that O'Connell, who aimed to please the crowd, always had the crowd's affection to fall back on, while the more solitary Parnell, like a tragic hero, was finally stripped of all resources save those he had within himself? Or that O'Connell, to gain power, would promise to bring about a happy ending, whereas Parnell, according to a possibly apocryphal story Yeats put into verse, was capable of saying to a man cheering him, 'Ireland shall get her freedom and you still break stone'? To settle on a definition, let us say 'comic' politics are based on popular appeal and flattering promises, 'tragic' politics on an opposed, Coriolanus-like stance.

The contest of opposites Yeats saw in the Irish political life of his early maturity, and used to interpret Irish history since the Elizabethan wars, was a contest fought not over who would rule Ireland, but over who would rule the nationalist movement. Very early on, he notes in his autobiography, Yeats had the idea that the nationalist movement would fare best if led by a small elite, and wondered if the '98 Commemoration Association might transform itself into 'some few men controlling some form of administration', to which the whole movement, including the Home Rule Irish members at Westminster, would be answerable.[66]

Instead, the movement was 'democratised',[67] and, as we have seen, this change alienated Yeats from the movement for many years. With the end of the Anglo-Irish war, however, the question of who ruled the nationalist movement turned into the question of who would rule Ireland. In Ireland as elsewhere in Europe the old institutions had disintegrated, and no one knew yet what might replace them. Yeats saw his opportunity to argue again on behalf of rule by the educated and able, and took it. In 'If I were Four-and-Twenty', published in 1919, he put before Ireland as persuasively as he could the advantages of maintaining a privileged, hereditary aristocracy. This essay differs from Yeats's earlier defences of aristocracy in its preoccupation with evil and human fallibility, matters which we will have to take up again in the following chapter, and in the authoritarian tone it slips into in its conclusion:

> With Christianity came the realisation that a man must surrender his particular will to an implacable will, not his, though within his, and perhaps we are restless because we approach a realisation that our general will must surrender itself to another will within it, interpreted by certain men, at once economists, patriots, and inquisitors.[68]

In 1922, both the Republicans' rejection of the voter-approved treaty and the Free State's harsh suppression of the Republicans seemed to Yeats proof that the old ideals of liberal democracy had finally dissolved – an idea he put into poetry in 'Nineteen Hundred and Nineteen'. He wrote to Sturge Moore in 1922, 'I wonder how the future of European civilisation will be affected by the rejection of majority rule, first in Russian and now in Ireland. It may lead to a Military Government or at any rate to a powerfully armed Civil Government.'[69] In a letter of the same year to Olivia Shakespear he again compared the Irish Republicans to the Russian Bolsheviks who had 'dissolved the constituent assembly', and saw in the emergent Free State a rejection of democracy of a stabler and sounder kind: 'On the other hand I hear that the Free State party will bring in a constitution especially arranged to give power to the heads of departments as distinguished from politicians, and with a second chamber so arranged as to put power into the hands of able men who could not expect election in the ordinary way.'[70] Later that year, he noted 'everywhere one notices a drift towards Conservatism, perhaps towards Autocracy'.[71] 'Oxford,' he said to Lady Gregory, 'being the home of lost causes is now violently democratic.'[72] By November 1922 he was writing of the change with even more confidence, and felt involved enough in it to use the first person plural:

> We are preparing here, behind our screen of bombs and smoke, a return to conservative politics as elsewhere in Europe. . . . The return will be painful and perhaps violent, but many educated men talk of it and must soon work for it and perhaps riot for it.[73]

In the same letter Yeats mentioned that his old friend George Russell was 'suffering some slight eclipse because of old democratic speeches', while he himself was now finding 'hearers' because 'I have been of the opposite party'. It crossed Yeats's mind that he might now obtain the actual power that he had been shut out of years ago by the democratisation of the nationalist movement. In a 1922 journal entry in the form of an exchange between Hic and Ille, Yeats weighs the possibility of entering public life with the task of imposing form on the revelations that became *A Vision* and seems to conclude that his esoteric text fulfils the greater need, being the map without which the helmsman of the ship of state is directionless, but when offered a seat in the Irish Senate (the aforementioned second chamber of able men), he accepted, according to Hone, 'with alacrity'.[74]

In a 1924 interview with a reporter from the *Irish Times*, Yeats spoke of a movement in Ireland towards 'authoritative government . . . towards the creation of a nation controlled by highly trained intellects':

> Authoritative government is certainly coming, if for no other reason than that the modern State is so complex that it must find some kind of expert government, a government firm enough, tyrannical enough if you will, to spend years in carrying out its plans.[75]

Yeats saw the Senate as potentially just such a body of 'highly trained intellects', 'expert government'. The Senate, created by the treaty to guarantee southern unionists a voice in the new government and at first filled mainly by appointment, actually possessed little real power. It could not initiate legislation, only revise what had been passed by the other house, the Dail; it could not veto legislation passed by the Dail, only delay its enactment by 270 days. Yeats knew of these limitations, but expected the Senate's responsibilities to grow once it had had a chance to prove itself: 'We are a fairly distinguished body, much more so that the lower house, and should get much government into our hands', he wrote to Olivia Shakespear.[76] In his earliest Senate speeches he tended to emphasise that the Senate's authority rested not on its representing the people, but on the knowledge and ability of its members. 'We do not represent constituencies; we are drawn together to represent certain forms of special knowledge, certain special interests', he noted in an early speech in the Senate.[77] He became notorious, indeed, for repeatedly asking that arguable matters be referred to a committee of appointed experts.[78]

To judge from the fullest account Yeats wrote of his experience in the Senate, that contained in a letter to Ezra Pound in 'A Packet for Ezra Pound', he did not live up to his own expectations as a Senator. However, the account also shows that he admired those fellow-Senators he did admire for the same reasons he had admired Parnell, Lady Gregory and John O'Leary: self-sufficiency, self-imposed duty, a sense of connection with the past. The letter begins by advising Pound not to enter the Senate of his country, for Yeats considers himself 'well out of' his. 'Neither you nor I, nor any other of our excitable profession, can match those old lawyers, old bankers, old business men, who, because all habit and memory, have begun to govern the world.'[79] Before we jump to conclusions about the dislike Yeats, a poet, must have felt for lawyers, bankers and business men, we ought to note the words 'habit and memory', the very words ('a rich world of memories and habits of thought') Yeats had used twenty years before to describe the aristocratic mind. As the account continues, we see the same distinction between formed-from-within and formed-from-without that Yeats had previously used to characterise the difference between aristocracy and democracy, the same insistence that the former leads to self-possession and the latter to shrill insincerity:

> They lean over the chair in front and talk as if to half a dozen of their own kind at some board-meeting, and, whether they carry

their point or not, retain moral ascendancy. When a politician follows, his thought shaped by newspaper and public meeting, it is as though somebody recited 'Eugene Aram' as it used to be recited in my youth.

Yeats then relates an anecdote. One day during the Civil War, he was in a Dublin bank when a street battle broke out. No one was allowed to leave the bank, and Yeats was invited to have lunch with the directors. Throughout the lunch he was anxious over the progress of the battle and the safety of the bank, but the bankers 'talked of their ordinary affairs', though 'they had to raise their voices a little as we do when we have selected a restaurant where there is an orchestra'. This is not insensibility, but self-possession in a crisis, Parnell impassive while answering his accusers, Lady Gregory in her last year keeping 'an unmoved face amid great pain',[80] John O'Leary refusing to complain of the treatment he had received as a prisoner of the British. Yeats admits to the sense of failure he felt in being unable to match their 'unperturbed lucidity', to the lack of confidence he felt save when he was speaking of art, which he knew thoroughly, or, embarrassingly enough one supposes, when he was relying on what he had heard people saying.

> Whenever I stood up to speak, no matter how long I had pondered my words, unless I spoke of something that concerned the arts, or upon something that depended not upon precise knowledge but upon public opinion – we writers are public opinion's children though we defy our mother – I was ashamed until shame turned at last, even if I spoke but a few words – my body being somewhat battered by time – into physical pain.[81]

As obvious as Yeats's unhappiness with his own performance as a Senator is his respect for those non-'politician' Senators who seemed to know intuitively how to govern. Had the Senate's power grown as Yeats believed it deserved to, it might have become just such a body of the able and educated as Yeats had been hoping for. Its power did not grow, however, and what was worse, the nominated Senators – the old lawyers, bankers, business men – were gradually replaced by elected Senators. Yeats's last Senate speech touched on his dislike of the change: 'I think we should not lose sight of the simple fact that it is more

desirable and more important to have able men in this House
than to get representative men into this House.'[82] Ten years later,
by which time de Valera had abolished the original Senate, Yeats
expressed the same disappointment more bluntly in *On the Boiler*:

> The thirty men nominated by President Cosgrave were plainly
> the most able and the most educated. . . . As the nominated
> element began to die out – almost all were old men – the Senate
> declined in ability and prestige. In its early days some old
> banker or lawyer would dominate the House, leaning upon the
> back of the chair in front, always speaking with undisturbed
> self-possession as at some table in a board-room. My imagination
> sets up against him some typical elected man, emotional as a
> youthful chimpanzee, hot and vague, always disturbed, always
> hating something or other.[83]

Throughout the twenties, Yeats's interest in authoritarian
government included an interest in Italian fascism. As early as
1922 he considered Italy a possible model for Ireland: 'The Ireland
that reacts from the present disorder is turning its eyes towards
individualist Italy', he wrote to a correspondent in that year.[84] In
1924, after describing to an interviewer the applause that had
greeted Mussolini's promise to 'trample upon the decomposing
body of the Goddess of Liberty' and suggesting that that applause
signalled a change in the climate of European opinion, he
remarked, 'I see the same tendency here in Ireland towards
authoritarian government.'[85] In a speech delivered the same year
which argued that the task of future generations would be 'not
the widening of liberty, but recovery from its errors – the building
up of authority, the restoration of discipline', he again noted
Mussolini's promise and the applause that had greeted it.[86] About
this time Italian education particularly interested him, and he
worked to make the ideas of Mussolini's Minister of Education,
the philosopher Gentile, known in Ireland.[87] What made Yeats
interested in Mussolini? First and most importantly, Mussolini
was ordinarily presented in these years as one who saw and
knew the 'bent and current' of his nation both more quickly and
more clearly than the nation did itself. If Yeats did not pick this
up from his friend Pound, who once wrote that Mussolini's
'authority comes . . . "from right reason" and from the general
fascist conviction that he is more likely to be right than anyone

else is',[88] or from J. S. Barnes, who called Mussolini 'a genius . . . with that medium-like gift of intuitioning and interpreting the vast subconscious ideals of historical Italy dormant in the heart of every true Italian',[89] he might have picked it up from nearly any account of Mussolini written before his alliance with Hitler.[90] Not only did Mussolini seem an 'antithetical' ruler, but he also seemed clear-eyed enough to see and hard-headed enough to employ to his advantage the cruelty, or barbarity, that seemed to have permanently entered European life with the events of 1914–1920. Those events had eroded the myths of progress and revealed us as 'weasels fighting in a hole',[91] and those who ruled in the aftermath of those events had to have a harshness that had seemed vicious and unnecessary only a few years earlier. They had to be 'inquisitors', 'implacable', 'firm', 'tyrannical', even 'surgical', to use the words Yeats was using in these years. Yeats did not think, though, that Ireland would turn to a single figure as Italy had turned to Mussolini. When he first came across the Swift passage on 'bent and current', he noted in his diary that the work in which the passage occurs (*Discourse of the Contests and Dissensions between the Nobles and the Commons in Athens and Rome*) 'might be for us what Vico is to the Italians, had we a thinking nation',[92] that is, it might be the philosophical base of an authoritarian government. Whereas Italy now had a 'government of one man surrounded by just such able assistants as Vico foresaw',[93] however, Ireland would look to a small company, what Swift called 'the Few'.

Thus, when a potentially fascist Irish political movement arose, a movement containing some of the 'ablest ministers'[94] of the government Yeats had worked with in the Senate, at a time when, as we saw in the first chapter, Yeats was particularly anxious over Ireland's future, he was naturally interested in it and inclined to lend it his support.

To move from Yeats's ideal of the able and educated and those individuals and institutions he believed best embodied that ideal to the Blueshirts themselves may prove a disappointment to the reader. The Blueshirts were not a particularly distinguished body, achieved no brilliant success, and by the end seemed almost a Gilbert and Sullivan version of a fascist party – I am thinking of their unlikely salute, 'Hail O'Duffy', and their foolish, ineffectual intervention on Franco's behalf in Spain. For much of 1933, however, they seemed about to transform Ireland, and it was in those months when they were full of untapped potential that Yeats was drawn to them.

The Blueshirts came into being in February 1932 as the Army Comrades Association, a fraternal organisation for veterans who had taken the Free State side in the Civil War.[95] The ACA's birth virtually coincided with the electoral victory, a month later, of Eamon de Valera and Fianna Fail over William T. Cosgrave and Cumann na nGaedheal, a victory which amounted to a reversal of the outcome of the Civil War. De Valera was intent on legally dismantling the Anglo-Irish Treaty over which the war had been fought, and which had been the foundation of the Free State. Naturally, old passions reawakened, as did some of the old violence. The IRA, a legal association once again after the new government suspended the old government's Public Safety Act, began breaking up meetings of Cumann na nGaedheal. Members of the ACA, which had close though unofficial ties to Cumann na nGaedheal, responded by acting as bodyguards and keepers of the peace at party rallies. In the brief but emotional campaign that preceded the national election of January 1933, in which de Valera triumphed again, the ACA and the IRA fought several small-scale battles with sticks and fists.

The *United Irishman*, which served as the Cumann na nGaedheal party organ and as counterweight to de Valera's *Irish Press*, had praised the ACA in the autmn of 1932 as 'sprung from the urgent needs of the hour' and 'representing the best and cleanest elements of the youth',[96] the organisation having by that time decided to admit not only veterans but also the right sort of young men. After de Valera's re-election, the editors seized on the organisation as Ireland's last best hope and grew wilder in their praise and expectations. On 11 February 1933 an article titled 'The Hope of the Future' stated that the ACA was 'going to go fearlessly forward and become the greatest regenerative force in the political life of this country'.[97] A week after that, an editorial, 'The A.C.A.'s New Phase', repeated the theme. On 18 March, a writer expressed his conviction that the ACA, succeeding where others had failed, would restore the Irish language and end Partition.[98] On 24 March, the ACA announced that it had adopted a uniform: blue shirt, black tie and black beret.

For several reasons – the uniform, the salute they later adopted, their praise of Italy, the cult of discipline, hygiene, youth and racial purity that colours their reports of themselves – the Blueshirts were suspected of fascist leanings. They denied this, both at the time and ever after, and most responsible historians dismiss their dress and slogans as the superficial aspect of a movement that was actually an after-effect of the Civil War. We can not simply label the Blueshirts 'fascist'. Still, some members, including some of the leadership, entertained the idea that the Blueshirts could become a non-political, paramilitary group that would dominate Irish public life. Some of these leaders, including Ernest Blythe, the former Cosgrave minister who had arranged the Abbey's state subsidy, consulted Yeats, and Yeats considered the conception fascist even if no one else did. In April 1933, soon after the inauguration of the ACA's 'new phase', he wrote to Olivia Shakespear:

> At the moment I am trying in association with an ex-Cabinet Minister, an eminent lawyer, and a philosopher, to work out a social theory which can be used against Communism in Ireland – what looks like emerging is Fascism modified by religion.[99]

'Fascism modified by religion' probably refers to the idea of the corporate state, the feature both of Mussolini's Italy and of Pope Pius's encyclical *Quadragesimo Anno*. Several articles about the system had recently appeared in the *United Irishman*. It was intended to alleviate class conflict and hatred by replacing horizontal economic associations – labour, management and capital – with vertical associations – workers, managers and owners of a given industry or trade uniting in a common body, as in a medieval guild. Each industrial or vocational organisation would send representatives to a national assembly which would assume the functions of a parliament, so making the nation's government a microcosm of its economic life. A similar idea had occurred to Yeats when a young man,[100] and may well have appealed to him. What probably appealed to him most, however, was not the new movement's complicated parliamentary reform proposals, but its clear anti-democratic bias.

Blueshirt pronouncements took on this bias not long after the organisation adopted its uniform. An article in the *United Irishman* of 15 April had speculated on the possibility of a 'great national

patriotic association', representing the cream of the nation, gaining
veto power over the parliament.[101] In the spring and summer of
1933, such seemed to be the ambition of the Blueshirts, particularly
as expressed by 'Onlooker', a regular columnist in the *United
Irishman*, usually assumed to have been Ernest Blythe. 'Onlooker'
wrote on 10 June:

> As matters are developing in this country I think everyone will
> soon see how ridiculous it is to talk of any party running the
> A.C.A. The A.C.A. will be obliged to run the political parties.[102]

A week later, writing of the younger members of the ACA,
'Onlooker' takes the idea up again:

> They think that all parliaments gabble too much and they are
> not at all sure that the national will can be properly ascertained
> by merely counting heads. They are generally without respect
> for an electoral system which enables men without ability,
> industry, patriotism, or common honesty to become members
> of the Nation's parliament more readily than the best men in
> the community.[103]

One almost senses Yeatsian influence here, both in the echo
(leaden though it is) of the Swift passage and in the assumption
that young Irishmen are always ready to do something new and
dramatic. Two weeks after this, 'Onlooker' calls for the ACA to
set policy in anticipation of the time when it will have 'sufficient
influence over political parties and public opinion'.[104] In mid-
summer of 1933 the ACA underwent a further transformation,
changing its name to the National Guard, naming as its leader
former chief of Irish Free State police Eoin O'Duffy, and
establishing its own newspaper, the *Blueshirt*. In its second issue,
the *Blueshirt* announced that the corporate state would 'bring the
political institutions of the state into harmony with the realities of
national life, rather than the whims and vagaries of the electorate
viewed as an aggregation of street mobs'.[105] Another article in the
same issue declared:

> Democracy, in the short space of a year, has gone mad and
> committed suicide, and a rapid choice between Communism
> and some system with discipline and authority as its first
> principles is facing the young generation here.[106]

This period of confident anti-democratic rhetoric was also the period of Yeats's greatest excitement over the Blueshirts, as documented in a series of letters to Olivia Shakespear. He wrote on 13 July:

> Politics are growing heroic. De Valera has forced political thought to face the most fundamental issues. A fascist opposition is forming behind the scenes should some tragic situation develop. I find myself constantly urging the despotic rule of the educated classes as the only end to our troubles. . . . Our chosen colour is blue, and blue shirts are marching about all over the country, and their organiser tells me that it was my suggestion – a suggestion I have entirely forgotten – that made them select for their flag a red St Patrick's cross on a blue ground – all I can remember is that I have always denounced green and recommended blue. . . .[107]

This letter marks the only time Yeats refers to the Blueshirts using first person plural pronouns, and the last time he writes as if he were actively involved in the group, but in subsequent letters he continues to write of new developments with enthusiasm ('The great secret is out – a convention of blue-shirts – "National Guards" – have received their new leader with the Fascist salute and the new leader announces reform of Parliament as his business'[108]) and sometimes even with intimations that he is somehow at the bottom of it all, the spark that touched off the conflagration. In an August letter he writes, 'Three months ago there seemed not a trace of such a movement and when it did come into existence it had little apparent importance until that romantic dreamer I have described to you pitched on O'Duffy for a leader.'[109] The 'romantic dreamer' is Yeats's friend Captain Dermot MacManus. In a later letter, Yeats writes that MacManus chose O'Duffy with 'his head full of vague Fascism, got probably from me'.[110] As Yeats then saw the movement, O'Duffy had inspired the transformation of the Blueshirts, MacManus had inspired O'Duffy, and he himself, likely as not, had inspired MacManus. Yeats was of course not responsible for the movement itself, but the anti-democratic ideology that was hastily heated up and served in the summer of 1933 may owe something to the influence he had on Blythe and MacManus.

It was Captain MacManus in whose company Yeats could be

seen 'gloating in the Kildare Street Club over the prospects of a really virile fascist Irish State',[111] who wrote the sentence about 'the whims and vagaries of the electorate' quoted above, who brought O'Duffy to meet Yeats, and who served as Yeats's chief liaison with the Blueshirts all through the summer of 1933. Yeats's assessment of him tells us a good deal about Yeats's expectations for the Blueshirts. In a 1933 letter Yeats wrote of him:

> He is an old friend of mine, served in India, is crippled with wounds . . . and therefore dreams an heroic dream. 'We shall be assassinated,' he said, 'but others have been chosen to take our place' – his dream perhaps but possibly not.[112]

In a 1935 letter to Margo Ruddock Yeats gave a fuller account:

> . . . I invited yet another guest to dine, a lame ex-British officer and Free-State general. His wound had given him my inhibition and several others. He had cured himself by Oriental meditations. Every morning he stands before his mirror and commands himself to become more positive, more masculine, more independent of the feelings of others. Six months ago he was ordered off the hunting field by a political enemy. He turned his horse and rode the man down. If he goes on with those meditations he will be murdered.[113]

In all that Yeats chooses to tell his correspondents of Captain MacManus – his heroism (born of an inward 'dream'), his self-imposed discipline, his willingness to risk death, his recklessness, even his horsemanship – we see the signs of the 'antithetical' hero. He possessed the virtues, in military cast, that Yeats desired of his company of the educated and able. So long as MacManus represented to Yeats the potential of the Blueshirts, it seemed to him they might indeed change Ireland in the way he hoped.

Compared to MacManus, O'Duffy himself was a disappointment. MacManus brought the Blueshirt leader to meet Yeats in July, 'that I might talk my anti-democratic philosophy', as Yeats said in a letter.[114] To judge from a note on the meeting Yeats left in his journal, Yeats spoke of Swift's 'bent and current' and the laws of history, argued that 'every government is a tyranny that is not government by the educated classes and that the state must be hierarchical throughout', and urged that the Blueshirts not precipitate a crisis, but 'prepare themselves by study to act without hesitation should the crisis arise'.[115] Apparently most of this went over O'Duffy's head, and after the interview, according to MacManus, Yeats declared O'Duffy an 'uneducated lunatic'.[116] To Olivia Shakespear Yeats expressed himself more reservedly and more hopefully. 'I did not think him a great man though a pleasant one, but one never knows, his face and mind may harden or clarify.'[117] The ultimate question, which Yeats posed in a letter of the following month, was whether O'Duffy would form himself from within or be formed from without:

> He seemed to me a plastic man but I could not judge whether he would prove plastic to the opinions of others, obvious political current, or to his own will ('Unity of Being'). The man plastic to his own will is always powerful. The opposite man is like a mechanical toy, lift him from the floor and he can but buzz.[118]

It is arguable whether obeying his own will would have made O'Duffy powerful, but inarguable that he was easily influenced and easily misled and in the event did but buzz. The leading historian of this period has written of him: 'A good police chief, he was a child in politics and, being a vain man with no judgment, was easily betrayed into wild language and false positions.'[119]

The Blueshirts began to run into difficulties in August. They had planned a parade through Dublin in honour of the memories of Arthur Griffith, Michael Collins and Kevin O'Higgins, which was to end in a ceremony on Leinster Lawn, virtually on the government's doorstep. O'Duffy predicted that 20 000 Blueshirts would participate. The planned parade seemed to the government too reminiscent of Mussolini's March on Rome, and de Valera banned the parade and called in armoured cars to ensure that it did not take place. O'Duffy called off the march. A little over a week later, the National Guard was proclaimed an illegal association. Curiously the Blueshirts responded by entering into partisan politics, which they had earlier disdained. They changed their name to 'Young Ireland' and together with Cumann na nGaedheal and the National Centre Party formed a new parliamentary opposition party, Fine Gael. O'Duffy, though not a member of the Dail, was made leader. In a letter of that September to Olivia Shakespear Yeats reports these doings and seems not unhappy with them, but the report begins in an hitherto unheard key: 'I wonder if the English newspapers have given you any idea of our political comedy.' He goes on to chronicle the events under the headings 'Act I', 'Act II' and so on.[120] We can put only so much weight on a single word, but if we recall that a few months earlier he had described the Blueshirts as standing in readiness 'should some tragic situation develop'; and recall as well the distinction he made between Parnell and O'Connell, the word 'comedy' seems significant. Did Yeats take their decision to enter electoral politics as a decision to abide by the old, worn-out rules of liberal democracy rather than invent their own, to play to the crowd, to grin through a horse-collar?

It was at this time, at least, that Yeats began to lose interest. His letters carry no mention of the Blueshirts again until February 1934, and then only by way of embroidering a story of how Mrs Yeats believed a dog belonging to some Blueshirt neighbours to have devoured one of her hens, and the unlikely events that followed. '"Blue shirts" are upholding law, incarnations of public spirit, rioters in the cause of peace, and George hates "Blue shirts"', Yeats explains.[121] The bald tone of this definition – 'incarnations of public spirit' – is sign enough that Yeats no longer took the group entirely seriously, for at the height of his interest he tended to be more guardedly obscure: 'There is so little in our stocking that we are ready at any moment to turn it inside out, and how can we not feel emulous when we see Hitler juggling with his sausage of a stocking', he had written in July.[122] He published the marching songs he had written for the Blueshirts in the *Spectator* of February 1934, and in the note that accompanied them he made plain that the 'mood' in which they had been written had passed, and that the song to which the Blueshirts actually marched, 'that is all about shamrocks and harps or seems all about them', was none of his doing.[123] In the summer of 1934 he wrote the postscript to the 'Commentary on the Three Songs' which we quoted at the beginning of the chapter, in which he said he had been mistaken in thinking the group for which the songs had been written could share 'some such aim' as his. About the same time he wrote the conclusion of 'Parnell's Funeral', with its contemptuous dismissal of O'Duffy and the two leading figures of post-treaty Ireland for failing to live up to the example of the tragedian Parnell, for taking their cues not from their own minds but from the crowd they tried to please:

Had even O'Duffy – but I name no more –
Their school a crowd, his master solitude;
Through Jonathan Swift's dark grove he passed, and there
Plucked bitter wisdom that enriched his blood.[124]

Before we discuss in detail what alienated Yeats from the Blueshirts in particular and Fascism in general, we need to consider some of the previously advanced explanations. Conor Cruise O'Brien has argued that Yeats withdrew from the Blueshirts because, by February 1934, they 'were beginning to look a little silly' and had 'proved a flop'. Yeats, being 'no lover of hopeless causes', severed his ties to the moribund organisation.[125] However persuasive one finds O'Brien's perceptive and informed essay, which twenty years after its writing remains the best single effort on the subject of Yeats's politics, one has to pull up at this. The man who wooed Maud Gonne, tried to revive poetic drama, battled the Irish Catholic Church over divorce, sang the greatness of the vanishing Protestant Ascendancy, wrote 'The Two Titans' at the beginning and 'The Black Tower' at the end of his career, no lover of hopeless causes? Yeats loved hopeless causes to distraction. If the Blueshirts had represented what he wished them to represent, he would have been prouder of his association with them with every setback they suffered. It was in September 1933, when the Blueshirts had arrived as near as they ever would to ordinary political success, and long before they had been embarrassed by name changes, legal squabbles, electoral defeats and O'Duffy's erratic leadership, that Yeats became capable of irony about them.

Many have followed T. R. Henn in arguing that while Yeats, like others of his time, may have thought that 'the discipline of fascist theory might impose order upon a distintegrating world', certainly 'nothing could be farther from Yeats's mind than its violent and suppressive practice'.[126] Yeats's attitude towards political violence was not so simple as this. Certainly, in 'Nineteen Hundred and Nineteen', in 'The Stare's Nest at my Window' and in 'Reprisals' he drew its terrors as well as anyone ever has. However, violence did not make him queasy, he did not believe mankind would ever be able to do without it, and he believed governments could legitimately employ it. He took pains to free

himself of every kind of cant about violence, and so often
appeared to speak of it with unnecessary relish. We can say he
was merely being outrageous when, during the Civil War, he was
asked by an English statesman whether he supported Cosgrave
and answered, 'Oh, I support the gunmen – on both sides.'[127] We
can say he was merely dealing in metaphysics when he startled
an interviewer by picking up Sato's sword, swinging it over his
head, and crying, 'Conflict! More conflict!'[128] We can say he was
merely speaking from a poetic persona when he wrote 'a good
strong cause and blows are delight' or the third section of 'Under
Ben Bulben'.[129] We can even say he was merely fantasising when
he predicted a civil war in the near future between the 'educated
classes' and the 'uneducatable masses', with 'the victory of the
skilful, riding their machines as did the feudal knights their
armoured horses'.[130] At other times, however, he addressed the
problem more plainly and more seriously.

> If human violence is not embodied in our institutions the young
> will not give them their affection, nor the young and old their
> loyalty. A government is legitimate because some instinct has
> compelled us to give it the right to take life in defence of its
> laws and its shores.[131]

So Yeats argued in 1938, and so he had argued in 1930:

> Much of the emotional energy in our civil war came from the
> indignant denial of the right of the State, as at present
> established, to take life in its own defence, whether by arms or
> by process of law, and that right is still denounced by a
> powerful minority. Only when all permit the State to demand
> the voluntary or involuntary sacrifice of its citizens' lives will
> Ireland possess that moral unity to which England, according to
> Coleridge, owes so large a part of its greatness.[132]

Yeats went so far as to base the legitimacy of the Free State not on
(as Free State spokesmen preferred to maintain) its having won a
democratic election, but on its having passed 'the only effective
test: it has been permitted to take life'.[133] That Yeats defended in
principle and practice the Free State's incarceration and execution
of its political enemies by no means implies that he would have
looked tolerantly upon what took place in Germany and Russia. It

does show, though, that we are presumptuous in thinking he must have shared our dislike for the Blueshirts' tactics.

In the 1930s, we ought to remember, people occupied with politics took force and violence for granted, whether their allegiance was to right, left or centre. The liberal E. M. Forster disliked violence intensely, but by 1939 felt compelled to admit that 'all society rests upon force', that force was 'the ultimate reality on this earth', that violence was the 'major partner' in the 'muddled establishment' of human violence and human creativity.[134] When the young Stephen Spender, on first meeting T. S. Eliot, asked for an opinion on 'the future of Western civilisation', Eliot 'indicated . . . there was no future "except" – I remember the phrase because I did not quite understand it – "internecine conflict". I asked him what exactly he meant by this, and he said: "People killing one another in the streets." '[135] In the catalogue of duties dictated by the needs of the hour in 'Spain 1937', Auden included 'the deliberate increase in the chances of death' and 'the conscious acceptance of guilt in the necessary murder' along with 'the expending of powers / On the flat ephemeral pamphlet and the boring meeting'.[136] George Orwell objected to what he considered the intellectual's pose in the matter-of-factness of these lines, saying, 'It could only be written by a person to whom murder is at most a *word*.'[137] Orwell himself, though, in a review of Arthur Koestler's *Spanish Testament*, had written, 'The only apparent alternatives are to smash dwelling houses to powder, blow out human entrails and burn holes in children with lumps of thermite, or to be enslaved by people who are more ready to do these things than you are yourself; as yet no one has suggested a practicable way out.'[138] George Watson, in his *Politics and Literature in Modern Britain*, has gathered example upon example of intelligent leftist Englishmen out-doing each other in steely-eyed pragmatism as they explain the necessity of the Stalinist purges.[139] Yeats was only one of many to conclude that politics could not be divorced from violence, and though he did not encourage the violent tendencies of the Blueshirts, if we are to judge from the advice he gave O'Duffy, it is not likely that those tendencies repelled him. At the time he became interested in the group, it had made what reputation it possessed by cracking heads and was given to boasting of its 'strong hands and stout sticks'.[140] In a letter to Olivia Shakespear Yeats mentions that 'The chance of being shot is raising everybody's spirits enormously.'[141] After he had abandoned his hopes for the Blueshirts, still hoping that some party might yet transform Ireland, he wrote:

> If any Government or party undertake this work it will need force, marching men (the logic of fanaticism, whether in a woman or a mob is drawn from a premise protected by ignorance and therefore irrefutable); it will promise not this or that measure but a discipline, a way of life. . . .[142]

Once again Yeats expresses his preference of the strength derived from obeying a self-created, self-imposed code to the strength derived from obeying the dictates of a 'mechanically' produced argument. Besides that, he says as plainly as possible that the one kind of strength will not triumph over the other without using force. It was not, then, the cracking of heads that did the most to dissuade Yeats from his belief that the Blueshirts were the party of his hopes.

It has been much more pertinently suggested that Yeats ended by detecting a democratic bias in the Blueshirts, by seeing in those who would impose order on the mob the worst traits of the mob – the theme of the short poem 'Church and State'. In 1947, Grattan Freyer wrote that Yeats eventually saw in both Italian and German fascism 'indications of a faith in numbers, an uncritical emphasis on quantity irrespective of quality, even cruder than that which he despised under democracy'.[143] In the 1960s Donald Torchiana made much the same point, with especial reference to the Blueshirts, when he described the differences between Yeats's ideal of a modern Grattan's Parliament and 'the grubby, thick-witted pomposities of over 100 000 marching farmers, firebrands, backwater attorneys, auctioneers, and disgruntled merchants, who looked to an uninspiring megalomaniac for their leadership'.[144] In 1981, Gratten Freyer added that Yeats 'dreamed of the eighteenth-century elitism' and fell away from the Blueshirts when he saw they represented only 'clerical autocracy'.[145] As the way I have approached the topic shows, I too believe this was the case. To say Yeats looked for eighteenth-century virtues in the Blueshirts, however, is to portray him as somewhat more naive than he was. Moreover, it leaves the door open for such mistaken conclusions as those of George Watson, who has written that 'fascism was too vulgar a phenomenon to attract Yeats consistently and for long. Snobbery, that supreme discriminator, always held him back where the fervour of political conviction might have pressed him onwards into final commitment.'[146] Yeats did not begin by thinking fascism a modern version of aristocracy and end by thinking it mob rule. Rather, he began by thinking it the stage succeeding communism in the breaking-up of democracy, and ended by thinking it the last, hysterical constriction of democracy, a finale rather than a prelude. A detailed but sometimes obscure record of how he arrived at his earlier assessment can be found in some notes on politics and history he made in the spring and summer of 1933.[147]

It was at this time that Yeats was trying, supposedly in association with others, 'to work out a social theory which can be used against Communism in Ireland . . .'. The notes take for granted that liberal democracy is no longer practicable and that Ireland and Europe must now choose between the authoritarianism of the left, communism, and that of the right, fascism. The chief difference, Yeats decides, lies in the attitude each takes toward history. In Yeats's understanding of the Hegelian dialectic as interpreted by Marxism, each ruling dispensation gave rise to and eventually was destroyed by a succeeding dispensation which contained all the strengths of its predecessor and wholly new strengths of its own. Each era was characterised by some lack which its successor remedied, creating a slow progression towards the society which would have all and require no successor. To the Marxist, Yeats thought, history was a record of imperfections, and the achievements of past civilisations were to be regarded with some condescension; he sees in the anecdote that Lenin never entered a museum in all his years of exile a logical consequence of Marxist principles. The ravages of the Red Guard and the authority granted to children by the Khmer Rouge would not, presumably, have surprised Yeats either, since one who assumes that only the class that wielded no power in the past, the proletariat, is clear of the past's guilt, might well go on to assume that only those who did not participate at all in the past are wholly innocent. The fascist – Yeats here follows the idea, much current at the time, that Croce's criticism on Hegel formed the philosophical base of the Italian state[148] – sees not a linear succession of classes and eras, each representing an advance over the last, but a continual, cyclical conflict in which a class rises to power, falls before another, then perhaps rises again, waxing and waning in relation to its 'distincts' the same way the 'antithetical' and 'primary' gyres do in *A Vision*. Each class's triumph is temporary, but unique, and later triumphs will differ from it without necessarily improving upon it. As in *A Vision*, the conflict never concludes, never reaches a stasis. Yeats explains this most fully not in these notes, but rather in a note he added to the second edition of *A Vision*:

A similar circular movement fundamental in the works of Giovanni Gentile is, I read somewhere, the half-conscious foundation of the political thought of modern Italy. Individuals and classes complete their personality and sink back to enrich the mass. Governments must, it is held, because all good things have been created by class war, recognise that class war though it may be regulated must never end. It is . . . the converse of Marxian Socialism.[149]

Plainly, Fascist Italy's intuition as to the nature of history (in his 1933 notes, Yeats attributes it not to Gentile, but to Croce) lies much closer to Yeats's own than did the Marxist intuition, and throughout these notes Yeats assumes that fascism, being wiser in its appreciation of the past and its expectations of the future, will everywhere triumph over communism. In Ireland, though, he wished to see the creation of political institutions that would take the fascist idea of history a step further by founding themselves on the human institution that best represented the mysterious totality-in-diversity of past, present and future – by founding themselves, that is, on the family.

Yeats's hope that events would develop in this direction becomes visible, if only dimly, in the schematic outline into which the notes were eventually organised, Yeats's 'Genealogical Tree of Revolution'.[150] Part I of the 'Tree' is a quick and cryptic account of western thought from Nicholas of Cusa to Hegel, and concludes with the statement that Hegel believed he had solved Kant's antinomies and made 'all things transparent to reason'. From the belief that all was transparent to reason grew 'Dialectical Materialism (Karl Marx and School)' and 'Italian Philosophy (influenced by Vico)', which are compared in parts II and III of the 'Tree' by means of two columns of opposed, parallel phrases. According to the first set of opposed phrases, Dialectical Materialism holds that external, material circumstances form the individual, and that change is our outgrowing the errors of the past. Italian philosophy holds that the individual creates his external, material circumstances, and that various past periods are the realisations of possibilities that still exist within us.

(a) Nature creates Spirit.
Brain creates Mind.
Only the reasonable
   should exist.
Evolution.
	(a) Spirit creates Nature.
	Mind creates Brain.
	All that exists is
	   reasonable.
	Platonic reminiscence.

For the Dialectical Materialist, history thus becomes the story of how material circumstances have shaped men and societies, of how men and societies have evolved as each class rose and was defeated by a succeeding, more efficient class. For one who follows Italian philosophy, history becomes the story of how one social possibility came to fruition and receded before the flowering of another possibility. Each past flowering and fruition is a gift to us in the present, one we ought duly to value.

(b) Dialectic as conflict of
   classes.
Each class denied by
   its successor.
History, a struggle for
   food; art, religion, but
   the cries of the hunting
   pack.
	(b) Dialectic rejected.
	Conflicts are between
	   positives ('distincts').
	Civilisation, the rise of
	   classes and their return
	   to the mass bearing their
	   gifts.

Basing his present politics on this view of history, the Dialectical Materialist may think of all institutions as the lingering effect of past errors, hence guilty, worthy of hate, and of his own political party, being new-born, as the only institution free of taint and fit to exercise authority. When the follower of Italian philosophy turns to present politics, his respect for the past and his refusal to see in every opposition one right term and one wrong one keep him from considering his party superior to the institutions that pre-date it and from hate.

(c) The past is criminal.
Hatred justified.
The Party is above the
   State.
	(c) The past is honoured.
	Hatred is condemned.
	The State is above the
	   Party.

The Dialectical Materialist, of course, is a communist, set on levelling what distinctions remain from the corrupt past, and sees as the great agent of our age the class that participated least in the guilt of the past. The follower of Italian philosophy is a fascist, for whom the past and what has been transmitted from the past (art, religion, class, state) have been justified by reason.

(d) Final aim: Communism.   (d) Final aim: Fascism.
Individual, class,   Individual, class, nation
   nations lost in the   a process of the whole.
   whole.

(e) The Proletariat justified,   (e) History, now transparent
   because, having nothing,   parent to reason, justified.
   it can reject all.

Yeats's idea of the fascist corresponds in some obvious ways to his idea of the aristocrat. Like the Yeatsian aristocrat, the Yeatsian fascist is formed from within rather than from without, honours the past, scorns hatred. A fascist society, having arrived by reason at these virtues, would be prepared to honour the inexplicable, unfathomable 'forces' that actually produce society, the family and the individual. This is why he tells Olivia Shakespear, 'We are about to exhaust our last Utopia, the State.'[151] Fascism represents our civilisation's last attempt to construct, by reason, the ideal society. Yeats outlines what must supersede this attempt in Part IV of the 'Tree', titled 'A Race Philosophy'. 'Communism, Fascism are inadequate because society is the struggle of two forces not transparent to reason – the family and the individual.' The world would realise this, and hierarchical society would return, founding itself on the mysteries of birth and ability. Fascism was on the other side of some catastrophe from this realisation and return, but it seemed able to prepare the soil for the change as communism would never be able to. For this reason, Yeats thought it likely to triumph. Yeats can hardly even be said to have endorsed fascism. It excited him because it made a prospect he longed for seem nearer.

Irish fascism, Yeats discovered, could not be made to take the philosophical stance he believed Italian fascism had adopted. There was nothing in it of the completed 'antithetical' personality, whether of the company or the individual. Instead, they seemed too interested in conformity, in letting themselves be moulded. The decision to enter electoral politics signalled a willingness to play to the crowd. O'Duffy was susceptible to any and every influence, particularly (and ominously, so far as Yeats was concerned[152]) clerical influence. The marching Blueshirts sang not Yeats's song about past Irish heroes, but one about harps and shamrocks – that is, gave themselves up to conventional (and, Yeats thought, sterile) patriotism.

His interest in fascism briefly survived his interest in the Blueshirts. This is discernible, for instance, in the 'Commentary on the Three Songs' that signalled the end of his association with the Blueshirts. The commentary describes, with considerable anger, the ruin that has come to Irish art because of the apathy of the upper class, who care 'nothing for Ireland except as a place for sport', and, most of all, the ignorance and ill-will of the 'mob'.[153] By contrast, Italy and Poland, both fascist countries, honour past intellectual achievements and foster present ones. A sentence about Poland is particularly telling: 'Poland is a Catholic nation and some ten years ago inflicted upon the national enemy an overwhelming, world-famous defeat, but its fanaticism, if it has any, thwarts neither science, nor art, nor letters.' Ireland, a Catholic nation that had inflicted defeat upon the national enemy eleven years before, could not claim as much, and the difference lay in mode of government. In Ireland, 'the mob reigned'. Ireland needed a government that would offer 'a discipline, a way of life', and could back that discipline with 'force, marching men'. The Blueshirts had the men, but not the chosen, internal discipline. Elsewhere in Europe, certain of the fascist parties still seemed to hold out such a possibility. In *Wheels and Butterflies*, published, as was the 'Commentary', in 1934, Yeats advised young Dublin intellectuals to consider 'the demand of the black, brown, green, and blue shirts, "Power to the most disciplined"', and 'ask themselves whether D'Annunzio and his terrible drill at Fiume' might not prove as potent a symbol of the power of literature to the coming generation as Shelley's life had been to Yeats's generation.[154] Only fascism, of all Europe's competing ideologies, seemed to recognise the power of those 'antithetical' individuals sufficiently in command of themselves to shape events.

In time, however, the Blueshirts seemed to Yeats more typical of fascism than did D'Annunzio's unlikely adventures as a military commander. It appeared less and less a movement founded upon the self-sufficient few, more and more a way for men to abandon their conscience by losing themselves in something large, powerful and external. Its faith in 'marching men' was too great. As early as 1902, as it happens, Yeats had used 'marching feet' as a figure for the intellectual cowardice that takes refuge by identifying with the mass:

> The thoughts that we find for ourselves are timid and a little secret, but those modern thoughts that we share with large numbers are confident and very insolent. We have little else today, and when we read our newspaper and take up its cry, above all, its cry of hatred, we will not think very carefully, for we hear the marching feet.[155]

In the middle thirties, he summed up what seemed to him the desire of Spender, Auden and Day-Lewis to submerge their own fears and anxieties by losing themselves in the mass of the proletariat with the phrase, 'they want marching feet'.[156] By 1936 Yeats saw in fascism, as in communism, this wish to abandon selfhood by joining a mass. Fascism – despite deceptive initial appearances – represented not the beginning of a new 'antithetical' cycle, but the decadence of the old 'primary' cycle:

> The antithetical is creative, painful – personal – the Primary imitative, happy, general. It is this imitativeness in which there is always happiness, that makes the Movements of our time attract the young. The art and politics of the antithetical age expressed a long maturing tradition and were best practiced by old men. That age has ended in the old political jugglers of liberal Democracy. I insist upon the paradox, that the old age of our civilisation begins with young men marching in step, with the shirts and songs that give our politics an air of sport.[157]

Yeats revised his opinion of fascism considerably in the time between the 'Genealogical Tree of Revolution' and this passage. The fascist of this passage lacks the inward self-sufficiency founded on the idea 'Spirit creates Nature' and has no awareness of the past. Even here, though, Yeats appears to expect fascism to win out over its rivals. It was not what he thought it was, but it seemed likely to outlast communism or democracy. In the conclusion of *A Vision*, he both condemns it as an imposed unity (if, that is, we read the bundle of dry sticks as a parody of the *fasces*, as Elizabeth Cullingford has acutely suggested[158]) and predicts its ascendancy: 'What discords will drive Europe to that artificial unity – only dry or drying sticks can be tied into a bundle – which is the decadence of every civilisation?'[159]

In giving up on fascism, Yeats did not give up the conviction that a nation ought to be led by the educated and able – not the many, nor the elected representatives of the many, but those few who by birth and training were able to govern by living up to their own rather than others' standards. In *On the Boiler* he told Ireland, 'Think first how many able men with public minds the country has . . . and mould your system upon those men.' These individuals, 'whether six or six thousand, are the core of Ireland, are Ireland itself'.[160] Nor did he give up the conviction that sooner or later, probably violently, the few would 'claim again their ancient omens'.[161]

3
Yeats, Socialism and Tragedy

In his later years, despite having been when young a follower of William Morris, Yeats disliked both utopian and Marxian socialism. In the thirties, this dislike placed him as variance with most of his artistic contemporaries. 'The dominance of the Left in universities and literary London was powerfully sensed and widely accepted at the time; and by the end of the decade the Left was often felt to be in total possession,' George Watson has written of the thirties, supporting the generalisation with a remarkable 1940 comment by George Orwell: 'there is now no intelligentsia that is not in some sense "left" '.[1] Many of Yeats's friends and fellow-artists had markedly leftist sympathies: Sean O'Casey, Frank O'Connor, Ethel Mannin, Liam O'Flaherty, Constance Markiewicz and of course Madame MacBride and her daughter. Why did Yeats choose to resist the tide? What did he think socialism was, and why did he dislike it so intensely? The answers to those questions are less apparent in Yeats's scattered remarks on socialism than they are in three decisions he made as an arbiter of the arts: the decision not to produce Sean O'Casey's *The Silver Tassie* at the Abbey, the decision to exclude Wilfred Owen from the *Oxford Book of Modern Verse* and the decision in the same anthology to identify the main movement in contemporary poetry not with Auden, Spender and Day-Lewis, but with W. J. Turner, Herbert Read, Dorothy Wellesley and Oliver St John Gogarty. In these decisions Yeats was not just battling the tide, but, like Cuchulain, hopelessly battling against it, and in all three decisions he is ordinarily accounted to have misjudged. However, by understanding the reasons behind those decisions, we can see how Yeats's antipathy to socialism derived from more than a detestation of levelling and a regret for the vanished aristocratic order, though he greatly detested the one and greatly regretted the other. It derived also from his idea of how the individual should respond to the existence of evil and the suffering it causes, and how evil and suffering should be presented in art, especially tragic art.

Yeats first became acquainted with socialism through William Morris, and in the late 1880s attended some of the debates held by the Socialist League in the stable behind Morris's house. He was personally impressed by Morris, whom he always called 'my chief of men'.[2] Sharing Morris's contempt for the ill-made and Morris's conviction that men's hearts were on the brink of a great and important change for the better, he 'turned socialist because of Morris's lectures and pamphlets'.[3] This political attachment, though his high regard for Morris continued, proved incomplete and temporary. Early in his acquaintance with Morris Yeats had written to Katharine Tynan, 'However, though I think Socialism good work, I am not sure that it is my work.'[4] After a violent argument at one of the debates, in which he had maintained that only religion could truly change men's hearts, and only slowly at that, he stopped attending the League's meetings. To judge from his letters of this time, which concern themselves almost entirely with getting his and other Irish poets' work published, his enthusiasm for socialism never ran high. When he came to write about Morris and the League in his autobiography, he praised Morris, but the other socialists, including Yeats's youthful self, appeared in anecdote after anecdote as vague, hot-headed, impractical eccentrics temporarily brought into alliance by a shared vague, hot-headed and impractical faith in progress. Yeats ends the chapter that covers his socialist phase by describing the argument on religion that brought that phase to an end, and by suggesting that the argument marked the beginning of the end of his own faith in continual human progress, that he 'gradually gave up thinking of and planning for some near sudden change for the better'.[5]

The group's faith in progress stemmed, Yeats thought, from Morris himself, and Morris's optimism stemmed from his having willed himself into innocence, made himself unconscious of evil. In a 1902 essay on Morris, 'The Happiest of Poets', Yeats noted and gently criticised the consistently pre-lapsarian tone of Morris's poetry:

> His poetry often wearies us as the unbroken green of July wearies us, for there is something in us, some bitterness because of the Fall, it may be, that takes a little from the

sweetness of Eve's apple after the first mouthful; but he who did all things gladly and easily, who never knew the curse of labour, found it always as sweet as it was in Eve's mouth.[6]

After some years had passed, Morris's willed innocence seemed to Yeats a graver fault. In his 1919 essay 'If I were Four-and-Twenty' he goes so far as to name this willed innocence as the common characteristic, and the downfall, of most nineteenth-century literature:

> The strength and weight of Shakespeare, of Villon, of Dante, even of Cervantes, come from their preoccupation with evil. In Shelley, in Ruskin, in Wordsworth . . . there is a constant resolution to dwell upon good only; and from this comes their lack of the sense of character, which is defined always by its defects or its incapacity, and their lack of dramatic sense; for them human nature has lost its antagonist. William Morris was and is my chief of men; but how would that strong, rich nature have grasped and held the world had he not denied all that forbade the millennium he longed for?[7]

Yeats makes virtually the same point about Morris in 'Four Years: 1887–1891', a section of his autobiography written, as was the above, soon after the first World War: 'The dream world of Morris was as much the antithesis of daily life as with other men of genius, but he was never conscious of the antithesis and so knew nothing of intellectual suffering.'[8] Taking these passages together, we see that Yeats held the artist responsible for recognising the unbridgeable gap between the imagined ideal and the imperfect real, and for recognising the evil in men, in nature and in himself that creates the gap. This recognition brings with it 'intellectual suffering', but in the greatest art that suffering redeems itself in taking on form. To 'dwell upon good only', as Morris did, or to conceive evil negatively as the absence of good, a wrong to be rectified, as many nineteenth-century writers did, makes art shallow and exhortatory, renders tragic affirmation, what Yeats called tragic joy, impossible. We see also, if we take Morris as Yeats's type and emblem of socialism – a fair enough assumption, since in 'If I were Four-and-Twenty' his name occurs alongside those of Shelley the radical, Ruskin the anti-capitalist, Wordsworth the one-time sympathiser with revolution and (in an unquoted part of the passage) Shaw the Fabian – that Yeats believed socialism blind to all that was evil in men, all that made heaven on earth impossible. Nor did he limit this criticism to utopian socialism. Conceding that Shaw's socialism was more practical than Morris's, he went on to argue that Shaw's politics nonetheless compelled Shaw to deny the evil in human nature, and so led to the 'slightness and shadowiness' of his drama. To the Irish, 'who have faith – whether heathen or Christian – who have believed from our cradle in original sin, and that man lives under a curse, and so must earn his bread with the sweat of his face', Shaw's plays would always seem to be 'blotting out one half of life'.[9] As for Lenin, in whose economics Yeats claimed to notice 'much that I applauded as a boy when Morris was the speaker', Yeats recommended that young Irishmen read instead the entire *Comédie humaine*: 'Balzac is the only modern mind which has made a synthesis comparable to that of Dante', that is, he has understood the part evil plays in human affairs, and so can clear away 'Utopian vapours'.[10]

The 'one half of life' that consisted of evil, suffering and destruction often occupied Yeats's mind in the late 'teens and early twenties. The mass destruction of the First World War, the brutality of the Black and Tan War and the Irish Civil War, the class warfare of the Russian Revolution, all of what he called 'the growing murderousness of the world'[11] had eroded what remained of the nineteenth-century liberal faith in which he had been raised, of his belief in progress and the innate goodness of man. In a 1922 letter to Olivia Shakespear, after describing a Black and Tan atrocity that had occurred near Coole, he wrote, 'I wonder will literature be much changed by that most momentous of events, the return of evil.'[12] He had already insisted, in 'If I were Four-and-Twenty', that literature became slight and shadowy when it refused to admit the persistence of evil, and two years earlier, in *Per Amica Silentia Lunae*, had asked that literature begin to change: 'Neither must we create, by hiding ugliness, a false beauty as our offering to the world. He only can create the greatest imaginable beauty who has endured all imaginable pangs, for only when we have seen and foreseen what we dread shall we be rewarded by that dazzling, unforeseen, wing-footed wanderer.'[13] By the early twenties, what he had previously called 'ugliness' and 'what we dread' was now called the 'Vision of

Evil', an idea that figures largely in *A Vision* and *The Trembling of the Veil*.[14]

Yeats's own response to the 'return of evil' was the great poem 'Nineteen Hundred and Nineteen' (originally published under the title 'Thoughts on the Present State of the World'[15]), which Yeats thought directly contradicted the claims of the socialists: 'I am writing a series of poems. . . . They are not philosophical but simple and passionate, a lamentation over lost peace and lost hope. My own philosophy does not make brighter the prospect, so far as any future we shall live to see is concerned, except that it flouts all socialistic hope if that is a brightening.'[16] Men are not innately good, but 'weasels fighting in a hole'. Progress is not continual, for nothing stands outside 'the circle of the moon / That pitches common things about'.[17] History was cyclical, not linear. War must follow peace, the rule of the few follow the rule of the many, destruction follow creation. Sato's 'changeless sword',[18] presented to Yeats in 1920, symbolised the eternal recurrence of war. 'We do not believe that war is passing away, and we do not believe the world is growing better and better', Yeats said in a 1924 speech, calling such hopes 'our opium dream'. Taking for granted the bankruptcy of the ideal of progress, the speech went on to declare related nineteenth-century ideals – democracy, equality, civil liberty – equally bankrupt, and named the task of the coming generation 'the building up of authority, the restoration of discipline, the discovery of a life sufficiency heroic to live without the opium dream'.[19] When Yeats uses the word 'heroic', we must remember, he has martial bravery not so much in mind as he has the tragic hero, who affirms the value of life while fully conscious of its imperfection, its wrongs, even of the fact that it will inevitably destroy him. A happy ending now out of the question, western civilisation ought to emulate the tragic hero – we should not press such an analogy too far, but it does illustrate what Yeats believed mistaken in socialist thought, and in 1934 he came close to using it himself. Writing of Spengler, Henry Adams and other historians who had insisted that history was cyclical rather than linear, he said that they had 'deepened our sense of tragedy and somewhat checked the naiver among those creeds and parties who push their way to power by flattering our moral hopes'.[20]

Both utopian and Marxian varieties of socialism mistook the nature of evil and suffering, but Yeats held the Marxian variety the more pernicious of the two because it insisted that all societies and civilisations were materially based. Yeats was inclined to believe that the human mind had made the material world by an act of imagination:

> Death and life were not
> Till man made up the whole,
> Made lock, stock and barrel
> Out of his bitter soul,
> Aye, sun and moon and star, all . . .[21]

Marxian socialism, however, ordinarily held that the human mind had been formed by material circumstances, a position exactly the reverse of Yeats's. Yeats would have come across this idea in Harold Laski's *Communism*, a book he had in his library:

Material conditions do not stand still. New markets, new methods, and new raw materials are discovered; organisation, whether of production or distribution, is improved; and the economic system becoming obsolete, a change in its foundations becomes essential. But its essentials are the whole structure of society, its ranks and classes, its laws and form of State, its religious institutions and intellectual systems.[22]

And its art, we might add, though Laski does not. To argue that 'religion, art, philosophy, expressed economic change' was, Yeats thought, to argue that 'the shell secreted the fish'.[23] Man created by expressing an inward idea, not by responding to stimuli. Morris's utopian socialism had at least possessed the advantage of having been born of an inward vision ('. . . his mind was illuminated from within and lifted into prophecy in the full right sense of the word, and he saw the natural things he was alone gifted to see in their perfect form . . .'[24]), but that vision failed as a social idea and was vitiated as an artistic one because it lacked the 'Vision of Evil'. The Marxian social idea failed even more grievously because it not only lacked the vision of evil, but denied the authenticity of vision itself by granting external, material actuality supremacy over immaterial mind. Since, as we shall see later, Yeats thought the autonomy of the mind enabled the individual to accept and even in a way affirm the necessity of evil in earthly life, materialist Marxism did more damage than merely naive utopian socialism. It did further damage by drawing the attention of artists away from what was internally realised to what was externally perceived, so trivialising art. It did still worse damage when, by denying the existence of the immaterial, it legitimised envy, justified hatred. Yeats made this point particularly in a 1919 letter:

> I consider the Marxian criterion of values as in this age the spear-head of materialism and leading to inevitable murder. From that criterion follows the well-known phrase 'Can the bourgeois be innocent?'[25]

In all the artistic controversies we are about to consider, Yeats insisted not only that great art must not pretend that evil and suffering can be finally done away with, but also that it comes first of all from an inner, immaterial inspiration.

In 1921, Yeats condemned Sean O'Casey's *The Crimson in the Tri-Colour* (an early, eventually rejected submission to the Abbey) for its 'loose and vague' dramatic construction and especially for its propagandistic bent, thanks to which 'all truth' was 'considered as inseperable [sic] from spite and hatred'. His critique concluded: 'If Robinson wants to produce it let him do so & be damned to him. My fashion has gone out.'[26] Ill at ease though Yeats was with O'Casey's well-advertised Communist sympathies, he wisely approved of the productions of *Shadow of a Gunman*, *Juno and the Paycock* and *The Plough and the Stars*, plays which proved the Abbey could still provide excellent, controversial new drama and which rescued the theatre financially. O'Casey's next play, *The Silver Tassie* (1928), abandoned Irish themes for a more universal one: the horror of war. Its protagonist, football hero Harry Heegan, is crippled on the Western Front, his life ruined and permanently embittered. The Abbey rejected the play, setting off a controversy that was carried on for months in the Dublin press.[27]

The director whose opinion mattered most, both in the newspaper debate and to O'Casey personally, was Yeats. Yeats wrote O'Casey a long letter at the time of the rejection, detailing what he considered the faults of the play. Chief of these was that

O'Casey, having no first hand experience of the war, had written
out of his 'opinions', had in effect written a 'leading article'.[28]
(Yeats expressed the same point more succinctly in a letter to
Olivia Shakespear in which he called the *Tassie* 'all anti-war
propaganda'.[29]) O'Casey made Yeats's letter public and responded
publicly, declaring that he was profoundly interested in the war
and that all writers, especially the greatest, wrote out of their
beliefs or 'opinions'. O'Casey's letters from this time indicate he
thought all this blather about opinions so much smoke Yeats was
blowing to avoid saying outright that he thought the *Tassie* a bad
play, and bad mainly for its experimental technique.[30] Although
Yeats had no higher praise for the expressionist second act than
that it was 'an interesting technical experiment',[31] there is no
reason to doubt that the anti-war bent of the play was what he
most disliked about it. 'Abstract', a word he routinely applied to
any political opinion he disagreed with, is the word he applies to
the last three acts. The *Tassie* is certainly an anti-war play: O'Casey
wished to 'set down without malice or portly platitude the
shattered enterprise of life to be endured by many of those who,
not understanding the bloody melody of war, went forth to fight,
to die, or to return again with tarnished bodies and complaining
minds', to 'silently show the garlanded horror of war'.[32] Why
would Yeats have objected to such a theme?

Yeats objected to O'Casey's presentation of war's horror because
tragic drama, to him, did not consist in the pain, suffering and
evil to which the protagonist fell victim, but in the inward act by
which the protagonist overcame or affirmed that pain, suffering
and evil and so reached 'tragic joy'. On this point, he often
quoted a remark of Lady Gregory: 'Tragedy must be a joy to the
man who dies.'[33] He might well, though he did not, have quoted
Nietzsche, who had written that 'it is precisely the function of
tragic myth to convince us that even the ugly and discordant is an
artistic game which the will, in the eternal fulness of its joy, plays
with itself'.[34] Yeats sometimes compared this inward act – as he
often did the translation from the incarnate to the eternal[35] – to a
light-giving fire, as if the pain and suffering of tragedy were no
more than sticks of kindling to be consumed in the burning. By
standing in this fire the protagonist came to self-knowledge, and by
emerging from it came into full selfhood, even in death.[36]
Oedipus, Lear, Hamlet and Cleopatra were Yeats's types:

The arts are all the bridal chambers of joy. No tragedy is legitimate unless it leads some great character to his final joy. Polonius may go out wretchedly, but I can hear dance music in 'Absent thee from felicity awhile', or in Hamlet's speech over the dead Ophelia, and what of Cleopatra's last farewells, Lear's rage under the lightning, Oedipus sinking down at the story's end into an earth 'riven' by love?[37]

Harry Heegan, the protagonist of the *Tassie*, never passes beyond self-pity: he exits on the line, 'The Lord hath given and man hath taken away!'[38] Heegan, indeed the entire play, gives way before suffering, rather than consuming it and turning it to light. In his letter to O'Casey, Yeats made just this objection:

> . . . there is no dominating character, no dominating action . . . and your great power of the past has been the creation of some unique character who dominated all about him and was himself a main impulse in some action that filled the play from beginning to end.
>
> The mere greatness of the world war has thwarted you; it has refused to become mere background, and obtrudes itself upon the stage as so much dead wood that will not burn with the dramatic fire. Dramatic action is a fire that must burn up everything but itself; there should be no room in a play for anything that does not belong to it; the whole history of the world must be reduced to wallpaper in front of which the characters must pose and speak.[39]

Yeats is here developing an idea he had described nine years before in an open letter to Lady Gregory titled 'A People's Theatre': Shakespeare 'could only write his best', Yeats then wrote, 'when he wrote of those who controlled the mechanism of life. Had they been controlled by it, intellect and emotion entangled by intricacy and detail could never have mounted to that union which . . . is a conflagration of the whole being.'[40] If a tragedy shows a noble mind mastering even the worst of all possible circumstances and so achieving a terrifying affirming joy, then the *Tassie* does not achieve the tragedy to which it aspires, for it is a play about a victim unable to see past his victimage. That Yeats rejected the play for being unequal to those of Shakespeare and Sophocles may seem unfair to O'Casey, but his doing so also shows how tremendous he thought O'Casey's gift potentially was.

Later in the letter, Yeats's complaint that O'Casey had let the outward circumstances of war overmaster the inward being of his characters allied itself to a complaint that O'Casey had let the outward circumstances of a political conviction overmaster his inward artistic vision.

> Among the things that dramatic action must burn up are the author's opinions; while he is writing he has no business to know anything that is not a portion of that action. Do you suppose for one moment that Shakespeare educated Hamlet and King Lear by telling them what he thought and believed? As I see it, Hamlet and Lear educated Shakespeare, and I have no doubt that in the process of that education he found out that he was an altogether different man to what he thought himself, and had altogether different beliefs.[41]

O'Casey had written his play not from the inside out but from the outside in – he had begun with the conviction that war was a horror wrongly imposed by the few on the many and constructed situation and character to fit that conviction, rather than letting characters and situations arrive at their own particular truth. The play's own voice had been silenced that it might speak what was, to Yeats, a journalist's platitude. by giving itself to a belief that had been warmed in many mouths, by becoming a vehicle for something external it itself, the play lost its uniqueness. Yeats concluded by advising O'Casey to drop his theme entirely and write instead on something 'you have found and no newspaper writer has ever found. What business have we with anything but the unique?'[42] 'Could anything equal the assumption of Zeusian infallibility,' was O'Casey's private reaction to Yeats's attitude,[43] and his resentment is easy to understand. Yeats's advice was given from hard-won knowledge, however, for all through the Abbey's controversial years he had learned the cost of making one's art jump through others' hoops, especially when the hoops disguised themselves as one's own heartfelt convictions.

Yeats sometimes went so far as to say that Irish art characteristically served an inward vision while English art characteristically reflected or served as vehicle for something external to itself. English art followed the philosophy of Bacon,

Newton and Locke, who had argued that the world formed the
mind by material impressions received through the senses.
Irish art followed Berkeley, who had countered his English
contemporaries by claiming that the mind of the perceiver created
the world. Yeats called this table-turning by Berkeley 'the Irish
Salamis', and held that it had created the Irish national intellect.[44]
In his diary, Yeats alluded to the central flaw of the *Tassie* by
saying O'Casey had 'caught the London contagion'.[45] In rejecting
the play, the Abbey directors had been 'biased . . . by the Irish
Salamis':

> The war, as O'Casey has conceived it, is an equivalent for those
> primary qualities brought down by Berkeley's secret society, it
> stands outside the characters, it is not part of their expression.
> . . . The English critics feel differently, to them a theme that
> 'bulks largely in the news' gives dignity to human nature, even
> raises it to international importance. We on the other hand are
> certain that nothing can give dignity to human nature but the
> character and energy of its expression. We do not even ask that
> it shall have dignity so long as it can burn away all that is not
> itself.[46]

The distinctions we have been discussing here, between the
protagonist who is overwhelmed by event and the protagonist
who overcomes event and arrives at complete expression, between
art formed from without and art formed from within, obviously
run parallel to the crucial Yeatsian distinction we discussed in the
second chapter, that between 'antithetical' and 'primary'. As
political faiths went, socialism was 'primary'. In the first place, as
we have already mentioned, it focused on what was material,
actual and external to the self. Yeats traced its descent, as he did
that of English art, to the philosophy of Bacon, Newton and
Locke, which in the form of dialectical materialism had worked
'all the mischief Berkeley foretold'.[47] The influence of Berkeley,
Yeats thought, made (or should have made) Irishmen proof
against not only false forms of tragedy, but also false political
systems. In the second place, the socialist, looking outward to the
want and suffering of others besides himself, will neglect himself,
abandon himself, even sacrifice himself to improve the lot of
those others. Being partly founded on this kind of pity, which
Yeats once said 'is fed by observation instead of experience'[48]

(again distinguishing between outward and inward), socialism has an affinity with Christianity, also categorised by Yeats as 'primary'. Indeed, they seemed to him different manifestations in different historical circumstances of one impulse. The socialist looked beyond himself to the forces of history, as the Christian looked beyond himself to divine power, to impose solutions and right all wrongs. Yeats described a 'primary' historical dispensation as 'dogmatic, levelling' like socialism, 'feminine, humane, peace its means and end' like Christianity.[49] Comparing Christianity to socialism is a commonplace, but Yeats may have been particularly following Nietzsche, who also contrasted the self-fleeing Christian to the self-sufficient (Yeats's 'antithetical') man:

The Christian seeks to *get rid* of himself. *Le moi est toujours haïssable.* – Noble morality, master morality, has, reversely, its roots in a triumphal *self*-affirmation – it is the self-affirming, the self-glorifying of life; it likewise requires sublime symbols and practices, but only 'because its heart is too full'.[50]

The most important part of that self-affirmation was the overcoming of one's own suffering, which Nietzsche called the 'discipline that has produced all the elevations of humanity hitherto'.[51] To wish 'to do away with suffering', out of Christian charity or the desire to establish a perfectly just society, was not only to wish the impossible, but to commit a positive mistake:

The tension of soul in misfortune which communicates to it its energy, its shuddering in view of rack and ruin, its inventiveness and bravery in steadfastly enduring, interpreting, and exploiting misfortune, and whatever depth, mystery, disguise, spirit, artifice, or greatness has been bestowed upon the soul – has it not been bestowed by suffering, through the discipline of great suffering?[52]

Yeats's ideal aristocrats, like his ideal tragic heroes, saw to the bottom of their suffering and somehow reached an inward affirmation in its despite. Hence Yeats found something almost anti-democratic in the tragic sense, something that made its possessors 'hated by journalists and groundlings'.[53] Hence he called Parnell a 'tragedian'.[54] If we consider the *Tassie* controversy with a comprehensive understanding of the 'antithetical'/'primary' dichotomy, we can see that Yeats would have perceived a perfect continuity in O'Casey's socialism, in his having come to socialism through Christianity and in his theme and artistic practice in the *Tassie*.

It is common to mention Yeats's rejection of *The Silver Tassie* together with his exclusion of Wilfred Owen from *The Oxford Book of Modern Verse*. Both O'Casey and Owen emphasise war's horror and portray war's human casualties as innocent victims; the *Tassie* dramatises the same situation described in Owen's 'Disabled'. Taken together, the two decisions reveal not only Yeats's dislike of art that served as vehicle for anti-war ideas, but also his complaint against art that justified itself by claiming to mirror the actual. Yeats believed that an artist who reflected the material and external, rather than expressing the immaterial and internal, thereby surrendered the autonomy of his imagination. Surrendering that autonomy eliminated any chance of a right response to evil: a choice or affirmation that included evil, an affirmation like that of the tragic hero through which the immaterial mind regained its supremacy over the material world.

Yeats's exclusion of Owen tells us also something about Yeats's understanding of socialism. Owen was not an official, publicly-avowed socialist as O'Casey, Spender and Day-Lewis were, though what political sympathies he had were on the side of the poor and underprivileged.[55] By the mid-thirties, however, he had become what Yeats called 'a revered sandwich-board man of the revolution'.[56] Owen's war poems served the left-leaning English poets of the thirties as models for the poetic expression of the hardships of the oppressed. Spender and Day-Lewis in particular praised Owen for his awareness of and responsiveness to the suffering of the many, sometimes with reference to Yeats's apparent aloofness to that suffering.[57] Some, like Edgell Rickword, thought that had Owen lived he would eventually have described the hardships of the working class as eloquently as he had those of his men.[58] Owen's poems served also as a document of the unmitigated brutality of warfare at a time when the English left was particularly interested in promoting peace.[59] Finally, in poems like 'The Parable of the Old Men and the Young', Owen contributed to the idea that in the Great War a whole generation had been wilfully slaughtered by an elder generation that had stayed safely at home, an idea that began to assume considerable weight with the English left in the late twenties and early thirties.[60] So, aside from his poetic merit, Owen's sense of the suffering of the masses, his pacifism and his place as a generational spokesman had combined to make his reputation unassailably high among the left-leaning English literati of the thirties. For this reason, perhaps, Yeats's judgment of Owen ran on a track parallel to those he took in judging the *Tassie* and Auden, Spender and Day-Lewis, and clarifies his opinion of socialism.

It was not the case, however, that Yeats discerned anything like merit in Owen's poetry. Rather, he experienced an immediate and irreversible aversion to it. The Oxford University Press vainly advised him against Owen's exclusion, and Dorothy Wellesley vainly urged that he include at least 'Strange Meeting'.[61] In his letters, Yeats had many hard things to say about Owen's language: 'unworthy of the poet's corner of a country newspaper', 'all blood, dirt & sucked sugar stick', 'clumsy', 'discordant'.[62] In the introduction to the *Oxford Book*, however, he rested his case for exclusion on a phrase formulated from an idea Matthew Arnold had expressed in making another exclusion, that of *Empedocles on Etna* from the 1853 edition of his poems: 'passive suffering is not a theme for poetry'.[63] Some have objected to this dismissal on the grounds that the suffering Owen took for theme was not his own, but that of the men in his command, and that Owen's attitude was not at all passive, but active, engaged, selfless, even Christlike.[64] To understand Yeats's point, though, we must remember that he ordinarily used the word 'passive' (which did not occur in Arnold's 'Preface') in a particular sense, to mean the shaping of mind from without, as in a 'primary' temperament, as opposed to the shaping of experience by mind, as in an 'antithetical' temperament. Yeats used the word this way as early as 1882, coincidentally soon after meeting Morris, in writing to Katharine Tynan: 'And I am anxious to look about me and become passive for a while too. I have woven about me a web of thoughts. I wish to break through it, to see the world again.'[65] Yeats here equates fabricating a personal mythology with being 'active' and being receptive to the outer world with being 'passive', even at a point when he feels he has over-indulged himself in mythologising. Six months later, when the appeal of the actual has paled, he is ready to be 'active' again: 'Indeed' all this last six

months I have grown more and more passive, ever since I
finished "Oisin", and what an eater-up of ideals is passivity, for
everything seems a vision and nothing worth seeking after.'[66] In
one of the charts of *A Vision*, Phase 15, the central 'antithetical'
phase, is labelled 'Unity of Being' since in that phase the self
achieves its truest, most complete expression, and Phase 1, the
corresponding 'primary' phase, is labelled 'Passivity'.[67] Phase 1 is
the phase of perfect receptivity and self-negation, the phase at
which 'mind and body take whatever shape, accept whatever
image is imprinted upon them, transact whatever purpose is
imposed upon them . . .'.[68] The materialist philosophy of Bacon,
Newton and Locke was another form of passivity: 'The mischief
began at the end of the seventeenth century, when man became
passive before a mechanized nature . . .' wrote Yeats in the
introduction to the *Oxford Book*.[69] Marxian socialism, with its
materialist foundation, is also 'passive' in this limited sense.
Owen's passivity, accordingly, lay in the failure of his imagination
to do more, when confronted by suffering, than receive
impressions, than observe and record.

To Yeats, art that did no more than observe and record could
never attain to tragedy, and so fell short of the highest. Yeats
made exactly this point about Owen, in a not too direct way.
Throughout his prose of the thirties, and particularly in his
introduction to the *Oxford Book*, Yeats used the word 'mirror' as
shorthand for art created out of passivity, most often with
reference to Stendhal's definition of the novel as a mirror that
dawdled down the road.[70] In the 'Introduction', he even makes
the broad claim that what 'ailed' post-Romantic literature was its
tendency to be only a mirror, to take whatever shape and image
actuality imposed upon it:

> Or I may dismiss all that ancient history and say it ['the
> mischief'] began when Stendhal described a masterpiece as a
> 'mirror dawdling down a lane'. There are only two long poems
> in Victorian literature that caught public attention; *The Ring and
> the Book* where great intellect analyses the suffering of one
> passive soul, weighs the persecutor's guilt, and *The Idylls of the
> King* where a poetry in itself an exquisite passivity is built about
> an allegory where a characterless king represents the soul. I
> read few modern novels, but I think I am right in saying that in
> every novel that has created an intellectual fashion from

Huysmans's *La Cathédrale* to Ernest Hemingway's *Farewell to Arms*, the chief character is a mirror.[71]

Yeats uses the image of the mirror again when discussing the exclusion of Owen:

> In all the great tragedies, tragedy is a joy to the man who dies; in Greece the tragic chorus danced. When man has withdrawn into the quicksilver at the back of the mirror no great event becomes luminous in his mind; it is no longer possible to write *The Persians*, *Agincourt*, *Chevy Chase*: some blunderer has driven his car on to the wrong side of the road – that is all.[72]

The word 'luminous' takes us back to the very point Yeats had made in his letter to O'Casey through the imagery of fire and burning. Like O'Casey's, Owen's art had only recorded suffering, had been passive before fact. Since mind had surrendered its transforming power, it could never reach the inexpressible cognition Yeats described as illumination or fire, and ended by seeing the necessary consequences of evil as lamentable, unnecessary accidents. In the greatest art – and Yeats includes not only tragedy as it is ordinarily defined, but folk lyrics that looked on human suffering with a kind of strange gaiety modern art seemed incapable of – the mind's transforming power turned suffering to joy, the mirror became a lamp. Yeats saw this quality – though it must be said few others have – in the poetry of Dorothy Wellesley: '. . . that soul must become its own betrayer, its own deliverer, the one activity, the mirror turn lamp'.[73]

Passivity of the mind before actual fact, as we have already noticed in discussing O'Casey, allied itself naturally in Yeats's mind with Christian pity. Christian pity as a response to evil occupies the centre of Owen's work, and lends it much of its peculiar strength. The 'Memoir' by Edmund Blunden which introduces the 1931 edition of Owen's poems that Yeats read when preparing his anthology not only reveals this quality in Owen, but insists upon it. For instance, Blunden quotes the following from a letter of Owen to his mother:

> Already I have comprehended a light which never will filter into the dogma of any national church: namely, that one of Christ's essential commands was: Passivity at any price! Suffer

dishonour and disgrace, but never resort to arms. Be bullied, be outraged, be killed; but do not kill.[74]

Blunden later quotes from an account of Owen by a Mrs Mary Gray, who knew Owen at Craiglockhart Hospital:

> The bond which drew us together was an intense pity for suffering humanity – a need to alleviate it, wherever possible, and an inability to shirk the sharing of it, even when this seemed useless. . . . His sensitiveness, his sympathy were so acute, so profound, that direct personal experience and personal development can hardly be said to have existed for him.[75]

Blunden also quotes another of Owen's letters to his mother, written shortly before he was killed, in which Owen writes that he considers it his duty to observe the sufferings of his men that 'I may speak of them as well as a pleader can'.[76] The 'Memoir' concludes with Owen's famous preface to his poems, containing the lines:

> My subject is War, and the pity of War.
> The Poetry is in the pity.[77]

Yeats's insensitivity to and undervaluation of this quality of Owen has been taken as evidence that 'Yeats knows nothing of humanity, of pity, of humiliation, of suffering or of love'.[78] To Yeats, though, pity and love were not the same thing. In a letter to Dorothy Wellesley on the anger of the reviewers at Owen's exclusion Yeats made exactly this point – 'love is not pity'[79] – but he was only repeating what he had written eleven years earlier, in *A Vision*, about Christ:

> The sacrifice of the 22nd Phase is voluntary and so we say of Him that He was love itself, and yet that part of Him which made Christendom was not love but pity, and not pity for intellectual despair, though the man in Him, being *antithetical* like His age, knew it in the Garden, but *primary* pity, that for the common lot, man's death seeing that He raised Lazarus, sickness seeing the He healed many, sin seeing that He died.
> Love is created and preserved by intellectual analysis, for we

love only that which is unique, and it belongs to contemplation not to action, for we would not change that which we love.[80]

For Yeats, pity seemed almost vampirism, one being enhancing itself by dissolving another: the Lazarus of Yeats's *Calvary* feels that Christ's love, which robs him of the peace of death, is a curse. In contrast to Christ, Yeats wrote in *A Vision*, 'the Good Samaritan discovers himself in the likeness of another, covered with sores and abandoned by thieves upon the roadside, and in that other serves himself. The opposites are gone; he does not need his Lazarus; they do not die the other's life, live the other's death.'[81] Love, as distinct from pity, is the regard one distinct, unique self holds for another because of the other's very uniqueness, requiring neither flight from self nor the usurpation of another self. In so far as Owen's pity was either a species of self-surrender or a fastening on to another's suffering, it would have struck Yeats as something other than love, and as an inadequate response to evil. Natural as it was for Owen to have been moved to pity by the destruction he saw, poems written so exclusively from that emotion could not be great poems. As Yeats wrote to Dorothy Wellesley about Owen, 'There is every excuse for him but none for those who like him.'[82]

At first glance, the war poems Yeats did include in his anthology – Julian Grenfell's 'Into Battle', Herbert Read's 'The End of a War' and Edward Shanks's 'High Germany' – seem to achieve the high end of tragic joy less than they celebrate bloodlust disguised as patriotism, perpetuate the myths of war that Owen exposed as lies.[83] Joseph Cohen has written that 'Yeats was apparently always attracted to the view, broadly conceived, that the only valid military theme for poetry was the *joy of battle* theme, i.e., the ancient, Romantic, exultant glorification by the combatant in his strength in arms and his willingness to sacrifice all, whatever the cause.'[84] Since we now ordinarily think of Owen as the typical Great War poet, and of the horrific contrast between patriotic myth and war's bloody reality as the major theme of the poetry of that war, Yeats's decision to enshrine poetry of a diametrically opposed character may appear wilfully reactionary, even perverse. Yet Yeats's 'joy' was no simple joy, and went past considerations of pride, strength and cause to a complex emotion, born of suffering and achieved by coming to terms with evil, that was the making of a soul. The English officer of Read's 'The End of a

War' moves toward such a clarification near the end of that poem, and his conclusion that suffering somehow makes man's soul recalls Yeats both in thought and language:

> Evil can only to the Reason stand
> in scheme or scope beyond the human mind.
> God seeks the perfect man, planned
> to love him as a friend: our savage fate
> a fire to burn our dross
> to temper us to finer stock
> man emerging in some inconceivèd span
> as something more than remnant of a dream.[85]

Read's English officer reaches this conclusion once the fighting has stopped, but similar revelations may occur when the fighting has only begun, and may come not from 'beyond the human mind', but from a match struck within the mind itself. Knowing that war has nothing in store for him but pain and death, the individual soldier may yet turn his assigned fate into a free choice by an act of the mind and so create a self. So the soldiers in Shanks's 'High Germany', whom the first stanza declares bound for 'the cruel wars / In Low Germany', march off in the second stanza singing, 'We're going to the merry wars / In Low Germany'. So Julian Grenfell's soldier goes gladly into battle. So the 'affable Irregular' in Yeats's own 'The Road at my Door' appears 'cracking jokes of civil war / As though to die by gunshot were / The finest play under the sun'.[86]

'As though' and 'play' deserve notice, suggesting as they do a consciously-chosen role. Yeats had written in 1909:

> There is a relation between discipline and the theatrical sense. If we cannot imagine ourselves as different from what we are and assume that second self, we cannot impose a discipline upon ourselves, though we may accept one from others. Active virtue as distinguished from the passive acceptance of a current code is therefore theatrical, consciously dramatic, the wearing of a mask.[87]

In a subsequent journal entry, Yeats distinguished between the self-expression or self-discovery of this 'active virtue' and the self-knowledge achieved by 'the ideal of culture expressed by Pater' in which 'the soul becomes a mirror not a brazier'.[88] The self generates its own light in cultures like that of the Italian Renaissance, 'founded not on self-knowledge but on knowledge of some other self, Christ or Caesar, not on delicate sincerity but on imitative energy'. 'Sincerity' was a word Yeats came virtually to associate with pacifism, as in *Per Amica Silentia Lunae*, in which if he wonders if modern culture's 'doctrine of sincerity' has 'made us gentle and passive', and decides that the hero wears always that hollow image of desire (the mask, the assumed self) that the artist wears only intermittently.[89]

A soldier's immediate, natural and sincere terror at finding himself in circumstances which dictate that he kill, be killed or both might be wholly transformed, Yeats felt, by the assuming of a second self that embraced those circumstances as something deliberately chosen, an antithesis of one's instinct that paradoxically seemed more one's true self than had that instinct. Yeats's own attempt to place himself imaginatively in the Great War, 'An Irish Airman Foresees His Death', turns on this kind of deliberate choice. The Irish Airman does not see himself as the victim of forces and fates that have compelled him to an early, violent death. Knowing that action in a fallen world includes evil, he still chooses to act, and so freely affirms the accident that threw him into the fallen world. He turns his fate into a free choice, a joyful choice, and makes his soul.[90]

This conjunction of chance and choice occupies dead centre of the antithetical mind. At Phase 15, 'Chance and Choice have become interchangeable without losing their identity'.[91] At that hour, says Owen Aherne in 'The Phases of the Moon', 'all is fed with light and heaven is bare'[92] – the light is not a reflection of divinity, but self-generated, and so the image of the conjunction of chance and choice is fire. In 'Solomon and the Witch', one of several poems produced by the conjunction of chance and choice that was Yeats's marriage, Solomon speaks of the 'cruelties of Choice and Chance':

> Yet the world ends when these two things,
> Though several, are a single light,
> When oil and wick are burned in one . . . .[93]

In the great elegy on the original of the Irish Airman, Robert Gregory's mind and life are compared to a sudden conflagration:

> Some burn damp faggots, others may consume
> The entire combustible world in one small room
> As though dried straw . . . .[94]

When desire and circumstance momentarily coincide for Yeats in the unwarlike setting of 'a crowded London shop', it is as if he too were ablaze:

> While on the shop and street I gazed
> My body of a sudden blazed;
> And twenty minutes more or less
> It seemed, so great my happiness,
> That I was blessed and could bless.[95]

Part of the conjunction of chance and choice at Phase 15 is a final coming to terms with evil. For the 'primary' mind, this coming to terms means sharp grief at how man suffers on earth; for the 'antithetical' mind, it means realising how great is the joy of man's whole incarnate life on earth, including its evil:

Even for the most perfect there is a time of pain, a passage through a vision, where evil reveals itself in its final meaning. In this passage Christ, it is said, mourned over the length of time and the unworthiness of man's lot to man, whereas his forerunner mourned and his successor will mourn over the shortness of time and the unworthiness of man to his lot; but this cannot yet be understood.[96]

The conjunction of chance and choice means that the mind gains ascendancy over the world, even in a way creates the world. For this self-created world to attain more than the tenuousness and fragility of the self-created world of Swift's spider, it must include the vision of evil. Yeats often invoked Swift's spider as an example of what he wished to avoid, as we saw when he referred to *The Wanderings of Oisin* as a 'web'.[97] He nevertheless maintained always that the self made its own world. The 'Vision of Evil' made the difference. The soul progressed from 'The world has proceeded from me' to 'The world is evil' to 'I would not have it otherwise'. We are reminded again of Nietzsche, of his 'yea-saying', of his motto *amor fati*, of the words of Zarathustra: 'To redeem what is past, and to transform every "It was" into "thus would I have it"! – that alone do I call redemption!'[98] All the threads we have tried to gather here – Swift's spider, the deliberate choice of a 'second self' to redeem chance, the affirmation of life without excluding evil – come together in a passage of the autobiography:

> Among subjective men (in all those, that is, who must spin a web out of their own bowels) the victory is an intellectual daily re-creation of all that exterior fate snatches away, and so that fate's antithesis; while what I have called 'the Mask' is an emotional antithesis to all that comes out of their internal nature. We begin to live when we have conceived life as tragedy.[99]

Mind does not gain its right ascendancy over the world, the self does not become complete, until by including its opposite it becomes able to affirm the whole, evil with good, as the Irish Airman does. To stop at grief or to speculate over regaining what ineluctable circumstance had snatched away, as Yeats believed Owen and the socialists did, was a kind of failure.

Yeats saw the editing of the *Oxford Book* as a chance to examine and arrive at an opinion about the poets who, in the years following the war, seemed to represent modernity, the 'Ezra, Eliot, Auden' school.[100] In the work of all three, Yeats eventually decided, the external and material had gained ascendancy over the internal and immaterial. In Eliot's work, particularly the earlier work, poetry had been forbidden to create an imaginary world and had been required instead to register the blemished, undecorated facts of urban life, or so Yeats claimed in his 1936 broadcast on modern poetry: 'Poetry must resemble prose, and both must accept the vocabulary of their time; nor must there be any special subject matter. Tristram and Isoult were not a more suitable theme than Paddington Railway Station.'[101] The selections from Eliot in the *Oxford Book* begin with 'Preludes', as if to buttress this hypothesis. Pound, too, Yeats thought, was more a poet of the actual than a poet of the imaginary, though for Pound the hard lines of the actual had dissolved until only flux was perceptible. The artist in these circumstances was more a 'swimmer' than a mirror, yet even so his art was more a response than a creation. Yeats described Pound's *Draft of XXX Cantos*, along with *Ulysses* and *The Waves*, as 'a deluge of experience breaking over us and within us, melting limits whether of line or tint; man no hard bright mirror dawdling by the dry sticks of a hedge, but a swimmer, or rather the waves themselves. In this new literature . . . as in that which it superseded, man in himself is nothing.'[102] Passivity and objectivity, in the limited Yeatsian sense of those words, prevailed in the arts when Auden and the other young English poets of the thirties began their careers, and Yeats thought passivity and objectivity prevailed in their work as well. Their passivity and objectivity, however, were of a more rarified kind, as we shall see.

Auden, Spender, Day-Lewis and Macneice attracted Yeats's interest because he was always interested in what young writers were doing, because they had already won a considerable reputation as the next important poetic movement and because they afforded him an opportunity to take a reading of the temper of the times. As a school, they impressed Yeats, though he had expected to dislike them. In his introduction to the *Oxford Book*, he called them 'a school which . . . I greatly admire', and said he had read their work 'with some excitement'.[103] Exactly what the source of that excitement was is difficult to tell, for in that section of the 'Introduction' which takes up the new poets Yeats's prose is even more allusive and elliptical than usual:

Many of these poets have called themselves communists, though I find in their work no trace of the recognized communist philosophy, and the practising communist rejects them. The Russian government in 1930 silenced its Mechanists, put Spinoza on his head and claimed him for grandfather; but the men who created the communism of the masses had Stendhal's mirror for a contemporary, believed that religion, art, philosophy expressed economic change, that the shell secreted the fish. Perhaps all that the masses accept is obsolete – the Orangeman beats his drum every Twelfth of July – perhaps fringes, wigs, furbelows, hoops, patches, stocks, Wellington boots start up as armed men; but were a poet sensitive to the best thought of his time [to] accept that belief, when time is restoring the soul's autonomy, it would be as though he had swallowed a stone and kept it in his bowels. None of these men have accepted it, communism is their *Deus ex Machina*, their Santa Claus, their happy ending, but speaking as a poet I prefer tragedy to tragi-comedy.[104]

The question Yeats is apparently addressing through this multiplicity of references is whether or not the poetry of Auden, Spender and the others is antithetical art, in which the mind imposes form on the world, or primary art, in which the world imposes form on the mind. This question naturally leads to the question of what one is to make of these poets' professed communism. 'Recognized communist philosophy', apart from a recent trend to the reverse,[105] had always held that the material world (specifically, the means of production and distribution of wealth) ultimately shaped men's minds and determined culture. This assertion, Yeats thought, obviously hailed from the same era in which art had decided its main purpose was to reflect the actual, to depict how men really lived. Did these poets, professedly communist, accept that supremacy of world over mind, of the material over the immaterial? That conclusion had grown so overwhelmingly popular that it seemed to be common sense, but Yeats thought it obsolete, and popular (he suggests) by reason of its very obsolescence. No poet could 'accept that belief' and write great poetry. The new poets did not accept it. Although their poetic models, Eliot and Owen, were 'objective' in the way Marxism was – Eliot because he had effaced himself the better to record the facts of urban life, Owen because he had effaced himself the better to record others' suffering – the objectivity of the new poets was of another order. Alert to the surrounding, actual world, sensitive to the suffering of the mass of men, they yet responded as individual intellectual beings, retaining a self-consciousness they sometimes wished to be rid of. Yeats's discussion of them begins:

> The years after the war certain poets combined the modern vocabulary, the accurate record of the relevant facts learnt from Eliot, with the sense of suffering of the war poets, that sense of suffering no longer passive, no longer an obsession of the nerves; philosophy had made it all part of the mind.[106]

'We have been gradually approaching this art through that cult of sincerity, that refusal to multiply personality which is characteristic of our time,' he notes, and a page later adds: 'I have read with some excitement poets I had approached with distaste, delighted in their pure spiritual objectivity as in something long foretold.'[107]

When Yeats describes something as 'foretold', most likely it was foretold by the Instructors. He may have discerned in these poets something that reminded him of the pure spiritual objectivity that characterises the culminating phases of the 'primary' gyre as described in *A Vision*. The six phases following the 'Breaking of Strength' at Phase 22 were defined, Yeats wrote, by two different kinds of 'Objectivities': 'From Phase 23 to Phase 25 is Physical Objectivity. From Phase 26 to Phase 28 is Spiritual Objectivity.'[108] In Phase 23 'the external world is 'for the first time studied and mastered for its own sake'.[109] At Phase 24 the self gives itself to 'a code . . . formed from social or historical tradition' to gain 'moral strength', at Phase 25 to 'some social order, some condition of life, some organized belief' that brings with it 'one overwhelming passion'. In the following three phases, though, the self seeks less the actual world, or a code, or a systematised belief than it does something infinitely removed, and the seeking is less social, more personal. These are the phases of the Hunchback, too sensible of the evil that always shadows good to 'pardon' himself or others, who 'stands in the presence of a terrible blinding light, and would, were that possible, be born as worm or mole'[110] – tragic revelation in which the self's annihilation cannot become the self's affirmation – the phases of the saint, of the Fool or 'Child of God', all leading to Phase 1, the phase of 'complete objectivity' in which mind and body become perfectly submissive, 'the final link between the living and more powerful beings'.[111] The desires of the new poets for the relief of human suffering, for stability amid flux, for escape from the contradictions of the self resemble the spiritual longings of these closing 'primary' phases. Their 'refusal to multiply personality', their refusal to find, as Yeatsian soldier and tragic hero do, a second self that freely chooses the evil imposed on the first self, ended by their finding their individual selves inadequate to their circumstances. They adopted communism as a means of salvation from the original sin of their bourgeois origins, as their '*Deus ex Machina*, their Santa Claus, their happy ending', as much as they adopted it out of political or philosophical conviction. They looked for an answer from above and beyond themselves, unlike the tragic hero who found an answer in himself; hence Yeats's remark that he prefers 'tragedy to tragi-comedy'. Yeats concluded that a longing to escape the self and the earth, not communism, defined the school:

> Spender has said that the poetry of belief must supersede that of personality, and it is perhaps a belief shared that has created their intensity, their resemblance; but this belief is not political. If I understand aright this difficult art the contemplation of suffering has compelled them to seek beyond the flux something unchanging, inviolate, that country where no ghost haunts, no beloved lures because it has neither past nor future.[112]

He then quotes the first seven lines of Auden's 'This Lunar Beauty'. He had made the same point about this school, more bluntly, in a letter to Dorothy Wellesley:

> When there is despair, public or private, when settled order seems lost, people look for strength within or without. Auden, Spender, all that seem the new movement *look* for strength in Marxian socialism, or in Major Douglas; they want marching feet.[113]

The socialism of this school of poets, compared to the socialism of a Shaw or a Wells, signalled to Yeats that Europe was a phase or two nearer an era's conclusion.

Yeats may have regarded these poets in this way because, having *A Vision*'s historical scheme in mind, he desired to see them in this way, but his analysis of this school, idiosyncratically couched though it was, was in some ways uncommonly acute. It has become almost commonplace to say, for instance, that Auden, Spender and Day-Lewis made their brand of communism a repository for desires that were not as political and social as they were spiritual and psychological. Samuel Hynes has noted how often these poets assumed that the desired leader would also be a healer, an amalgam of V. I. Lenin and D. H. Lawrence whose righting of society would necessarily involve the curing of individual neuroses.[114] Robin Skelton has noticed the same conjunction of the political and the psychological in the poets of the thirties: 'To some revolutionaries it seemed that, though Marx was God, Freud was his Prophet.'[115] Auden's biographer Humphrey Carpenter has written that the typical landscape of Auden's early poems, with its abandoned mines, closed factories and crumbling pylons, 'soon reveals itself as not really concerned with the present state of the country but with the defective emotional condition of the middle-class intellectual, for which the ruined industrial landscape is a symbol'.[116] Stephen Spender wrote in his autobiography that his politics of the thirties came almost entirely out of his own pity and guilt, and that he sometimes wondered what would become of his politics if he allowed Freudian analysis to remove his guilt.[117] In sum, this group's politics were so bound up with hopes for deliverance from the trials of selfhood that one might argue that Yeats had them pegged. As Yeats mentioned in the long passage quoted above, official communists in England viewed the poet-converts with suspicion.[118]

Even though Yeats concluded that these professedly communist poets were not, properly speaking, communists, his opinion of them is of a piece with his opinion of socialism and communism in general. In his view, Morris, O'Casey, Owen and socialists generally shared the assumption that evil, or whatever the thing was that set the workings of society so horribly askew and caused so much suffering, could be identified, exposed, isolated and eventually eliminated. The reforming impulse born of this assumption caused the individual soul to surrender its autonomy and become diffused in the world outside itself: a thing not necessarily bad in itself, but bound to empty any artist's work. In Auden, Spender, Day-Lewis and perhaps Macneice a greater attention to individual personality had not neutralised the reforming impulse, but instead inspired the hope that the wrong in the personality, like the wrong in society, could be identified, exposed, isolated and eliminated, if possible simultaneously with the wrong in society. Since they looked for a cure for these wrongs to be imposed from somewhere above and beyond themselves, their art also ran the risk of losing the centre that the autonomy of the artist's self could provide. To Yeats, evil was permanent, and the self dealt with it best by retaining its autonomy. Every reformer must sooner or later face the unreformable, and the great test of the imagination was to face the unreformable and remain whole: 'No matter how great a reformer's energy a still greater is required to face, all activities expended in vain, the unreformed.'[119] That greater energy is the energy of the tragic hero, and its object is not flight from the self, but the final making of self. In the above-quoted letter to Dorothy

Wellesley in which Yeats wrote that the new poets looked 'without' for strength, he went on, 'The lasting expression of our time is not this obvious choice but in a sense of something steel-like and cold within the will, something passionate and cold.'[120] This something passionate and cold is what emerges from the 'dramatic fire' Yeats described to O'Casey, what follows the choice made within the mind of the Irish Airman. It is what all the greatest – that is, tragic – art attains, as Yeats claimed in 'A General Introduction for my Work':

> . . . no actress has ever sobbed when she played Cleopatra, even the shallow brain of a producer has never thought of such a thing. The supernatural is present, cold winds blow across our hands, upon our faces, the thermometer falls. . . . There may be in this or that detail painful tragedy, but in the whole work none. . . . Nor is it any different with lyrics, songs, narrative poems . . . imagination must dance, must be carried beyond feeling into the aboriginal ice.[121]

To ask of art that deals with human suffering that it be too deep for tears is asking much. Recall, though, the exacting criterion Yeats set for his own work:

> No longer in Lethean foliage caught
> Begin the preparation for your death
> And from the fortieth winter by that thought
> Test every work of intellect or faith,
> And everything that your own hands have wrought,
> And call those works extravagance of breath
> That are not suited for such men as come
> Proud, open-eyed and laughing to the tomb.[122]

The widespread belief that Auden and the others constituted the genuine poetic movement of the day – a belief that began to spread while they were still undergraduates – may explain why Yeats mounted a countercampaign to promote a different group of poets as the genuine poetic movement of the day. He did this in a small way by championing Edith Sitwell, whose poetry was often ridiculed in the magazines that supported the new poets,[123] and in a larger way by using the *Oxford Book* to exhibit extensively the work of W. J. Turner, Herbert Read, Dorothy Wellesley and

Oliver St John Gogarty, and devoting much of his introduction to establishing these poets as a movement and explaining their importance. Like the Auden group, Turner, Read and Wellesley had moved a step beyond Eliot and Pound, though not in the same direction as had the Auden group. If Eliot mirrored reality, if Pound swam in it, if the Auden group sought to cure or transcend it, Turner, Read and Wellesley thought all reality was created by the mind, believed that 'what we call the solid earth was manufactured by the human mind from unknown raw material'.[124] This 'antithetical' assertion of the power of the mind over actuality was, as we have seen, a precondition of Yeatsian tragic joy. Yeats devotes a section apiece to these poets in this introduction, and the sequence of those sections follows the model of the tragic moment we have been using: the mind takes control of the actual, fire and light follow, and the individual arrives at knowledge and joy.

Section XI of the Introduction, parts of which we quoted in discussing Owen, argues that since the Renaissance, 'with the exception of a brief period between Smart's *Song to David* and the death of Byron, wherein imprisoned man beat on the door' and the less significant exception of the Rhymers' Club, literature has been dominated by copyists of nature, Stendhal's mirror. The section concludes, 'the moment had come for some poet to cry "the flux is in my own mind" '.[125] Section XII begins, 'It was Turner who raised that cry, to gain upon the instant a control of plastic material, a power of emotional construction, Pound has always lacked.'[126] Turner, Yeats explains, abandoned conventional wisdom, refused to let others do his thinking for him, realised the power of his own imagination, and so attained the self-sufficiency of a Renaissance poet: 'I think of him as the first poet to read a mathematical equation, a musical score, a book of verse with an equal understanding . . . .'[127] Yeats admits that Turner's poetry is flawed, but nonetheless considers his poetry a harbinger of an imminent change in the relation of world and mind: 'Generations must pass before man recovers control of event and circumstance; mind has recognized its responsibility, that is all; Turner himself seems the symbol of an incomplete discovery.'[128] Section XIII, which is strikingly brief, deals with Read's 'The Mutations of the Phoenix', a poem not included in the anthology. Yeats offers by way of comment that for Read 'the flux is in the mind, not of it perhaps, but in it', mentions what light signified to Berkeley and to Robert Grosseteste, and concludes with a quotation from the poem, ending with the line, 'Light burns the world in the focus of an eye.'[129] The few sentences of this section offer little to hang interpretation upon, but occurring where they do, they suggest the internal illumination-through-destruction that follows the realisation that all the mind knows of good or evil is somehow of its own making. That illumination takes place in Dorothy Wellesley's work, and there wins through to joy. Section XIV describes how a 'new positive belief has given her, as it gave to Shelley, an uncheckable impulse', with the result, as we have seen, that 'soul must become its own betrayer, its own deliverer, . . . the mirror turn lamp'.[130] Yeats brings this section to a close by comparing his excitement in discovering Turner and Wellesley to his excitement in discovering Dowson, implicitly establishing a tradition that connects the great Romantics, the Rhymers' Club, and his two new discoveries.

Gogarty's case differs from that of Turner, Read and Wellesley because action, not philosophy, brought his soul to self-sufficiency. 'We cannot become philosophic like the English, our lives are too exciting,' said 'a distinguished Irish poet' to Yeats after hearing him read a poem by Turner.[131] In both the *Oxford Book* and his 1936 broadcast on modern poetry Yeats told the story of how Gogarty escaped IRA justice by plunging into the Liffey (in December) and swimming away. By virtue of that self-sufficiency Gogarty sang a 'heroic song'[132] – 'heroic' signifying again not only bravery, but also the heroism of the tragic hero – and so belonged, with the other three, to the 'true poetic movement of our time', which 'is towards some heroic discipline'.[133]

Yeats's conviction that this group of poets formed the 'true poetic movement' of the time appears several times in his correspondence with Dorothy Wellesley. He speaks of her work and Turner's as 'the most typical movement in recent poetry', of her work and his own as 'the main road, the road of naturalness and swiftness and we have thirty centuries upon our side'.[134] He gave much attention to Turner, Read and Wellesley in his 1936 broadcast on modern poetry, attributed their unifying belief (that mind had originally created the earth) to 'something that has got into the air', and left the impression that this something was intimately allied to the turning of Europe's gyres, and would end by establishing these three as the important poets of their time.[135] In Yeats's last prose writings he is less ready to promote particular poets, but in 'Whither?', the concluding section of 'A General Introduction for my Work', he still expected some counter-movement to that of 'the young English poets' to arise, and in *On the Boiler*, he again linked together realistic art, psychological art and art based on socialist 'pity', and blamed the failure of the English tragic drama on the source of all three, English objectivity:

> The English are an objective people; they have no longer a sense of tragedy in their theatre; pity, which is fed by observation instead of experience, has taken its place; their poets are psychological, looking at their own minds from without.[136]

Irish dramatists had accordingly come to dominate the English stage since the Renaissance, and as long as they remained Irish, would continue to do so.

Poetry did not alter its course towards the ancient, imaginative and heroic as Yeats predicted it would, nor have the reputations of Turner, Read or Wellesley, despite Yeats's efforts, surpassed those of Eliot, Owen or Auden. However, one of the greatest of Yeats's own poems, 'Lapis Lazuli', can serve as an example of how the sense of tragedy he missed in O'Casey, Owen and the poets of the twenties and thirties can be achieved in a lyric poem, and of what he held to be the right response to evil, including the greatest evil of war. Evil, the poem argues, neither increases nor diminishes, and our share of it is neither greater nor less than the share suffered by past civilisations. One may seek solutions, but 'the unreformed', that which can never be solved, must eventually be faced. One may feel pity for others, sorrow for oneself, but the noblest response, and the great artist's response, is to accomplish the Irish Airman's choice, to achieve joy by turning the necessity of living as a mortal in a world of evil into something freely chosen.

The poem begins with the declaration of the 'hysterical women' that history having reached its crisis, art must now address the crisis. The hysterical women remind us of the young socialist women who accosted Yeats and other members of the Rhymers' Club at parties and asked their opinion of the latest strike, 'or declared that to paint pictures or write poetry at such a moment was to resemble the fiddler Nero',[137] and they remind us of Maud Gonne, who had no patience with any poetry that did not serve the cause of Irish independence, but they remind us as well of poets like Spender and Day-Lewis, who had also insisted that art, if it were not to be naive or immorally negligent, must address the present crisis. As Samuel Hynes has pointed out, the reference to aerial bombardment makes the women's declaration not merely contemporary, but topical, for the destruction of cities by airplanes was thought the most horrible potentiality of the war that already, in 1936, seemed inevitable.[138] The telescoped reference to William of Orange and Kaiser Wilhelm, on the other hand, suggests that there is nothing new in the destruction of cities, though it may be accomplished in new ways, and that we cannot pretend we will be the first to have to endure it.

The hysterical women having been given their say, the poem turns to a discussion of tragedy – a turn entirely to the point, since to Yeats the suffering and destruction through which tragic characters struggle to reach affirmation were apposite to the suffering and destruction every nation or civilisation must endure. Neither sorrow nor self-pity will answer – Hamlet and Lear do not weep. The self, or the civilisation, must be equal to and encompass its despair, and find in that despair the fire and light discussed so often above:

> All men have aimed at, found and lost;
> Black out; Heaven blazing into the head:
> Tragedy wrought to the uttermost.[139]

'It cannot grow by an inch or an ounce': it is perverse pride to imagine our lot the worst that history has ever tossed out.

The poem then considers civilisations that have previously gone to wrack. The coming aerial bombardment can destroy nothing more precious than the 'handiwork of Callimachus,/Who handled marble as if it were bronze,/Made draperies that seemed to rise/When sea-wind swept the corner'. As he did in 'Nineteen Hundred and Nineteen', Yeats uses the disappearance of the great art objects of antiquity to make the point that even the most admired, most accomplished civilisations fall, and that we have no reason to suppose ours will, or even ought to be, excepted. Again, neither sorrow nor hasty patchings-up will answer. Only tragic affirmation, and the austere joy it inspires, can overcome this loss.

> All things fall and are built again,
> And those that build them again are gay.

Tragic affirmation, the inner decision that chooses mortal, incarnate life with all its accidents, evil, and suffering, is achieved by the imagined Chinamen in the poem's final section. The flaws of the sculpture itself become to the poet the natural catastrophes that have visited the represented mountainside:

> Every discoloration of the stone,
> Every accidental crack or dent,
> Seems a watercourse or avalanche.
> Or lofty slope where it still snows
> Though doubtless plum or cherry branch
> Sweetens the little half-way house
> Those Chinamen climb towards . . .

Starting on 'the mountain and the sky,/On all the tragic scene', the Chinamen reach affirmation. Full of wrong though the world is, they would not have it otherwise: 'Their eyes,/Their ancient, glittering eyes, are gay.' The verb 'sweetens' reminds us of the conclusion of 'A Dialogue of Self and Soul', in which Yeats himself chooses incarnate life with its attendant evils:

> When such as I cast out remorse
> So great a sweetness flows into the breast
> We must laugh and we must sing,
> We are blest by everything,
> Everything we look upon is blest.[140]

In a letter to Dorothy Wellesley that mentioned the lapis lazuli status celebrated in this poem, Yeats described the emotion of the Chinamen as 'the heroic cry in the midst of despair', yet added the qualification, 'But no, I am wrong, the east has its solutions always and therefore knows nothing of tragedy. It is we, not the east, that must raise the heroic cry.'[141] This letter, as it happens, also contains the above-quoted passage about Auden and Spender looking 'without' for strength in 'Marxian socialism'. The Chinamen of the poem, putting aside their Oriental nature for the moment, do not look beyond themselves for strength or for solutions. They have chosen 'the unreformed'. That 'accomplished

fingers begin to play' at this moment calls to mind Yeats's remark
that the tragic sense can inhabit not only drama, but also 'lyrics,
songs, narrative poems': it evidently inhabits the song the
Chinamen hear. The action of fingers on strings calls also to mind
an earlier Yeats poem about loss, loss without hope of recovery,
loss that can be mastered only if the soul turns chance into choice:

> Bred to a harder thing
> Than Triumph, turn away
> And like a laughing string
> Whereon mad fingers play
> Amid a place of stone,
> Be secret and exult,
> Because of all things known
> That is most difficult.[142]

That poem, 'To a Friend whose Work has Come to Nothing', was
addressed to an aristocrat, and so gives us some idea why Yeats
preferred aristocracy to socialism. An aristocrat was bred to a
harder thing than triumph, was not bound to think of history as
Santa Claus, was not obliged to expect a happy ending or to blink
at all that made a happy ending impossible. The aristocrat, like
Parnell, was a 'tragedian'.

4
Yeats and Balzac

'Lionel Johnson held that a man should have read through all good books before he was forty and after that be satisfied with six', Yeats told one of his American lecture audiences in 1932. When asked the inevitable question, he answered that he wanted not six books but six authors, two of whom he had forgotten, and named Shakespeare, Powys Mather's translation of the Arabian Nights, William Morris and Balzac.[1] No other novelist stood so high in Yeats's estimation for so long as did Balzac. While Yeats was still a boy, his father told him 'plots of Balzac novels, using incident of character as an illustration for some profound criticism of life'.[2] He read the *Comédie humaine* through in the years between 1905 and the First World War, and later wrote that this reading had 'changed all my thought'.[3] He re-read most if not all of this gigantic work in the early 1930s, and wrote that Balzac 'has fascinated me as he did thirty years ago. In some ways I see more in him than I did thirty years ago.'[4] His letters and essays of the thirties often reveal this deepened fascination with Balzac. 'I was educated upon Balzac and Shakespeare and cannot go beyond them,' he wrote in a letter of 1932, and in a letter of 1933 he included *Louis Lambert* and *Séraphita* in a list of his 'sacred books'.[5] He devoted one of his last essays entirely to Balzac, and suggested in another late essay devoted to Shelley that Balzac had 'saved' him from Shelley.[6] Even had Yeats refrained from making such testimonials as these, his frequent, usually off-hand allusions to Balzac novels – he cites, exclusive of those novels mentioned solely in his Balzac essay, *La Peau de chagrin*, *Les Comédiens sans le savoir*, *Le Chef d'oeuvre inconnu*, *Cousin Pons*, *Sur Catherine de Médicis*, *L'Illustre Gaudissart*, *Une Ténébreuse Affaire* and *Illusions perdues* – would attest to an intellectual debt to the great French novelist.

What fascinated Yeats most was what he called Balzac's 'philosophy': 'His philosophy interests me almost more than his drama', he wrote to his father in 1908,[7] and by the thirties the qualifying 'almost' was unnecessary. In a 1937 letter to Mrs

Llewelyn Davies he stated more definitely his idea of what Balzac's philosophy was, and suggested the consonance of that philosophy with his own: 'My poetry is generally written out of despair – I have just come out of a particularly black attack. . . . Like Balzac, I see decreasing ability and energy and increasing commonness, and like Balzac I know no one who shares the premises from which I work.'[8] The two resemblances Yeats points to here – one concerned with historical decline and the political consequences of that decline, the other concerned with aesthetic first principles – will govern the following discussion.

As we have already seen, Yeats's assessments of other writers tend to be unorthodox and idiosyncratic, and for that reason we will mainly be discussing 'Yeats's Balzac', an entity who lies at some remove from the main current of Balzacian scholarship and criticism. The two aspects of Balzac which appealed to Yeats – Balzac the legitimist, propagandist for throne, altar and primogeniture, and Balzac the Swendenborgian, author of *Louis Lambert* and *Séraphita* – are ordinarily considered unlikely and even unbecoming excrescences of Balzac's major achievement.[9] Balzac's Marxist critics, naturally, have taken the political aspect seriously, but an old and influential tradition in Marxist criticism, begun by Engels and carried forward by Georg Lukács and Fredric Jameson, discounts Balzac's professed political opinions and maintains that in the novels the relentlessly truthful analyst triumphs over the partisan and presents honestly and accurately the exhaustion of the nobility, the rapacity of the bourgeoisie, the superstitious backwardness of the peasantry.[10] The central thesis of this point of view has been expressed with a kind of ferocity by André Wurmser:

> Ce pseudo légitimiste qui prétend – tardivement – écrire "à la lueur de deux Vérités éternelles: la Religion, la Monarchie", ne cesse de demontrer que "ce n'est pas le roi Louis-Phillippe qui règne" mais "la toute-puissante pièce de cent sous". . . . Si, sur sa tombe, Hugo le dira "de la forte race des écrivains révolutionnaires", si de Marx à Lukács les révolutionnaires l'admireront, ce n'est pas à la suite de je ne sais quelle "annexion" mais *parce qui'il dit vrai* et que "la vérité est révolutionnaire" (Gramsci).[11]

These assumptions about Balzac's occult and political interests resemble assumptions sometimes made about Yeats's own occult and political interests. One encounters often in the critical literature on the novelist or the poet the attitude that though Balzac's or Yeats's ideas on the supernatural are at best curious, though Balzac's or Yeats's political ideas are at worst loathsome, neither writer's opinions on these matters are so central to his work as to impede enjoyment or appreciation of that work by enlightened readers such as ourselves . . . failing that, one can argue that the real tenor of the work is altogether more humane, progressive and congenial than the writers' superficially held opinions, which we may justly ignore. In so labouring to make the great writers of the past uniformly digestible, we perhaps do ourselves a disservice. Examining Yeats's interest in Balzac brings into relief some of the thornier and less inviting aspects of his career, but doing so makes plainer what is at stake in his art, and how powerful its claims on us are.

From 1907 on, Yeats frequently enlisted Balzac as an ally in various Irish controversies,[12] the most important and most conspicuous of these occasions being his 1919 essay, 'If I were Four-and-Twenty'. At the time Yeats was worried that soon-to-be-independent Ireland might follow Russia's recent example. In June of that year he wrote to George Russell, 'What I want is that Ireland be kept from giving itself . . . to Marxian revolution or Marxian definitions of value in any form.'[13] 'If I were Four-and-Twenty', first published in Russell's *Irish Statesmen* in August 1919, calls on Ireland, particularly young Ireland, to abandon whatever interest it may have in Marx's social ideas and look instead to a writer whose social ideas are more consistent with Ireland's Catholicism: Balzac. That Ireland might hammer its thoughts into unity, Yeats declared he would, 'but for my disabilities', set 'some exceptional young man, some writer of Abbey plays perhaps, to what once changed all my thought: the reading of the whole *Comédie humaine*'.[14]

'Balzac is the only modern mind which has made a synthesis comparable to that of Dante, and, though certain of his books are on the Index, his whole purpose was to expound the doctrine of his Church as it is displayed, not in decrees and manuals, but in the institutions of Christendom.'[15] The chief of these institutions was the family. To Balzac, Yeats writes, 'social order is the creation of two struggles, that of family with family, that of individual with individual . . .'.[16] In the latter struggle, the individual seeks to triumph over his contemporaries, to gain power, wealth and status through his own talent and force of will – one thinks immediately of Rastignac and Lucien de Rubempré. In the former struggle, the family acts as a vessel that preserves over many generations the power, wealth and status won in the individual struggle, and so acts as a foundation for achievements impossible to attain in a single lifetime. From the vantage of the individual enmeshed in the individual struggle, hereditary privileges seems unjust because of the great advantages it grants to certain individuals who may be less talented or weaker than he. But Balzac, Yeats argues, saw the question from the other side:

> Throughout the *Comédie humaine* one finds – and in this Balzac was perhaps conscious of contradicting the cloudy Utopian genius of Hugo – that the more noble and stable qualities, those that are spread through the personality, and not isolated in a faculty, are the results of victory in the family struggle, while those qualities of logic and will, all those qualities of toil rather than of power, belong most to the individual struggle. For a long time after closing the last novel one finds it hard to admire deeply any individual strength that has not family strength behind it.[17]

As the liberal impulse to perfect society by making the individual's talent the sole limit and means of his ambition had drawn Balzac's fire, so the Marxist impulse to perfect society by limiting what one individual might gain at the expense of another drew Yeats's, and for the same reasons. By focusing exclusively on the individual, both impulses severed the familial bonds that connected the individual to the past and the future, rendered impossible the nurturing of those 'more noble and stable qualities' that mature only over many generations. While we read Balzac, Yeats writes, 'we must believe – and it is the doctrine of his Church – that we discover what is most lasting in ourselves in labouring for old men, for children, for the unborn, for those whom we have not even chosen'.[18]

As the just-quoted passage makes clear, Yeats is speaking not of founding the state on cheerful domesticity or the circle at the hearth, but of founding it, to use Lawrence Stone's definition of the older idea of the family, on 'the preservation, increase and transmission through inheritance and marriage of the property and status of the lineage, of the generations of ancestors stretching back into the remote past'.[19] Yeats does not exaggerate the importance this older idea of the family assumes in the *Comédie humaine*. In the 'Avant-Propos' Balzac pauses in an attack on democracy to insist, 'I regard the family and not the individual as the true social unit.'[20] 'The family is society', proclaims a character in *Modeste Mignon*, and the narrator of *La Cousine Bette* declares, 'In France, henceforth, there will be great names, but no great houses, unless there should be political changes which we can hardly foresee. Everything takes the stamp of individuality. . . . Family pride is destroyed.'[21] In *Mémoires de deux jeunes mariées*, the Duc de Chaulieu sketches the larger picture:

> The family has ceased to exist; we have only individuals. . . .
> But all this has paved the way for weakened authority, for the blind force of the masses, for the decay of art and the supremacy of individual interests, and has left the road open to the foreign invader. We stand between two policies – either to found the state on the basis of the family, or to rest it on individual interests – in other words, between democracy and aristocracy. . . .[22]

The erosion of generational continuity and the havoc caused by individuals so bent on present power and enjoyment as to forget what they owe their forebears and descendants come under indictment again and again in the *Comédie humaine*, in short studies like *Gobseck* and fantastic tales like *L'Elixir de longue vie* as well as in *Père Goriot*. Labouring 'for those whom we have not even chosen', but to whom we have a natural and inextinguishable tie, brings to each section of society and to the whole a stability and dignity that the free play of 'interêts' will never provide, or so Balzac believed.

As important as this stability, in Yeats's own vision of society – perhaps more important – was the nobility of mind and manner made possible when inherited family privileged freed an individual, from birth, of fear, want and necessity. Yeats was reading Balzac during the same years that he was sharpening his sense of the aristocratic with Castiglione, and he must have caught the full import of Balzac's uncountable parenthetical tributes to the women of the Faubourg St Germain, to the distinct mode of existence discernible in the way such a woman turns her head. Although a Balzacian family may owe its fortune and power, Yeats writes, to 'some obscure toiler' or to a 'notorious speculator' or even to 'some stroke of lawless rapacity', the darkness and brutality of the struggle of family with family finds a justification in the rich life it makes possible generations later:

> His beautiful ladies and their lovers, his old statesmen, and some occasional artist to whom he has given his heart . . . often have seemed to me like those great blossoming plants that rise through the gloom of some Cingalese forest to open their blossoms above the tops of the trees. He, too, so does he love all bitter things, cannot leave undescribed that gloom, that struggle, which had made them their own legislators. . . .[23]

In the image of the blossom that shoots clear of the tangled forest, as in that of the fountain in 'Ancestral Houses' that seems 'to choose whatever shape it wills', Yeats celebrates the family, 'that wing of the Historical Antinomy that best fosters fine manners, minds set too high for intrigue or fear', as he was to put it in his 1934 essay on Balzac. Since the spoils of the struggle of individual with individual were limited to what could be gathered in one lifetime, and excited jealousy in oneself and envy in others, the individual struggle could not, as could the family struggle, eventually redeem its crimes by attaining a sphere of life above fear or intrigue. Yeats illustrated this idea in a satirical sketch included in *The Bounty of Sweden*. After describing the Swedish court, he imagines 'some equivalent gathering to that about me, called together by the heads of some State where every democratic dream had been fulfilled, and where all men had started level and only merit, acknowledged by the people, ruled':

> The majority so gathered, certainly all who had supreme authority, would have reached the age when an English novelist becomes eligible for the Order of Merit. . . . In the conversation of old and young there would be much sarcasm, great numbers of those tales which we all tell to one another's disadvantage. For all men would display to others' envy the trophies won in their life of struggle.[24]

The number of minds 'set too high for intrigue or fear' will always be small, of course. Needing a doctrine of inequality to set against the radically egalitarian doctrine of Marxism, Yeats found in Balzac's opposition of the family to the individual a means of arguing that aristocratic privileges were earned and legitimate. Interestingly enough, however, the image Yeats uses to express the final, cumulative achievement of the family struggle – the Cingalese plant – comes not from Balzac but from Nietzsche:

> Its [an aristocracy's] fundamental belief must really be that society is *not* entitled to exist for its own sake, but only as a substructure and scaffolding, by means of which a select race of beings may elevate themselves to their higher duties, and, in general, to a higher *existence* – comparable to the sun-seeking, climbing plants in Java (they are called *Sipo matador*), which encircle an oak so long and so often with their arms, until at last, high above it, but still supported by it, they can spread their tops in the open light and manifest their felicity.[25]

Yeats's borrowing of this image suggests that while writing 'If I were Four-and-Twenty' he had in the back of his mind a more severe idea of aristocracy than any actually uttered in the essay. Yeats may have decided that he had a better chance of swaying his intended audience with Balzac than with Nietzsche: Balzac, Catholic and French, at least stood some chance of gaining a hearing in Catholic, Francophile Ireland. The Catholic doctrine of the fall gave weight to Balzac's suspicion and scorn of social reformers – in acknowledgment of which Yeats with some enjoyment cites Publicola Masson, the pedicurist of *Les Comédiens sans le savoir* who while cutting corns declares genius a privilege to be abolished. Balzac also suited the purposes of the essay, which begins by giving considerable attention to Claudel and Péguy, by having written that 'the sects of today – religious, political, humanitarian, and levelling – are the train of Calvinism', and by having particularly honoured Catherine de Medici, who having foreseen 'the future to which the Reformation was dooming Europe', took upon herself the cruel responsibility of ordering the St Bartholomew's Day Massacre.[26] Yeats, hoping to sway Catholic Ireland, takes exactly this line. 'Logic is loose again,' he writes, 'as once in Calvin and Knox, or in the hysterical rhetoric of Savanarola, or in Christianity itself in its first raw centuries, and because it must always draw its deductions from what every dolt can understand, the wild beast cannot but destroy mysterious life.'[27] In choosing to foreground Balzac rather than Nietzsche Yeats was not, however, simply being disingenuous, for he credited Balzac with having anticipated Nietzsche in several respects. In 'If I were Four-and-Twenty', for example, he writes, 'Nietzsche might have taken, and perhaps did take, his conception of the superman in history from his Balzac's *Catherine de Médicis*,' and he once announced in conversation that 'All Nietzsche is in Balzac'.[28] Perhaps, having learned from Nietzsche how to take an unrepentant stance on the question of degrees of human superiority, he found in Balzac, as he later found in Burke, a saner treatment of that question in the old idea of government as a family tradition. Since Balzac combined Nietzsche's intemperate arrogance with a sense of the tradition that stretched back before the French Revolution, he loomed large in all Yeats's subsequent efforts to justify the social inequality, the hereditary privilege, that best fostered the aristocratic personality 'for whose lack men are "sheep without shepherds when the snow shuts out the sun"'.[29]

In an unpublished conclusion to 'If I were Four-and-Twenty', Yeats drew from Balzac a further defence of social inequality, this one apparently inspired by the multiplicity of the *Comédie humaine* itself.[30] Since men were not equal, not 'all exactly alike, all pushable, arrangeable, or, as Blake said, all intermeasurable by one another', as Yeats wrote in *On the Boiler*,[31] society's good lay not in encouraging an impossible uniformity, but in encouraging variety, in allowing for the full play of each individual's uniqueness. For instance, the life of an aristocratic woman, possible only under certain rare conditions of birth and education, constituted a contribution to her community, a unique and irreplaceable contribution, one that enlarged her community's imagination. We ought to value that contribution at least as highly as we do the more tangible contribution of, say, a prolific if opportunistic journalist. But we may value both lady and journalist as unique departures from the bare norm, as tokens of human variety. Yeats makes this point with reference to Laurence de Cinq-Cygne, the proud, beautiful, aristocratic horsewoman who in *Une Ténébreuse Affaire* plots to overthrow Napoleon, to Raoul Nathan, the ambitious literary man who appears in many novels, and to Publicola Masson, corn-cutting advocate of the bare norm, and goes on to wonder whether the immaterial, unmeasureable contribution of a woman like Laurence de Cinq-Cygne would finally be recognised and understood, its necessary conditions granted as a right, if science finally turned its attention to the immaterial, as he always believed it ought presently to do. Yeats had, in the essay as published, asserted that 'a man devoted to his collection of Chinese paintings affects the mind even of men who do physical labour without spoken or written word',[32] and a redirection of scientific inquiry, proving that effect, might lead to a community that sought to foster an infinitely wide range of possible achievements – a community Yeats feels will be nearer to the long dreamt-of City of God than could possibly be any community founded on the belief that its members, abstractly conceived, are perfectly alike. In such a community, a Constance Gore-Booth – like Laurence de Cinq-Cygne, an excellent horsewoman – need not feel the privilege of her great gazebo as guilt, nor her sister Eva feel compelled to 'Climb on a wagonette to scream'. They would know instead that in perfecting their idleness they gave their community a kind of gift.

We have looked this closely at 'If I were Four-and-Twenty' because when Yeats, in the early thirties, tried again to formulate his political beliefs, he returned to the Balzacian ideas of that essay: the family struggle and the individual struggle, multiplicity *versus* uniformity. The first idea was now buttressed by a reading of Burke and given a dialectical rigour Balzac never gave it; the second idea, based on a non-materialist notion of value, was now deepened by the reading of Berkeley, Kant and Gentile. Both ideas now seem thoroughly Yeats's own, but they remain recognisably those Yeats attributed to Balzac in 'If I were Four-and-Twenty'.

In an early section of the diary later published as *Pages from a Diary Written in Nineteen Hundred and Thirty* Yeats returned to the idea that society might found itself on what individual members were uniquely capable of, rather than on what all were capable of, on variety rather than uniformity, inequality rather than equality.

The abrogation of equality of rights and duties is because duties should depend on rights, rights on duties. If I till and dig my land I should have rights because of that duty done, and if I have much land, that, according to all ancient races, should bring me still more rights. . . . Shall we grant the nun and the lady of fashion their leisure? Can we call their refinement duty and therefore the leisure essential to it a right?[33]

In a later section of the diary, Yeats made the point again, having arrived at a certainty about the importance of immaterial social contributions that needed no recourse to rhetorical questions:

> An idea of the State which is not a preparation for those three convictions [that is, 'the three things which Kant thought we must postulate to make life livable – Freedom, God, Immortality'], a State founded on economics alone, would be a prison house. A State must be made like a Chartres Cathedral for the glory of God and the soul. It exists for the sake of the virtues and must pay their price. The uneconomic leisure of scholars, monks, and women gave us truth, sanctity, and manners.[34]

Reducing men and women to economic units, producers and consumers, or to soulless matter justified organising the state on the principle of equality, but the state so organised would achieve only the confining cell-by-cell uniformity of a prison house. If, on the other hand, the state recognises its need of what is outside economics' ken, of the immaterial, invisible and uncomputable, it will organise itself on the principle of inequality, and so grow to resemble a cathedral – physically varied, with parts subordinate to other parts, but consecrate to a single purpose.[35] Balzac the 'social philosopher' is named but once in the 1930 diary, but given the similarity between these two passages and the passages on Balzac in the 1919 essay, he remains perfectly discernible in the middle distance.

Balzac figures more markedly in the 'Genealogical Tree of Revolution', written three years later. While at Coole during Lady Gregory's last illness in 1932, Yeats was re-reading Balzac,[36] and Balzac became a touchstone in Yeats's efforts to define his political principles and hopes for Ireland in the months following de Valera's coming to power and Lady Gregory's death. In the spring of 1933 he considered writing a note on *Catherine de Médicis*, that being the work in which Balzac had the most to say about the change in the family's social role between the sixteenth and nineteenth centuries.[37] The notes in which Yeats tried to define the opposed philosophies of fascism and Marxism, and which in the Blueshirt summer of 1933 became the 'Genealogical Tree', conclude by arriving at that old Balzacian crux: 'Communism, Fascism, are inadequate because society is the struggle of two forces not transparent to reason – the family and the individual.'[38] Communism, like the upstart individual, discounted the past. The honour fascism paid to the past lent it a strength that would ensure its triumph over communism, but even fascism did not adequately understand the power of the family, the means through which the past lives in us. Accordingly, fascism was a stage that would be succeeded by a stage in which society's two constitutive struggles, that of family with family and that of individual with individual, would be harmonised. 'The business of Government is not to abate either struggle but to see that individual and family triumph by adding to Spiritual and material wealth.'[39] This conclusion echoes a phrase Yeats had applied to Balzac, attributing Balzac's dismissal of the Fourieristes to impatience with 'those who would abate or abolish the struggle'.[40] Ideally, society draws sustenance from both the 'intellectual initiative' produced by individual strength and the 'good taste and good habits', or tradition, created by family strength, both Rastignac and the Marquise de Cinq-Cygne.

The social ideas Yeats found in Balzac – or, we might say instead, extrapolated from the drama of the *Comédie humaine* – constitute in a way his final position, for he never tried to reason so abstractly about society again. Instead, he lamented the passing, or hoped for the return, of aristocratic control, of all that these notes try to express in the word 'family'. Yeats saw in Balzac a political wisdom at once Nietzschean and Burkean, one that had the advantage of being dramatised rather than stated, one that had the further advantage of being attributable to a man who, like Yeats, was a titanic literary creator with a keen interest in the occult. Accordingly, Yeats's Balzac was not a historian of *mœurs* or the author of an enormous work the hero of which was the twenty-franc piece, but a sage. Yeats never writes of Balzac but with the respect one accords a master.

When I was a child I heard the names of men whose lives had been changed by Balzac, perhaps because he cleared them of Utopian vapours, then very prevalent; and I can remember someone saying to an old lion-painter: 'If you had to choose, which would you give up, Shakespeare or Balzac?' and his answering, 'I would keep the yellow-backs.'[41]

After the collapse of the Blueshirts, Yeats stopped speculating on how society and the state might be re-ordered, and devoted himself more to speculating on history itself. Democracy and egalitarianism were no longer for him a trend that might yet be reversed in his lifetime, but a late stage in western civilisation's long, irreversible, slow but accelerating slide towards its apocalypse. Yeats took up with a passion the Spenglerian idea that civilisations are born, mature and decline; western civilisation, slipping daily into greater shabbiness and brutality, was obviously in decline. Here, too, Balzac became an ally. In Yeats's 1934 introduction to his 1931 play *The Resurrection*, which dramatises the moment when a dying civilisation confronts a new-born one, he wondered if Balzac had given him an early, half-conscious glimpse of the idea that civilisations die, and so led him to write 'The Adoration of the Magi', a more mystical handling of *The Resurrection*'s theme: 'Our civilisation was about to reverse itself, or some new civilisation about to be born from all that our age rejected. . . . A passage in *La Peau de chagrin* may have started me, but because I knew no ally but Balzac, I kept silent about all I could not get into fantastic romance.'[42] Yeats does not identify the passage in the novel that may have started him, but the likeliest possibility is an observation tossed off by Balzac while recording, in the manner of the fifth chapter of *Gargantua*, several specimens of the drunken dinner conversation of a group of especially cynical young journalists:

Between the dreary jests of these children of the Revolution over the inauguration of a newspaper, and the talk of the joyous gossips at Gargantua's birth, stretched the gulf that divides the nineteenth century from the sixteenth. Laughingly they had begun the work of destruction, and our journalists laughed amid the ruins.[43]

The point of view taken in this passing comment is exactly that of the historical sections of *A Vision*. Balzac postulates a 'gulf' between the France of the Renaissance and the France of 1830, a descent into cheapness, mannerism, insignificance. The chapter of *A Vision* titled 'Dove or Swan' analyses more elaborately the same gulf by means of graduated gyres, historical 'Phases'. For both Balzac and Yeats the Renaissance is a high achievement lost, the nineteenth century its tawdry, degenerate heir. In *Sur Catherine de Médicis*, which, Yeats claimed, contained along with *La Peau de chagrin* Balzac's 'philosophy of History',[44] Balzac in several asides and a long introduction describes the sixteenth century as a time of unparalleled achievement in literature, architecture and the arts, a time when even the citizens were more 'great, free, and noble' than their nineteenth-century counterparts.[45] The meanness and mediocrity of nineteenth-century France he blames on the 'individualism' that rose with Protestantism in the sixteenth century, with its 'terrible texts of liberty, tolerance, progress, and philanthropy'.[46] As one kind of life reached its culmination in the Renaissance, another was born with the Reformation; thus the sixteenth century had 'begun the work of destruction' that created the 'ruins' of the nineteenth. Similarly, Yeats saw in the Renaissance our civilisation's nearest approach to Unity of Being, the Phase 15 of the second of our two 1000-year cycles. Similarly again, he saw as evidence of that moment's dissolution such phenomena as Protestantism, liberal individualism (men as isolated, interchangeable political and economic units, 'children of the Revolution'), and the commodification of art and ideas (Balzac's drunken journalists are celebrating the 'inauguration of a newspaper'; one thinks also of *Illusions perdues*). Yeats's discussion of 'the ninth gyre, Phases 19, 20 and 21' of European history, which he dated as lasting approximately from 1650 to 1875, could be read as a highly imaginative gloss on the passage from *La Peau de chagrin*:

> The beginning of the gyre like that of its forerunner is violent, a breaking of the soul and world into fragments, and has for a chief character the materialistic movement at the end of the seventeenth century, all that comes out of Bacon perhaps, the foundation of our modern inductive reasoning, the declamatory religious sects and controversies and first in England and then in France destroy the sense of form. . . . Men change rapidly from deduction to deduction, opinion to opinion, have but one impression at a time and utter it always, no matter how often they change, with the same emphasis. . . . Personality is

everywhere spreading out its fingers in vain, or grasping with an always more convulsive grasp a world where the predominance of physical science, of finance and economics in all their forms, of democratic politics, of vast populations, of architecture where styles jostle one another, or newspapers where all is heterogeneous, show that mechanical force will in a moment become supreme.[47]

Here, too, however, we might claim the influence of Nietzsche as well, who like Balzac attributed the French Revolution to the swelling influence of Protestantism, but found the common principle not in individualism, but in *ressentiment*. Yeats would have read in Thomas Common's anthology of Nietzsche that the 'thoroughly plebeian *ressentiment* movement (German and English)' of the Reformation had snuffed out the Renaissance, and that in the French Revolution the same *ressentiment* had overthrown 'the last political nobleness in Europe'.[48] Once again, though not as plainly as in the instance of the Cingalese plant, we see that Yeats's Balzac was a powerful presence partly because he contained Nietzsche. Yeats is not, however, simply disguising the powerful influence of Nietzsche by labelling it 'Balzac'. Balzac's intuitions about his historical moment confirmed Yeats's own intuitions about the course of Europe from the Renaissance to the early nineteenth century, and seemed to forecast the course Europe took between Balzac's time and Yeats's own. Men had been isolated by 'individualism', made uniform by science, economics, newspapers, mass production, democracy. This uniformity made real unity, that of Chartres Cathedral or of a 'perfectly proportioned human body', impossible.

Yeats's most thorough and most striking assimilation of Balzac's intuitions to his own occurs in an unlikely context: Yeats's 'Introduction' to *The Holy Mountain*, the story of a pilgrimage taken by Bhagwān Shri Hamsa, spiritual master of Yeats's friend Shri Purohit Swami. Most of the introduction is rightly devoted to the career of Bhagwān Shri Hamsa and the topic of Hindu mysticism, but in its ninth section Yeats turns unexpectedly to the subject of history, setting Hegel against Balzac. The section begins, 'In 1818 Hegel, his head full of the intellectual pride of the eighteenth century, was expounding History.' Hegel, Yeats writes, argued that civilisation progresses and will eventually reach perfection. Ancient Greece 'first delivered mankind from nature', a liberation symbolised by Oedipus' answering the riddle of the 'Asiatic and animal' Sphinx. Man's intellect having triumphed over nature, his civilisation would proceed unimpeded to its transfiguration:

> From that moment on, intellect or Spirit, that which has value in itself, began to prevail, and now in Hegel's own day, the climax had come, not crippled age [the 'three legs' of the Sphinx's riddle] but wisdom; there had been many rehearsals, . . . but the play itself had been saved up for our patronage. A few years more and religion would be absorbed in the State, art in philosophy, God's will proved to be man's will.[49]

Yeats then has Balzac, 'that great eater, his medieval humility greater than his pride', answer in the first person: 'Man's intellect or Spirit can do nothing but bear witness; Nature alone is active . . . I refuse to confine Nature to claw, paw, and hoof. It is the irrational glory that reaches perfection at the mid-moment, the Renaissance of every civilisation.' Yeats's Balzac goes on to describe European civilisation's ascent to its mid-moment, using the same examples Yeats had used in 'Dove or Swan': the change from Byzantine to Romanesque architecture, Mont Saint Michel, Raphael's paintings in the Camera della Signatura, Pope Julius II. At that moment, 'Europe might have made its plan, begun the solution of its problem, but individualism came instead; the egg instead of hatching burst. The *Peau de chagrin* and *Catherine de Médicis* contain my philosophy of History. Genius and talent have torn Europe to pieces.' Dante's *Divina Commedia*, Yeats's Balzac goes on, 'summed up and closed . . . the Europe that went upon its knees or upon all fours', his own *Comédie humaine* had 'closed the counter-movement, that kept her upon two legs', and the future held not a transfiguration but the grinding decline of old age: 'In my open letter to the Duchesse de Castries I foretell the future. What was, before man stood up, an impulse in our blood, returns as external necessity.' That is, the conformity and singleness of mind of a primitive civilisation (one prior to Yeats's Phase 8, 'The Discovery of Strength') returns in an exhausted civilisation (one following Phase 22, 'The Breaking of Strength') as the imposition of a rule. In our case, received ideas that replace experience and mass-produced goods will compel uniformity:

We shall become one through violence or imitation. . . . As we grow old we accumulate abstract substitutes for experience, commodities of all kinds, but an old pensioner that taps upon the ground is no wit [sic] the wiser for all his proverbs. You should have gone to Hugo with that romantic dream. . . . My *Comédie humaine* will cure the world of all Utopias, but you [Hegel] were born too soon.[50]

'That last sentence,' Yeats adds with noticeable bitterness, 'would have been untrue.' Although Balzac has influenced 'some exceptional men and women', Hegel's influence 'dominates the masses, though they have not heard his name, as Rousseau's philosophy did in the nineteenth and later eighteenth centuries, and has shed more blood'.[51]

The prophecy Yeats gives to Balzac in the *Holy Mountain* introduction, about the nature of our civilisation's old age, was one Yeats was virtually willing to let stand as his own. After several unsatisfactory attempts to write a section on the future with which to conclude 'Dove or Swan' and *A Vision*, Yeats eventually published the brief, allusive, non-committal section titled 'The End of the Cycle'. As he used Balzac previously to reject Hegel, he uses him in this section to reject, implicitly, the Marxist vision of the future: 'How far can I accept socialistic or communistic prophecies? I remember the decadence Balzac foretold to the Duchesse de Castries.'[52] The Duchesse (later Marquise) de Castries was the woman who persuaded Balzac to adopt the Legitimist cause, and the prophecy Yeats refers to here, in the *Holy Mountain* introduction, and finally in *On the Boiler* is that contained in the opening paragraph of 'L'Illustre Gaudissart', a short story dedicated to the Duchesse. The Gaudissart of the title is a commercial traveller, and Balzac begins even this relatively slight comic tale (in which the Parisian Gaudissart is outwitted by a Tourangeau villager) with a characteristically Olympian sweep of the eye, pegging the role played by the commercial traveller in the life of France and in the history of civilisation. Industrialisation having brought uniformity to the nation's material goods, the commercial traveller, who 'is to ideas what coaches are to men and things', was bringing uniformity to the nation's ideas, eliminating old differences between what people thought in Paris and what they thought in the provinces:

. . . is it not his peculiar function to carry out in a certain class of things the immense transition which connects the age of material development with that of intellectual development? Our epoch will be the link between the age of isolated forces rich in original creativeness and that of the uniform but levelling force which gives monotony to its products, casting them in masses, and following out one unifying idea – the ultimate expression of social communities. After the Saturnalia of intellectual communism, after the last struggles of many civilisations concentrating all the treasures of the world on a single spot, must not the darkness of barbarism inevitably supervene?[53]

Yeats paraphrased this passage in the conclusion of the Hegel-Balzac section of the introduction to *The Holy Mountain*; it is the only part of 'Balzac's' monologue that is as Balzacian as it is Yeatsian. The stultifying uniformity among both commodities and minds foreseen by Balzac had, Yeats thought, come to pass. In 1919 he had written of 'an historical necessity that has made the furniture and the clothes and the brains of all but the leisured and the lettered, copies and travesties', and Dorothy Wellesley records of his conversation in the thirties that his hatred of 'democracy' included 'a furious attitude toward the cheap, the trashy, the ill-made'.[54] This fury may owe something to William Morris's early influence, but its peculiar political dimension must not be missed: mass production meant the rule of the mass mind, which signalled the imminence of the 'darkness of barbarism'.

In 'Michael Robartes Foretells', an earlier, more elaborate, eventually abandoned attempt to foretell the future for *A Vision*, Yeats predicts, as did Balzac, that once all distinctions are overwhelmed our civilisation will end in violence.

Phase 24 will perform the task of Augustus [that of 'concentrating all the treasures of the world on a single spot'], but the end of our civilisation will differ from that of an antithetical civilisation; the imitation of those who seem to express most completely the mass mind, the discovery of the mass mind in ourselves, will create a political system, more preoccupied with the common good, more derived from the common people, than that of Rome and later Greece.[55]

Phase 25 'must see the completion of a public ideal, its assimilation in the common civilisation, where all, whatever degree of rank and station remain, will live and think in much the same way'.[56] At Phase 26, knowledge 'of a form of existence . . . opposite to any our civilisation has pursued' will affect a minority, who 'organising their disgust, will create a turbulence',[57] the war and barbarity that Michael Robartes elsewhere enjoins us to 'Love . . . because of its horror, that belief may be changed, civilisation renewed'.[58] Our 'primary' civilisation, approaching its conclusion, had come to value the common and indistinct over the rare and particular, and to choose its leaders not for their superiority, but for their conformity to what most people thought, felt, feared and desired. The turbulence to come would reverse this scale of values; and once again the Yeatsian Balzac has led us to the Yeatsian Nietzsche:

> When a civilisation ends, task having led to task until everybody was bored, the whole turns bottom upwards, Nietzsche's 'transvaluation of all values'. As we approach the phoenix' nest the old classes, with their power of co-ordinating events, evaporate, the mere multitude is everywhere with its empty photographic eyes.[59]

When the flat, unrelieved uniformity Balzac had foreseen had been achieved, the Platonic Year would whirl out the new right and wrong based on the common, whirl in the old right and wrong based on the rare.

From passing references in *La Peau de chagrin* and *Sur Catherine de Médicis* to differences between the sixteenth and nineteenth centuries, and from the brief glimpse into the future that opens 'L'Illustre Gaudissart', Yeats drew the substance of a 'philosophy of History' which, to judge from the frequency with which he cites it, impressed him as much as did the better-grounded efforts of Vico, Spengler and Henry Adams.[60] That this philosophy, like the social idea of the family and individual struggles, was sketchy, incomplete and dramatised rather than stated would constitute no objection for Yeats. As Yeats once wrote of Balzac's ideas on the supernatural: 'Balzac but touches and passes on, absorbed in drama. One could fill the gaps in his thought, substitute definition for vague suggestion, were not that to lose the bull-necked man, the great eater. . . .'[61] Since Balzac's ideas *were* incomplete, Yeats could supply enough of what was missing to make of a Balzac a titanic figure capable of standing with Dante and Shakespeare, capable of answering Hegel and Marx.

As western civilisation had moved from its 'antithetical' phases dominated by a controlling imagination and its 'power of co-ordinating events' to its 'primary' phases symbolised by the 'empty photographic eyes' of the 'mere multitude', so western literature had moved an aesthetic in which the imagination imposed its forms upon the world to an aesthetic in which the world imposed its forms upon the imagination.

Yeats elaborated his own history of the novel to illustrate this change. Balzac, who in Yeats's estimation had dramatised an internal vision rather than trying to mirror actuality, stood as the last great figure of the previous, 'antithetical' dispensation. After Balzac, the history of the novel was the history of the western mind's ever-deepening and ever more disastrous involvement in the delusory world of appearances, or of its levelling tendency to prefer the commonplace and ordinary to the rare and extraordinary. Yeats condemned Dickens, for instance, for the latter fault,[62] but the pivotal figure in Yeats's history of the novel was Stendhal, less for his work itself than for his definition of the novel as a mirror dawdling down the lane, which began what Yeats called 'the mischief'.[63] 'Stendhal created a modern art; the seminary in *Le Rouge et le noir*, unlike that described by Balzac in *Louis Lambert*, is of his own time and is judged according to its standards, is wholly reflected in the dawdling mirror that was to empty modern literature', wrote Yeats in 1934.[64] The strength of Yeats's conviction on this point may have surprised the interviewer who, having listened to Yeats's praise of Balzac, asked the natural follow-up question about Stendhal. 'Stendhal is the beginning of what I hate', Yeats answered. 'He says a novel should be like a mirror dawdling down the lane. Stendhal began the collapse of the human soul.'[65] Stendhal was to blame for this collapse because his maxim, rather than Balzac's example, had determined the course of nineteenth-century literature, as Yeats described it in *Wheels and Butterflies*:

Gradually literature conformed to his [Stendhal's] ideal; Balzac

became old-fashioned; romanticism grew theatrical in its strain
to hold the public; till, by the end of the nineteenth century, the
principal characters in the most famous books were the passive
analysts of events, or had been brutalized into the likeness of
mechanical objects.[66]

Flaubert differed from Stendhal in that his art was 'strangely
hard, cold, and invulnerable, that this mirror is not brittle but of
unbreakable steel',[67] yet Flaubert's imagination, like Stendhal's,
had been absorbed in the external and phenomenal, had lost its
autonomous power: at Phase 22, Flaubert's phase, 'We identify
ourselves in our surroundings – in our surroundings perceived as
fact – while at the same time our intellect so slips from our grasp,
as it were, that we contemplate its energies as something we can
no longer control. . . .'[68] The naturalism that followed Flaubert
combined the passivity of Stendhal's recording mirror with
Dickens's love of the commonplace, and when that movement
had exhausted its vogue, Stendhal's mirror dissolved into Virginia
Woolf's waves and Joyce's streams of consciousness. The swimmer
in the waves, however, was as much at the mercy of the external
as the mirror had been, and Balzac had foreseen it all: 'In this new
literature announced with much else by Balzac in *Le Chef-d'oeuvre
inconnu*, as in that which it superseded, man in himself is
nothing.'[69]

An artist might sacrifice the command he ought to have over
his work not only by becoming a passive recorder of what was
external to him, as nineteenth-century novelists had done, but
also by bending his work to serve a doctrine or to confirm the
opinions of his audience, as Irish artists in the early twentieth
century were continually tempted to do. Yeats continually argued
this point during the years of the worst Abbey battles, and here
too Balzac and Balzacian characters served as examples of the
imagination's need to maintain its autonomy. As the task Balzac
had set for himself in the *Comédie humaine* had required him to
describe much that the sexual code of his time considered
immoral, so the task of the Abbey, Yeats argued, required its
playwrights to write of Ireland in ways that might offend Irish
nationalist orthodoxy.[70] Worse than the possibility of the audience's
opinions stifling good art was the possibility that artists, labouring
under similarly restrictive opinions of their own, might for that
reason be unable to produce good art at all. Yeats took as example

Dubourdieu, the Fourierist sculptor of *Les Comédiens sans le savoir*, who 'made an allegorical figure of Harmony, and got into his statue the doctrine of his master by giving it six breasts and by putting under its feet an enormous Savoy cabbage', and who hoped to become famous once the new age dawned.[71] Yeats did not mean, he went on to insist, that 'the artist should not as a man be a good citizen and hold opinions like another', but that the artist's first obligations was to his work: 'The artist who permits opinion to master his work is always insincere, always what Balzac calls an unconscious comedian, a man playing to a public for an end, or a philanthropist who has made the most tragic and the most useless of sacrifices.'[72] In his 1909 journal, Yeats noted that 'certain disciples of A. E.' were just such unconscious comedians, adopting 'extreme politics' because 'like an artist described by Balzac, they long for popularity that they may believe in themselves'.[73]

Stendhal and these 'disciples of A. E.' are examples of the Yeatsian 'primary', in which the mind recognises and submits to the authority of something outside itself – matter for a scientist, dialectical materialism for a Marxist, God for a saint. Balzac's art came from the opposed 'antithetical' impulse, the one Yeats in most moods took to be his own, in which the mind imposes shape on experience and the world. A Balzacian anecdote Yeats recalls in *Reveries Over Childhood and Youth* illustrates the difference. Yeats, then in his early twenties, had attended a séance in Dublin and been visited by some power. His hands began to twitch, then his shoulders; he stilled the movements for a moment, then his back was suddenly thrown against a wall. He tried again to control his movements.

> Everybody began to say I was a medium, and that if I would not resist some wonderful thing would happen. I remembered that Balzac had once desired to take opium for the experience' sake, but would not because he dreaded the surrender of his will.[74]

The movements recommenced and 'became so violent the table was broken'. Unable to think of a prayer, Yeats invoked the power of poetry by reciting the opening lines of *Paradise Lost*, and the visitation ceased. Yeats stopped attending séances for some years after this, and wondered whether the power that had come over him was 'a part of myself – something always to be a danger perhaps; or had it come from without, as it seemed?' In the opposition of medium and agent, surrender of the will and assertion of the will, primary and antithetical, the Balzac who had denied himself opium stood at the antithetical pole. In 'Louis Lambert', his 1934 essay on Balzac, the largest part of which Yeats devotes to discussing Balzac the student of the supernatural, Yeats describes this opposition again:

Louis Lambert, having attributed to man two natures, one that of an angel, hesitates; perhaps, he says, man has not two natures, perhaps, though merely men, we are capable of incomprehensible acts which we, in our admiration for the incomprehensible, attribute to spiritual beings. Here are the two doctrines which dominate our psychical research – spiritualism and animism – the first in Anglo-Saxon countries where the Fox Sisters had so great an effect, the second upon the continent, where the Mesmerists, perhaps more through Balzac, George Sand, Dumas, than by direct influence, have accustomed students to think that a personal illumination or state of power can be aroused by experimental means.[75]

Discussing the evoking of images in *Per Amica Silentia Lunae*, Yeats writes of those adepts who to call up images 'suspend will and intellect' and 'seek to become, as it were, polished mirrors'. He himself, he found, 'had no natural gift for this clear quiet', so he 'invented a new process. . . . I elaborated a symbolism of natural objects that I might give myself dreams during sleep, or rather visions, for they had none of the confusion of dreams, by laying upon my pillow or beside my bed certain flowers or leaves.'[76] This is as much as to say that Yeats was an artist. *He* elaborated the symbolism, *he* made the suitable dispositions of matter, *he* orchestrated his visions. Balzac's 'animism' is the same realisation that an artist is more powerful as agent than as medium. Alone at night in a room bare of all but a writing table and a pot of hellishly-brewed coffee, dressed in a white monastic robe, Balzac had brought himself to a 'personal illumination or state of power' in which he accomplished by vision and imagination what he never could have accomplished by observation alone. On two different occasions Yeats cites a remark by an unnamed contemporary of Balzac: 'If I meet him at midday he is a very ignorant man, but at midnight, when he sits beside a cup of black coffee, he knows everything in the world.'[77] Like his characters Vautrin and de Marsay, who continually summon power from an electromagnetic source within and discharge it through their glances to bend others to their will, Balzac had drawn on some internal source for the strength that enabled him to bring the disorderly world into unity.

We might express Balzac's status in Yeatsian literary history by describing his achievement as the high water mark of romanticism. This assertion probably runs counter to the reader's intuitions, but if we trace the development of Yeats's assumptions about the nature of romanticism we are led with surprising directness to Balzac and his monumental work. What distinguished romantic art from most other art of the eighteenth and nineteenth centuries, Yeats believed, was that it was imaginative rather than mimetic, 'active' rather than 'passive' (to revive two terms from the third chapter), the mind shaping the world rather than the world shaping the mind. 'The romantic movement seems related to the idealist philosophy . . .' he wrote in his 1931 essay on Berkeley, thinking not of direct influence but of shared assumptions about the mind's capabilities.[78] In his long correspondence with Sturge Moore over the reality or unreality of Ruskin's cat, he cited Blake, Shelley and Coleridge as well as Berkeley and Gentile.[79] In his introduction to the *Oxford Book of Modern Verse*, describing Western civilisation since Bacon and Newton as the gradual imprisonment of man within his corporeal senses, he referred to the 'brief period between Smart's *Song of David* and the death of Byron' as a time when 'imprisoned man beat upon the door'.[80] The romantic movement, with 'its turbulent heroism, its self-assertion',[81] seemed to Yeats the soul's last, necessarily doomed attempt to regain right mastery of things before the final collapse of our 'primary' gyre, and for the most part he took its aesthetic means and ends for his own. However, once past the age of thirty-five – the age, it has been said, after which one is 'dead' as a romantic poet – Yeats grew increasingly impatient and uncomfortable with what we might call romanticism's utopian strain, its hope that the imperfect would be made perfect if it could cast off the accumulated crust of past mistakes. This change in Yeats's relations with the romantics is soonest understood by looking at his changing evaluation of Shelley.

To the young Yeats, Shelley was 'poetry itself'.[82] Looking back on his career in 1932, Yeats found it was not Blake, 'whom I had studied more and with more approval', but Shelley who 'had shaped my life' up until middle age.[83] George Bornstein has examined the pervasive Shelleyan influence in Yeats's work of the eighties and nineties,[84] a discipleship capped by the long essay 'The Philosophy of Shelley's Poetry' in *Ideas of Good and Evil*, a volume saturated with the Yeatsian interpretation of English romanticism. That book was no sooner out, however, than Yeats, fresh from his first acquaintance with Nietzsche, felt inclined to disavow it. 'The book is only one half of the orange for I only got a grip on the other half very lately', he wrote to George Russell, explaining that he wished to move from the 'Dionysiac' or 'sad and desirous' to the 'Apollonic' or 'joyful and self-sufficient'.[85] This same distinction, made without reference to Apollo or Dionysus but with special reference to Shelley, is taken up in the final essay of *Discoveries* (1906):

> A man of that unbroken day [of Homer and Hesiod] could have all the subtlety of Shelley, and yet use no image unknown among the common people, and speak no thought that was not a deduction from the common thought. Unless the discovery of legendary knowledge and the returning belief in miracle, or what we must needs call so, can bring once more a new belief in the sanctity of common ploughland, and new wonders that reward no difficult ecclesiastical routine but the common, wayward, spirited man, we may never see again a Shelley and a Dickens in the one body, but be broken to the end. We have grown jealous of the body, and we dress it in dull unshapely clothes, that we may cherish aspiration alone.[86]

Yeats is not speaking only of a reconciliation with the humble, familiar, warm and cosy, though the mention of Dickens and of 'common ploughland' suggests that he is. For Yeats, any re-evaluation of the physical and material involved a re-evaluation of wrong, imperfection, evil. What he goes on to call 'Shelley's dizzy . . . disdain with usual daily things' is one with the 'sad and desirous' state of mind he mentioned to Russell: sadness over the stain of evil on all the things we live among, desire to fly from them to the sphere of unalterable good. Yeats is here labelling as 'Shelley' a tendency of his younger self – one thinks of 'The Lover tells of the Rose in his Heart', for instance – and he continued to so label it as he developed the idea of the 'Vision of Evil' in the years of the first World War and the Irish Troubles. In 'If I were Four-and-Twenty' (1919), Yeats blamed Shelley's 'rhetoric and vagueness' on incomprehension of man's fall, and in *The Trembling of the Veil* (1922) wrote that Donne, possessing the Vision of Evil, 'could be as metaphysical as he pleased, and yet never seemed unhuman and hysterical as Shelley often does, because he could be as physical as he pleased. . . .'.[87] In *A Vision* Yeats assigned Shelley to Phase 17, thus identifying Shelley's mind and enterprise with his own, yet entered an important qualification: 'He lacked the Vision of Evil, could not conceive of the world as continual conflict, so, though great poet he certainly was, he was not of the greatest kind.'[88]

Harold Bloom writes that 'Yeats knew better' than this, since in his essay on Shelley 'he correctly understands the great myth of Demogorgon in *Prometheus Unbound* as the principle of continual conflict that turns over the cycle in the universe from Jupiter to Prometheus, and that threatens destruction again in a world that cannot by its nature be finally redeemed.'[89] This perhaps misses the point. Conceiving of the world as continual conflict does not mean conceiving of it as contention between good and evil, but as contention *tout court*. It means ceasing to dread the agents that 'threaten destruction', ceasing to long or look for final redemption. When Yeats writes that Shelley lacked the Vision of Evil, he means that Shelley could affirm but one, not both, of the contending forces, each of which is named 'Evil' by its opposite. According to Yeats, Shelley's love of the spiritual and perfect was so overwhelming it led to a distorting hate of the incarnate and flawed. That love, which in 1900 Yeats had considered the animating idea of Shelley's poetry, seemed to him in 1932 'the pursuit of a beauty that, seeming at once absolute and eternal, requires, to strike a balance, hatred as absolute'.[90] Demogorgon was an instance of this. 'Why . . . does Demogorgon, whose task is beneficent,' Yeats asks near the beginning of his 1932 essay on Shelley, 'bear so terrible a shape, and not to the eyes of Jupiter, external necessity, alone, but to those of Asia, who is identical with the Venus-Urania of the *Athanase*? Why is Shelley terrified of the Last Day like a Victorian child?' Yeats's answer is: 'Demogorgon made his plot incoherent, its interpretation impossible; it was thrust there by that something which again and again forced him to balance the object of desire conceived as miraculous and superhuman, with nightmare.'[91] Unable to affirm one of the contending forces without vehemently saying 'no' to the other, Shelley ended up with only half the orange, and even his 'yes', like the affirmations of the socialist writers discussed in the previous chapter, sounded shrill and strangled to Yeats's maturer ear. 'He could neither say with Dante, "His will is our peace", nor with Finn in the Irish story, "The best music is what happens".'[92] Yeats sees the same phenomenon in Shelley's life (the transformation of the 'admired Elizabeth Hichener' to 'the brown demon') and in his politics: an ideal of liberty so closely cherished that it could see only wrong, ugliness and oppression in every human institution, a corollary impulse to reform, regenerate, transfigure at any cost. Yeats had seen enough of this attitude among Irish nationalists to dislike it intensely in Shelley: 'vague propagandistic emotion', 'the cold rhetoric of obsession', 'Jacobin frenzies', are the phrases he falls into.[93]

As we have seen, Yeats juxtaposed Shelley with various other figures, such as Dickens and Donne, to try to name what it was he missed in Shelley. Among the most important are Nietzsche, an unnamed presence in the letter to Russell about *Ideas of Good and Evil*, and Dante, like Shelley a poet of Phase 17, but one whom Yeats credited with having attained the Vision of Evil.[94] In the conclusion of his 1932 essay on Shelley, he made another such juxtaposition and followed it up with a surprising avowal:

> Another study of that time [of Yeats's youth, when 'Shelley was much talked about'], less general, more confined to exceptional men, was that of Balzac as a social philosopher. When I was thirteen or fourteen I heard somebody say that he changed men's lives, nor can I think it a coincidence that an epoch founded in such thought as Shelley's ended with an art of solidity and complexity. Me at any rate he saved from the pursuit of a beauty that, seeming at once absolute and external, requires, to strike a balance, hatred as absolute.[95]

This is an unlikely turn for an essay by Yeats on Shelley to take – neither Bornstein nor Bloom, in their extensive discussions of Yeats and Shelley, mentions it – but Balzac was precisely the sort of literary predecessor Yeats needed. Since Balzac wrote out of imagination rather than observation, he was a romantic, one who contradicted Stendhal's infamous adage. Since in his historical vision and his political thought he 'was perhaps conscious of contradicting the cloudy Utopian genius of Hugo',[96] he acted as counterweight to Shelley's 'Jacobin frenzies'. We have already seen how Yeats's Balzac contains or confirms the two great figures with which Yeats tries to distance himself from Shelley, Dante and Nietzsche: in 'If I were Four-and-Twenty', Yeats within the space of a few lines compares Balzac to the earlier figure and declares him a precursor of the later. In Balzac Yeats found a romantic writer, one who shared 'the premises from which I work', who had disabused himself of political optimism, who saw as Yeats did 'decreasing ability and increasing commonness'.

Balzac had lived at the historical moment when the headiness of the antithetical phases was subsiding before a crushing hangover,[97] and so Yeats called him 'the voice of the last subjective phases, of individualism in its exaltation'. This is virtually to say that he was the voice of the age of romanticism. The unified community of the Renaissance being broken, certain individuals, full of 'turbulent heroism' and 'self-assertion', try, and of course fail, to reassemble that unity within their isolated selves: personality spreading out its fingers in vain, imprisoned man beating upon the door. Balzac's backward glances to the unified sensibility of the Renaissance led Yeats to place the novelist with Shakespeare and Napoleon at Phase 20, 'a phase of the breaking up and sub-division of the being', in which one sought 'a similitude of the old unity' by 'projecting a dramatisation or many dramatisations'.[98] The source of the internal, self-created power of multitudinous dramatisation thus capable of effecting a similitude of the old unity could be glimpsed, Yeats argued, in the beliefs about the supernatural collected by Balzac in *Louis Lambert*: his conviction that 'the human mind' was 'capable . . . of containing within itself all that is significant in human history and of relating that history to timeless reality', his conviction that man was 'self-sufficing and eternal'.[99] For this reason, *Louis Lambert* was, for Yeats, heart and soul of the *Comédie humaine*. Taking the Whistlerian doctrine that 'a picture must be perfect from the first sketch', and further asserting that 'what is true of the work of art is true of the painter's or dramatist's own life', Yeats argues that *Louis Lambert* is the 'first sketch' that made the *Comédie* possible:

Jane Austen, Scott, Fielding, inherited that other sketch in its clearest and simplest form, but Balzac had to find it in his own

mind. His sketch is *Louis Lambert*, the demonstration of its truth
is that it made possible the *Comédie humaine*.[100]

The names of Austen and of Fielding, if not that of Scott,
suggest that Balzac's task was a romantic one. A civilisation's
Unity of Being is something an artist can participate in, can in a
sense inherit, but by Balzac's time that unity or 'first sketch' had
been broken. He had to generate his own, 'find it in his own
mind'. But the imaginative world born of that self-generated 'first
sketch' was not – as it had been in the romantic works the
younger Yeats most admired, Shelley's vision, Morris's romances,
or in early works of his own like *The Shadowy Waters* – a
dreamland. It was dense, populated, noisy, composed of living
stuff. Rather than trying to imagine a distinct world, Balzac had
re-invented the actual one, with the peculiar result of his re-
invention eventually being accepted as the reality: 'And this world
of his, where everything happens in a blaze of light, and not the
France of the historians, is early nineteenth-century France to
thousands all over Europe.'[101] One of those thousands, Yeats
probably remembered, was Oscar Wilde, 'a Balzac scholar, perhaps
a Balzac disciple – so perhaps were we all', according to a Yeats
letter of 1932.[102] In 'The Decay of Lying' Wilde had written, 'The
nineteenth century, as we know it, is largely an invention of
Balzac.'[103] Another of those thousands, as Yeats might have been
surprised or intrigued to discover, was Frederick Engels, who
called Balzac's works 'a complete history of French Society from
which, even in economic details . . . I have learned more than
from all the professed historians, economists and statisticians of
the period together.'[104] Engels meant, of course, that Balzac had
seen the truth the historians had missed. Yeats attributed Balzac's
powerful persuasiveness to another cause: as a great artist, Balzac
had not so much seen the truth of his time as created it, rendering
whatever had actually happened insignificant. One feels Yeats
was attempting the same feat, on a smaller scale, in his later
works that deal with the Easter Rising, 'The O'Rahilly', 'Three
Songs to the One Burden', 'The Statues', *The Death of Cuchulain*,
trying to ensure that in future that ambiguous event would have
not a de Valeran but a Yeatsian meaning. If poetry is conscious of
its own power, it can outstare history and even become accepted
as history.

Balzac shared in the romantic faith in the imagination's

supernatural power and its participation in the eternal. At the same time, he had chosen, as Blake, Shelley and Morris had not, as Homer arguably had, to make his imagination engage the actual, historical and mundane. He had been, more nearly than any other post-Renaissance figure, a Shelley and a Dickens in the one body. Devoted to the body and to matter, he was yet a kind of visionary: Yeats called him 'the bull-necked man, the great eater, the mechanist and materialist who wrote upon the darkness with a burnt stick such sacred and exciting symbols'.[105] He was aware of both worlds, yet the flawed, incarnate world seemed to have the greater share of his love.

> . . . Balzac leaves us when the book is closed amid the crowd that fills the boxes and the galleries of the grand opera; even after hearing Séraphita amid her snows, we return to that crowd which is always right because there is so much history in its veins, to those kings, generals, diplomats, beautiful ladies, to that young Bianchon, to that young Desplein, to all those shabby students of the arts sitting in the galleries.[106]

A 'return' similar to that which leads us from Séraphita, spiritual and perfect, to the crowd at the opera, incarnate, flawed, but intoxicating, occurs in several later Yeats poems. The scholar of 'Sailing to Byzantium', purged by fire of his mortal dross and become a mechanical, immortal bird, chooses to sing of the time-bound and mortal. 'Byzantium', after describing the dance of the shades, gradually and finally turns toward 'That dolphin-torn, that gong-tormented sea': the animal body, pain, time, generation. The Soul in 'Dialogue of Self and Soul' falls silent as the self contemplates almost with joy another leap into the foul ditch of incarnation. The golden codgers of 'News for the Delphic Oracle' seem almost bored with Paradise, and the poem ends with images of generation. When in the middle 1930s Yeats was occupied with both the re-reading of the *Comédie humaine* and the study of Hinduism, these two pursuits seemed to him signs of the divergent tugs within himself, his vacillation between the incarnate and spiritual worlds:

> 'I know nothing but the novels of Balzac, and the Aphorisms of Patanjali. I once knew other things, but I am an old man with a poor memory.' There must be some reason why I wanted to

write that lying sentence, for it has been in my head for weeks. Is it that whenever I have been tempted to go to Japan, China, or India for my philosophy, Balzac has brought me back, reminded me of my preoccupation with national, social, personal problems, convinced me that I cannot escape from our *Comédie humaine*?[107]

Séraphita and *Louis Lambert* proved that Balzac had, as did Yeats, a longing for the eternal, but he possessed as well a counter-balancing fascination with the physical world before him that kept him, and Yeats, from a fatal embrace of 'All Asiatic vague immensities'.[108] Carl Benson, in his 'Yeats and Balzac's *Louis Lambert*', suggests Balzac may have shown Yeats the way to reconcile the occult systems of *A Vision* with his need to write of actual men, women and events:

It seems quite likely that *Louis Lambert* provided Yeats with his first suggestion of a means of confronting the bitter realities of actual life and, at the same time, of retaining an ordered view which allowed to man a genuine dignity and to creative imagination and individual will their rightful roles of control. . . .[109]

Benson's 'it seems quite likely' recognises the impossibility of saying whether Balzac led Yeats to or only confirmed Yeats in his late efforts to hold in one thought both what was eternal and what was fleeting. Certainly, though, it seemed to Yeats that Balzac had come near to solving the problem Yeats posed for himself in 'Vacillation':

The Soul. Seek our reality, leave things that seem.
The Heart. What, be a singer born and lack a theme?[110]

However, Benson's phrase 'the bitter realities of actual life' tends too much to suggest that the affirmation of the incarnate, the return to the crowd at the opera, was a dirty, distasteful, unfortunately necessary job. 'Bitter' might indeed have been Yeats's very word, but it had a peculiar meaning for him: ' "The passionate-minded," says an Indian saying, "love bitter food",' he once wrote apropos of Balzac.[111] Can the artist, having glimpsed the perfection of Séraphita amid her snows, then turn to the incarnate world with all its imperfection, wrong and evil and not judge that world, even love it? That Balzac had 'love[d] all bitter things'[112] set him, in Yeats's eyes, above all later novelists. As early as 1897, in an essay on Shakespeare, Yeats drew this distinction between Balzac and those who came after him:

> In *La Peau de chagrin* Balzac spends many pages in describing a coquette, who seems the very image of heartlessness, and then invents an improbable incident that her chief victim may discover how beautifully she can sing. Nobody had ever heard her sing, and yet in her singing, and in her chatter with her maid, Balzac tells us, was her true self. He would have us understand that behind the momentary self, which acts and lives in the world, and is subject to the judgment of the world, there is that which cannot be called before any moral judgment seat, even though a great poet, or novelist, or philosopher be sitting upon it. Great literature has always been written in a like spirit, and is, indeed, the Forgiveness of Sin, and when we find it becoming the Accusation of Sin, as in George Eliot . . . literature has begun to change into something else.[113]

In the essay 'Louis Lambert', after the already-quoted description of the crowd at the opera, Yeats made a similar point: 'Tolstoi, Dostoieffsky, Flaubert drew to their support scholars and sectaries, their readers stand above the theme or beside it, they judge and they reject; but there in the crowded theatre are Balzac's readers and his theme, seen with his eyes they have become philosophy without ceasing to be history.'[114] He made the same point more clearly, if more playfully, in a letter of this time to Olivia Shakespear: 'How one loves Balzac's audience – great ladies, diplomatists, everybody who goes to grand opera, and ourselves. Then think of Tolstoy's – all the bores, not a poor sinner amongst them.'[115] The word 'sinner', though lightly employed, leads us – 'What theme had Homer but original sin?' – to what distinguished Balzac's art from most art of the nineteenth century: the Vision of Evil.

> When we compare any modern writer, except Balzac, with the writers of an older world . . . we are in the presence of something slight and shadowy. It is natural for a man who believes that man finds happiness here on earth, or not at all, to

make light of all obstacles to that happiness and to deny altogether the insuperable obstacles seen by religious philosophy. The strength and weight of Shakespeare, of Villon, of Dante, even of Cervantes, come from their preoccupation with evil.[116]

In this passage from 'If I were Four-and-Twenty', Yeats goes on to name two romantics, Shelley and Wordsworth, and two romantic descendants, Ruskin and Morris, as subscribers to the Wordsworthian notion that 'man finds his happiness here on earth, or not at all'. To choose earthly existence was a hollow victory if one then judged or tried to wish away the evil that attended earthly existence, even if one then became absorbed in pity for evil's victims. Balzac seemed to realise that pity, wishing and judgment would not answer, that to affirm incarnate life meant affirming evil, affirming both sides of the antinomy. Balzac's all-encompassing affirmation was what had saved Yeats from Shelley's 'Jacobin frenzies' and 'brown demons', from a love that required a compensating hatred.

When Yeats, in the conclusion of his essay 'Prometheus Unbound', claimed that Balzac had 'saved' him, he entered a qualification: 'Yet Balzac is no complete solution, for that can be found in religion alone. . . . It was many years before I understood that we must not demand even the welfare of the human race, nor traffic with divinity in our prayers.'[117] Yet perhaps Balzac had phrased the question of evil as successfully as any artist relying on his own faculties could. The essay 'Louis Lambert', like 'Prometheus Unbound' named for the most admired of an admired author's works, immediately follows 'Prometheus Unbound' in the Cuala volume *Essays 1931–1936*, and like 'Prometheus Unbound' ends by describing Balzac's influence as redemptive. Balzac 'saved' him, Yeats writes, 'from Jacobin and Jacobite', that is, from destructive egalitarianism and from the most furious kind of Irish Catholic nationalism.[118] The penultimate section of the essay, that containing the already-quoted description of the crowd at the opera, ends with the suggestion that Balzac is one of a handful of writers who had realised that to love the incarnate world we must love it in its imperfection and evil. Yeats speaks of 'those passages in the *Comédie humaine* that suddenly startle us with a wisdom deeper than intellect and seem to demand an audience of the daring and the powerful'. He concludes:

> I have lived from boyhood in the shadow, as it were, of that
> enumeration of famous women in *La Recherche de l'absolu* ending
> with the sentence, 'Blessed are the imperfect, for theirs is the
> Kingdom of Love.' Dante might have made it or some mediaeval
> monk, preaching in Rheims, where the French kings lie
> buried.[119]

As he had in 'If I were Four-and-Twenty' and the introduction to
The Holy Mountain, Yeats again links Balzac with Dante, always
the touchstone for the idea of the Vision of Evil. In trying to
encompass the difficult idea that we must affirm evil to affirm life,
Yeats sometimes quoted the words on an old Irish countrywoman:
'God smiles alike when regarding the good and condemning the
lost.'[120] As God of the *Comédie humaine*, Balzac, too, as in the
instance of the cruel Foedora's beautiful voice, smiled on his lost.
In Balzac Yeats found a dense, articulated, teeming, roaring, cruel
but never heartless world, found a knowledge of evil that could
say, 'Blessed are the imperfect, for theirs is the Kingdom of Love',
found alive and laughing all that seemed to have disappeared in
Shelley. In chucking Shelley, he became a great poet, became, for
all the foolishness he was forever embracing, a wise man.

5

Yeats and Eugenics

In 1928, while visiting Ezra Pound in Rapallo, Yeats met the composer George Antheil. According to Hone, 'In conversation with Antheil, Yeats, the tone-deaf, rapidly and characteristically persuaded himself that his old theories of half-tones in verse-speaking were the dogmas of modern composers, and felt confident that he would be supplied in future with all the music he needed for his plays from this source.'[1] The trick of Yeats's mind illustrated by this anecdote partly explains his later interest in eugenics. In both cases, it seemed to him that pioneering modern minds had finally come around to establishing as fundamental principles truths he had intuited as a young man. Modern composers, in their experiments with ever more minute pitch intervals, had apparently arrived at the same conclusions Yeats had set out in 'Speaking to the Psaltery'. The eugenists confirmed, with their batteries of intelligence tests, Yeats's suspicion that Europe's stocks were degenerating, and strengthened, by their emphasis of genes and heredity, his conviction of the importance of lineage and the family. His acquaintance with the ideas of the eugenists, however, was certainly deeper than was his acquaintance with the theories of modern composers. He read much of the literature then available on the subject, attended at least one meeting of the Eugenics Society,[2] and devoted a full section of his last prose work to eugenics. Furthermore, eugenics – if we use the word broadly, to cover topics such as degeneration and proper breeding – amounts to a recurring theme of the last two volumes of poetry, *New Poems* (1938) and *Last Poems and Two Plays* (1939), which refer often to racial degeneration ('gangling stocks grown great, great stocks run dry'[3]) and the proper means to remedy same, even though those means are sometimes as superficially unscientific as Mannion the Roaring Tinker's promise to 'Throw likely couples into bed / And knock the others down'.[4]

Concern for lineage, degeneration and the right conditions for the continuation of the species – for what could, without great

145

exactness but fairly enough, be called eugenics – became noticeable in Yeats's work as early as 1904. As F. S. L. Lyons has noted, 1903 had marked a turning point for Yeats. In 1903 the controversy over Synge's *Shadow of the Glen* ruined Yeats's hopes for literature in the nationalist movement and presaged a split between the Catholic and Protestant sections of that movement, and Maud Gonne married Major MacBride, whom Yeats thought a decidedly inferior man. Added to these events was the influence of Nietzsche, the 'strong enchanter'[5] whom Yeats read for the first time in 1902. It was under the pressure of those events and that influence that Yeats, as Lyons has written, 'began that withdrawal into aristocratic contempt for what he saw as the base and squalid elements in Irish life which was to become so central to his later attitudes'.[6] Admiration of the aristocratic and dislike of the bourgeois accounted for the greatest part of this withdrawal into contempt, but at times the distinctions Yeats saw between classes seemed to him distinctions between races, distinctions in 'blood'. He implied such a distinction when, in defending *Shadow of the Glen* and noting that Ireland did not have a stage censorship as England did, he chose the word 'caste' rather than 'class' in describing Grattan's Parliament as a 'ruling caste of free spirits' who, 'being free themselves . . . left the theatre in freedom'.[7] Maud Gonne's marriage seemed to him a *mésalliance* between higher and lower breeds, as is plain from a poem in his 1907 journal:

> My love is angry that of late
> I cry all base blood down
> As though she had not taught me hate
> By kisses to a clown.[8]

Yeats's interest in Nietzsche likewise included an interest in breeding, an interest which surfaces briefly in *Where There Is Nothing*, a curious play of 1902 which sets a Nietzschean visionary hero among Irish monks and tinkers. In the third act, Paul Ruttledge, the hero, has his troop of drunken tinkers bind several civic leaders and hoist them on to barrels so that he may arraign them for hypocrisy. The arraignment concluded, he closes the scene by dismissing one of the leaders, his own brother, as follows:

> *Thomas Ruttledge:* You have nothing against me, have you,
>   Paul?
> *Paul Ruttledge:* Oh, yes, I have; a little that I have said against
>   all these, and a worse thing than all, though it is not in the
>   book.
> *Thomas Ruttledge:* What is it?
> *Paul Ruttledge:* (*Looking back from the threshold.*) You have
>   begotten fools.[9]

In two of Yeats's 1903–4 plays, *On Baile's Strand* and *The King's
Threshold*, questions of heredity and generation do more than
appear briefly and implicitly. They bear the main burdens of the
plays.

Thematically, *On Baile's Strand* turns on the tension between
Conchubar's bourgeois practicality and Cuchulain's heroic
sprezzatura, but its plot turns on the idea of degeneration, the
degeneracy of Conchubar's heirs inspiring both his fears for their
future and Cuchulain's unwillingness to obey them. Cuchulain
alludes to this degeneracy candidly and often. When Conchubar
complains that his children have found Cuchulain unbiddable,
Cuchulain answers:

> We in our young days
> Have seen the heavens like a burning cloud
> Brooding upon the world, and being more
> Than men can be now that cloud's lifted up,
> We should be the more truthful. Conchubar,
> I do not like your children – they have no pith,
> No marrow in their bones, and will lie soft
> Where you and I lie hard.[10]

'You rail at them,' Conchubar replies, 'Because you have no
children of your own.' Cuchulain answers:

> I think myself most lucky that I leave
> No pallid ghost or mockery of a man
> To drift and mutter in the corridors
> Where I have laughed and sung.[11]

But Conchubar presses the point. He has heard Cuchulain cry out
in his sleep that he 'had no son'. Cuchulain does feel keenly the

lack of an heir, as the play's end shows, yet he counters
Conchubar by insisting again on the inevitability of degeneration,
and declaring that it would take more than pithless offspring to
bind him to the obedience Conchubar desires:

> . . . you thought
> That I should be as biddable as others
> Had I their reason for it; but that's not true;
> For I would need a weightier argument
> Than one that marred me in the copying
> As I have that clean hawk out of the air
> That, as men say, begot this body of mine
> Upon a mortal woman.[12]

Conchubar never defends the abilities of his children. He answers
only that he must look to their security, and that Cuchulain
would do the same were he fortunate enough to have children
himself. Both men believe that in the course of nature their sons
will be weaker than they themselves are. Conchubar sees in this
the necessity of submitting individual strength and will to law
and government. Cuchulain sees instead an occasion for mockery,
bitter mockery since he nonetheless regrets that he has no son.

Conchubar then reminds Cuchulain that he, Cuchulain, has
previously expressed a wish to have had a child by 'that fierce
woman of the camp',[13] Aoife. At her name, Cuchulain goes into a
reverie which concludes with an admission of what Conchubar
has claimed: 'None other had all beauty, queen or lover, / Or was
so fitted to give birth to kings.'[14] Aoife, we discover later, has
been as exacting in her choice of a mate as Cuchulain. The Fool
reveals to Cuchulain at the climax of the play that Aoife had
'never but the one lover, and he the only man that had overcome
her in battle'[15] – that is, Cuchulain himself. She has put into effect
one of the ready-to-hand eugenical measures of which Irish
legend furnishes many examples, and consequently her son
Conlaoch, though not quite a match for Cuchulain himself, yet
carries more of the heroic strain than anyone else of his generation
and would certainly wreak havoc among the pithless heirs
of Conchubar. Cuchulain was likewise stronger than his
contemporaries, but they were still able to lead the life he led.
Conlaoch has no such fellows, and so constitutes a danger to the

community. The heroic age is ended, and the best must be sacrificed to the mediocre.

Everything about Conlaoch testifies to his breeding. When he appears in Conchubar's hall and is asked for proof of his nobility, he offers 'the signs about this body and in these bones'.[16] Cuchulain immediately sees the high descent of the young stranger, though he recognises that it is not quite so high as his own: 'That arm had a good father and a good mother, / But it is not like this.'[17] He offers the young stranger friendship, thus angering Conchubar, who cries, 'You cannot think as I do, who would leave / A throne too high for insult.'[18] Cuchulain naturally snorts at this – 'Let your children / Re-mortar their inheritance, as we have, / And put more muscle on'[19] – and repeats the offer of friendship, which Conlaoch seems ready to accept. The assembled kings protest, and for a moment it seems Cuchulain and Conlaoch will join forces against them all, the swift and strong in natural alliance against the stable and secure. Cuchulain says:

> Boy, I would meet them all in arms
> If I'd a son like you . . .
> . . . You and I
> Would scatter them like water from a dish.[20]

Yet Conchubar asserts his authority, persuades Cuchulain that he has been bewitched, and sends the two heroes out to combat. The combat takes place offstage, but one of the women who remain in the hall has a vision of the destruction of Cuchulain's 'house':

> I have seen Cuchulain's roof-tree
> Leap into fire, and the walls split and blacken.[21]

So the divinely-descended heroic race is blotted out, and the degenerate offspring of the patently bourgeois Conchubar are left in safety. *On Baile's Strand* shows how readily Yeats figured class differences as differences in race or kind, and how readily he imagined modern barrenness as a consequence of degeneration, the triumph of weak stocks over the strong by weight of numbers. This last tendency had much to do with his later interest in eugenics.

The King's Threshold, like *On Baile's Strand* first published in 1903, several times revised, and dated '1904' in the *Collected Plays*, has much to do with the disruptions then taking place in the Irish nationalist movement. The controversies of 1903–4 had displaced literature from the position of leadership it had assumed in the years after Parnell's fall, and *The King's Threshold* contains some of the bitterness Yeats felt over that displacement. It contains also, as virtually every commentator has mentioned, a brief for the case that the arts are not an ornament to society, but its very life. Commentators make next to nothing, however, of Seanchan's resting that case on an eccentric eugenical argument. When his oldest pupil disapproves of Seanchan's protest as too extravagant, Seanchan bids the pupil remember what the pupil once answered when Seanchan asked him why poetry is honoured.

> *Oldest Pupil:* I said the poets hung
>   Images of the life that was in Eden
>   About the child-bed of the world, that it,
>   Looking upon those images, might bear
>   Triumphant children. But why must I stand here,
>   Repeating an old lesson, while you starve?
> *Seanchan:* Tell on, for I begin to know the voice.
>   What evil thing will come upon the world
>   If the Arts perish?
> *Oldest Pupil:* If the Arts should perish,
>   The world that lacked them would be like the woman
>   That, looking upon the cloven lips of a hare,
>   Brings forth a hare-lipped child.[22]

Seanchan's point is made. He is protesting on behalf of 'some that shall be born in the nick o' time':

> And how could they be born to majesty
> If I had never made the golden cradle?[23]

Seanchan's claim that art justifies itself by bringing into the world 'triumphant children' is literal as well as figurative. He asserts several times that poetry physically transforms humanity. 'The mothers that have borne you mated rightly,' he tells two young girls, 'They'd little ears as thirsty as your ears / For many love songs.'[24] He asks of two cripples, 'What bad poet did your mothers listen to / That you were born so crooked?'[25] His last vision is of those unborn whose golden cradle his poetry has made:

> The stars had come so near me that I caught
> Their singing. It was praise of that great race
> That would be haughty, mirthful, and white-bodied,
> With a high head, and open hand, and how,
> Laughing, it would take the mastery of the whole world.[26]

Seanchan's defence of poetry and the poet claims no less than that the imaginings of poets created the human race as it now exists, and that the imaginings of poets will eventually create an even greater race, one apparently compounded of Nietzsche's superman and the world of faery. Hence Yeats's animus against realism. If art physically transforms the world, an age which demands of art what Pound called 'an accelerated image of its own grimace' will hasten its own degeneration. This notion of the power of art in right breeding crops up later in Yeats's work, particularly during the time of his interest in eugenics.

In the degeneration theme of *On Baile's Strand* and the transformation-of-man-through-art theme of *The King's Threshold* we have two of the three ideas most prominent in Yeats's later interest in eugenics. We should note here, since the matter will come up again, that these ideas combine a radically geneticist approach with a radically environmentalist approach. In *On Baile's Strand*, a race naturally goes to ruin unless the best mate with the best. Parentage is destiny. In *The King's Threshold*, a race is improved by an environmental force external to genes and chromosomes – art and poetry. Seanchan's argument for art and poetry is properly speaking euthenical, not eugenical, since it holds that a stock can be improved by environmental forces.[27] This combination of ideas does not indicate confusion of mind. Rather, Yeats entered an artist's qualification into his regard for lineage and heredity, allowing art the power, as we might put it, to decide which genetic variations would be most prized. In the nature-nurture question. Yeats leaned toward the side of nature, but never undervalued the kind of nurture provided by imaginative art.

The third of the three ideas that contributed to Yeats's later
interest in eugenics was that all states are rightly founded on the
continuity of the family. Yeats believed in breeds apart, inevitably
a small minority, who by innate superiority and inherited tradition
created order and significance in the community to which they
belonged. The younger Yeats had imagined the heroic races of
Irish legend, those of Cuchulain and the Tuatha de Danaan, as
such breeds apart, and had thought that making them living
figures in modern Irish literature would create order and
significance in modern Ireland. The older Yeats imagined the
families of Ireland's Protestant ascendancy as such a breed apart,
and appointed himself their champion. The privileged position
they had gained should remain theirs, he argued, for by virtue of
that position they gave to Ireland great if sometimes intangible
gifts. In 'If I were Four-and-Twenty', written when Ireland was
about to gain independence, and 'A Race Philosophy', written in
the early thirties when he was beginning to despair over the Free
State, Yeats asserted the family's importance and urged that the
state not allow the rights of individuals to overwhelm the rights of
families.

Yeats began 'If I were Four-and-Twenty' by advising Ireland to
hammer its thoughts into unity. Given that 'we are a religious
nation',[28] what form of social organisation will suit Ireland best?
Central to Christianity, he argued, was the family: 'When I close
my eyes and pronounce the word "Christianity" and await its
unconscious suggestion, I do not see Christ crucified, or the Good
Shepherd from the catacombs, but a father and mother and their
children, a picture by Leonardo da Vinci most often.'[29] How will a
Christian state embody the Christian principle of the family in its
government? There, as we have already seen, his chief authority
was Balzac, whose 'whole purpose was to expound the doctrine
of his church as it is displayed, not in decrees and manuals, but in
the institutions of Christendom'.[30] The *Comédie humaine*, Yeats
writes, shows that society is the evolving product of two struggles,

that of family with family, that of individual with individual,
and that our politics depend on which of the two struggles has
most affected our imagination. If it has been most affected by
the individual struggle we insist upon equality of opportunity,
'the career open to talent', and consider rank and wealth
fortuitous and unjust; and if it is most affected by the struggles

of families we insist upon all that preserves what that struggle has earned, upon social privilege, upon the rights of property.[31]

Balzac's imagination, and one supposes Yeats's own, were most moved by the struggle of families. Balzac shows, Yeats writes, that 'the more noble and stable qualities . . . are the results of victory in the family struggle',[32] and it is probably for that reason that Yeats claims that Balzac 'has explained and proved, even more thoroughly than Darwin, the doctrine of the survival of the fittest species'.[33]

In the otherwise impossible accomplishments that accumulated power and privilege make possible, the accomplishments figured by Yeats in the Nietzschean figure of 'those great blossoming plants that rise through the gloom of some Cingalese forest to open their blossoms above the trees', the cruelty of the struggle is justified. In the 1920s, Yeats found a like organic metaphor for the community's continuity and growth in time in Burke's comparison of the state to a tree. In 1919, not yet having the deep acquaintance with Burke he was to have later, or perhaps adhering to the self-imposed necessity of making his case on Christian grounds, he takes as his second authority not Burke, but the 'Christian economist',[34] Vladimir Soloviev, whose works he urged booksellers who were 'regular church-goers' to place in their shopwindows alongside those of Marx, which he noted were omnipresent.[35]

Soloviev, in Yeats's words, held that 'the desire of the father to see his child better off than himself, socially, financially, morally', is 'the main cause of all social progress, of all improvements in civilisation'.[36] Yeats admitted this idea into his essay as one more argument in favour of basing government on the family principle, yet qualified it by noting that Soloviev fixed his attention too much 'upon the direct conscious effects' of regard for ancestors and descendants 'and not enough upon its indirect unconscious effects, upon the creation of social species each bound together by its emotional quality'.[37] That is, Soloviev concerned himself more with the material progress caused by the family principle than with the more important though less tangible product of that principle, the creation over generations of a breed apart that is 'held together, not by a logical process, but by historical association, and possesses a personality for whose lack men are "sheep without shepherds when the snow shuts out the sun"'. In the past, before the privileges of governing families were toppled in the interests of the individual struggle, 'Men who did not share their privileges have died and lived for all these, and judged them little.'[38]

Although the words 'hereditary aristocracy' occur nowhere in the essay, it is abundantly clear that such is the polity Yeats had in mind, and near his conclusion wonders whether 'our will must surrender itself to another will within it, interpreted by certain men, at once economists, patriots, and inquisitors', whether 'we may be about to accept the most implacable authority the world has known'.[39] The Yeats who was later attracted to fascism is audible here, but he goes on to ask a question more related to his interest in eugenics: 'Do I desire it or dread it, loving as I do the gaming-table of Nature where many are ruined but none is judged, and where all is fortuitous, unforeseen?' The 'gaming-table of nature' is Yeats's phrase for the varying fortunes of inheritance, as becomes clear in an unpublished conclusion to this essay in which he proceeds to the topic of Mendel.[40] Would Mendel's research confirm Balzac's pre-Darwinian Darwinism, create a modern version of the ancient wisdom about breeding? Yeats was willing to imagine that it might. If a nation's constitution did not lend the individual struggle an unnatural advantage over the family struggle, those few family strains with the gifts that govern men would emerge without recourse to the mud-slinging campaigns of democracy or to the cumbersome examination apparatus of a meritocracy. Six years later, in *The Bounty of Sweden*, Yeats made this point explicit: 'The politic Tudor kings and the masterful descendants of Gustavus Vasa were as able as the American presidents, and better educated, and the artistic genius of old Japan continually renewed itself through dynasties of painters.'[41]

In a society based on heredity, the artist contributed by educating desire, perfecting the race by celebrating what was heroic and comely; 'If I were Four-and-Twenty' glances back not only to *On Baile's Strand*, but also to what Seanchan taught his pupils to do in *The King's Threshold*.

> If, as these writers affirm, the family is the unit of social life, and the origin of civilisation which but exists to preserve it, . . . it seems more natural than it did before that its ecstatic moment, the sexual choice of man and woman, should be the greater part of all poetry. A single wrong choice may destroy a family,

dissipating its tradition or its biological force, and the great sculptors, painters, and poets are there that instinct may find its lamp. When a young man imagines the woman of his hope, shaped for all the uses of life, mother and mistress and yet fitted to carry a bow in the wilderness, how little of it all is mere instinct, how much has come from chisel and brush. Educationalists and statesmen, servants of the logical process, do their worst, but they are not the matchmakers who bring together the fathers and mothers of the generations nor shall the type they plan survive.[42]

Yeats here brings Seanchan's argument on to firmer physical ground without altering its essential import. Artists have made the world, for they have decided what types will survive. It is their work that enables a family to preserve its 'biological force – the quasi-scientific note here struck will be amplified once Yeats discovers eugenics.

As we have seen, Yeats returned to the idea that society was based on the struggles of families and individuals in the notes on politics and society he composed in 1933 and titled 'Genealogical Tree of Revolution' and 'A Race Philosophy', concluding in the latter that neither communism nor fascism takes into account that 'society is the struggle of two forces not transparent to reason – the family and the individual',[43] and so neither will finally answer. Government must not act to 'abate either struggle', but must 'see that individual and family triumph by adding to Spiritual and material wealth'.[44] Government, in short, must reconcile the conflicting principles of equality of opportunity and hereditary privilege. Rather than spell out exactly how this could be done, Yeats suggests in the final note of 'A Race Philosophy' that Nature, which, according to another note, man cannot understand 'because he has not made it',[45] will settle all satisfactorily if the government does not interfere:

It must not be forgotten that Race, which has for flower the family and the individual, is wiser than Government, and that it is the source of all initiative.[46]

'A Race Philosophy' tries to be even-handed on the question of the family and the individual, but the word 'flower', reminiscent of the earlier Cingalese blossoming plant, makes one suspect that

Yeats's bias toward the family was intact, that he, like the hypothetical reader of the *Comédie humaine* described in 'If I were Four-and-Twenty', still found it 'hard to admire deeply any individual strength that has not family strength behind it'.[47] If the government will but forbear from egalitarian pruning, the breed apart, call it 'Family' or 'Race' or 'Nature', will flower, and the whole community, in ways no utilitarian would comprehend, will benefit in turn. In *The Bounty of Sweden*, Yeats referred to 'hereditary honour' as Nature's 'old arrangements', and wrote that Nature may have 'created the family with no other object' than that of preserving honour, and 'may even now mock in her secret way our new ideals – the equality of man, equality of rights – meditating some wholly different end'.[48] In a passage of his 1930 diary, he put great weight on the word 'kindred':

> Spengler is right when he says all who preserve tradition will find their opportunity. Tradition is kindred. The abrogation of equality of rights and duties is because duties should depend on rights, rights on duties.[49]

No person's duty is like another's, the passage goes on to argue, so the rights that accompany those duties will necessarily be inequal. Those who take on special duties – the landholder, the nun, even the 'lady of fashion' – require and deserve special rights. The sentence 'Tradition is kindred' suggest Yeats has in mind another kind of inequality as well: genetic inheritance, inevitably inequal, will make some families capable of larger duties and entitle them to larger rights, which will become as much a part of their inheritance as their genes are. Blood will tell, unless, as in *On Baile's Strand*, the law intervenes to enforce an unnatural equality. In the diary passage, Yeats speculates on the formation of a 'kindred' who will lead Europe's impending reversal, and in a 1937 essay imagined a 'rule of kindred' waiting on the other side of whatever disaster Europe was about to pass through.[50] The attention Yeats pays to the family in 'If I were Four-and-Twenty' and 'A Race Philosophy' suggests that Yeats meant nothing very vague in using the word 'kindred'. To his mind, a community's government, manners and civilisation rested, in the natural order of things, on the traditions and abilities preserved over the generations within a small number of particularly gifted families.

Yeats's belief in the power of genetic inheritance, and its importance to the social order, comes out plainly in an incident he related to Olivia Shakespear, in a letter of 1933:

> I have been reading Morris' *Sigurd* to Anne and last night when I came to the description of the birth of Sigurd and that wonderful first nursing of the child, I could hardly read for my tears. Then when Anne had gone to bed I tried to read it to George and it was just the same.[51]

Sigurd, in Morris's poem, is the fruit of careful breeding, 'the best . . . sprung from the best', and his nurses know him immediately for one belonging to a breed apart:

> Man say of the serving women, when they cried on the joy of
>   the morn,
> When they handled the linen raiment, and washed the king
>   new-born,
> When they bore him back unto Hiordis, and the weary and
>   happy breast.
> And bade her be glad to behold it, how the best was sprung
>   from the best,
> Yet they shrank in their rejoicing before the eyes of the child,
> So bright and dreadful were they; yea though the spring morn
>   smiled,
> And a thousand birds were singing round the fair familiar
>   home,
> And still as on other mornings they saw folk go and come,
> Yet the hour seemed awful to them, and the hearts within
>   them burned.
> As though of fateful matters their souls were newly learned.[52]

Morris may have meant that the nurses were strangely cognisant of Sigurd's destiny, not merely of his superior breeding, but it was the breeding that struck Yeats. He quoted the poem a year later in *Wheels and Butterflies* and asked, 'How can one fail to be moved in the presence of the central mystery of the faith of poets, painters, and athletes?'[53] That central mystery is the perfection in mind and body of a breed apart, celebrated by poet and painter, aspired to by the athlete. In the next paragraph, Yeats touched on the political implications of this faith. Since 'Science has driven out the legends, stories, superstitions that protected the immature and the ignorant with symbol', it must now 'take their place and demonstrate as philosophy has in all ages, that States are justified . . . because sustained by those for whom the hour seems "awful", and by those born out of themselves, the best born of the best'.[54] When in the late thirties Yeats became aware of the eugenics movement, he may have thought that science had taken on exactly that task.

The reputation of eugenics has never recovered from its association with the worst forms of state cruelty, particularly the genocidal policies of Nazi Germany. We think of eugenics as one of the horrific elements in an anti-Utopian novel, or as an example of the moral havoc science creates when it lacks a guiding humanist intelligence, or as a species of pseudo-scientific charlatanry, and interest in the subject seems to mark the interested person as at best naive and at worst vicious. At the time eugenics attracted Yeats's interest, however, its scientific basis appeared firm, and it numbered among its English promoters not only many eminent biologists and doctors, but also such reputable non-scientists as Dean William Inge, Havelock Ellis, Harold Laski, Goldsworthy Lowes Dickinson and John Maynard Keynes.[55] The word itself was first used by Sir Francis Galton in *The Inheritance of Human Faculties* in 1883. When anxiety arose over the supposed physical deterioration of the average Englishman, as evidenced by the surprisingly poor health and size of those recruited for the Boer War, and the newly rediscovered researches of Gregor Mendel seemed to offer an explanation of that deterioration, eugenics turned from field of speculation to public issue. The English Eugenics Education Society was formed in the winter of 1907–8 and set itself the task of educating the public and the lawmakers in the principles of eugenics and their possible applications to public policy. While members of the Society did not unanimously agree on the relative importance of heredity and environment or on what practical measures best conformed with eugenical principles, most were 'hereditarians' and thought the movement's immediate goal should be the correction of the 'differential birth rate', that is, the reversal of the tendency of inferior stocks to reproduce at a higher rate than did superior stocks.

Class bias accounted for most of the anxiety over the differential birth rate. Socially superior families, the assumption ran, had achieved their high status through innate superiority. Consequently, if upper class families tended to have only one or two children while lower class families tended to have seven or eight, the nation would gradually become almost entirely populated by the innately inferior. A recent development in psychology, the intelligence test, provided evidence in support of this argument. Since intelligence tests purported to measure innate intelligence, and since intelligence was usually assumed to be linked with health, size, strength, beauty and even the moral sense in one generative substance ('germ plasm' – this being before the discovery of chromosomes), the discovery that the prolific lower classes scored much lower on the tests that did the less prolific upper and middle classes indicated to eugenists that a national biological crisis was at hand. The greatest public impact of the eugenical movement was not, however, on the birth rate, but on policy regarding the 'feeble-minded'. Intelligence tests in England and America (particularly the tests given to US Army recruits in World War I by Charles Yerkes[56]) revealed alarmingly high numbers of the feeble-minded, and since many studies (Goddard's *The Kallikak Family*, for instance) had apparently proven that feeble-mindedness was hereditary, the eugenics movement lobbied for laws that prohibited reproduction among the feeble-minded, either by isolation, or by voluntary sterilisation, or by forced sterilisation. England's Mental Deficiency Act of 1913, which empowered the government to detain and sexually segregate the feeble-minded, resulted from this effort, as did the sterilisation laws that thirty American states had enacted by 1931.[57] The movement was international. By the time Germany passed its sterilisation laws in 1933, similar laws had already been enacted in Canada, Denmark, Finland, Sweden, Norway and Iceland.[58] This legislation, disturbing and even frightening as it is in the light of subsequent history, serves to show that in the years before World War II, when Yeats became interested in eugenics, it was respected, widely influential and had even started to seem orthodox. it had its public opponents, such as G. K. Chesterton and Josiah Wedgwood, but with the test scores and the laws of Mendel on their side, the eugenists could and did dismiss opposition as unscientific sentimentality.

However compelling the scientific evidence in favour of

eugenics may have been to some of Yeats's contemporaries, one would not have expected Yeats himself to have been much impressed by it. Science to him was the 'opium of the suburbs', and he normally exhibited a Blakean scorn for science's mania for quantification and its absorption in the merely material. However, he modified that scorn whenever there was a question of finding physical, scientifically valid proof for his own convictions. His countless psychic experiments and tireless efforts to verify psychic phenomena show this, as does the wide reading in the literature of the paranormal apparent in the footnotes to his essay on Berkeley. In the full version of the dig at science quoted above, Yeats makes just such a modification: 'Science, separated from philosophy, is the opium of the suburbs.'[59] Investigation into physic phenomena was science still wedded to philosophy since it did not begin by discarding ancient wisdom, the immortality of the soul, the reality of immaterial existences. Likewise, eugenics, however modern its veneer, seemed to spring from ancient wisdom about generation and the family, and to confirm convictions Yeats had long held.

Raymond B. Cattell's *The Fight for our National Intelligence*, the book on eugenics which most deeply impressed Yeats,[60] contains many passages which are strikingly congruent to Yeats's own ideas. While Yeats had intuited that degeneration had set in, Cattell had discerned that it had by correlating the results of intelligence tests with birth rate statistics, but given the same premise they drew the same conclusions. As early as 1901, and several times since then, Yeats had written of 'an inexplicable movement that was trampling out the minds of all but some few thousands born to cultivated ease',[61] and as early as 1904 had asked Ireland to 'look for leadership in matters of art to men and women whose business or whose leisure has made the great writers of the world their habitual company'.[62] Cattell wrote of the same 'movement', though to him it was not inexplicable, and made the same appeal for a leadership of an elite: 'An undue preponderance of low intelligence can swamp a minority and set a tone in our newspapers, films, novels and social recreations which makes life intolerable for that minority. . . . And we have to decide between making life intolerable for the group that is leading society onward or for the group that is dragging it to the dust.'[63] This debasement of culture was plainest in the popular press, which appeared to grow in influence as it lowered its standards. Cattell's strictures on contemporary journalism (such as, 'The tone of the newspaper with the record circulation may become a national menace'[64]) equal anything in *Samhain* or *Estrangement*. Since democracy depended upon an informed public, the debasement of the press raised the question of whether democracy could still function as it ought. 'We must get either a new press or a political organisation which does not need a press,' warned Cattell,[65] having earlier noted that 'democracy is only just practicable at the level of intelligence we now possess', and that it 'must give way to some less happy forms of authority if the landslide of intelligence continues'.[66] Yeats thought, as we have already seen, that society had long ago retreated from the level of intelligence at which democracy became practicable, if indeed society had ever attained it. To suggest, as Cattell did, or insist, as Yeats did, that the average man did not have the intellectual wherewithal to govern himself was not, both claimed, to hate humanity, but to love what was best in humanity. Cattell made this point in a three-page 'Note on Clarification of Moral Issues':

. . . Christianity is, *at first sight*, ruining the whole purpose of group survival ethics by extending love to all humanity. For, on closer analysis, we realise that evolution can proceed under the aegis of love as easily as that of hate; if that love is love of the best. With such love the less capable men and races vanish because they can extinguish themselves in the service of others whose greater nobility is no longer in doubt.[67]

Here, too, Cattell is unconsciously echoing Yeats, who, as we have already mentioned, had argued that 'States are justified, not by multiplying or, as it would seem, comforting those that are inherently miserable, but because sustained by . . . the best born of the best'.

Just as Yeats had insisted that 'Materially and Spiritually uncreative families or individuals must not be allowed to triumph over the creative',[68] so Cattell insisted that rather than let 'the more enterprising perish while the stall-fed multiply' governments should adjust 'the birth rate of parents to the magnitude of their contribution to civilisation and the need which society has of them'.[69] Since 'the best' was transmitted through the hereditary principle, and the natural locus of the hereditary principle was the family, Cattell praised and pleaded for the family almost as strongly as Yeats did. In the third paragraph of his book he writes, 'To create a civilisation, to let it burst forth in flower from a previous state of barbarism, the race concerned must first accumulate a rich crop of men – or rather of family strains – possessed of great natural mental capacity',[70] reminding us of Yeats's Cingalese bloom. Near the end of his book, in a chapter titled, 'The Way Out', Cattell writes of the importance 'pride of family' must assume in future societies:

> The most important habit of aristocracy which it has to take over is concern for the family breeding and the ideal of regarding mating, not as a sentimental incident in a musical comedy, but as a sacred trust involving more thought and sentiment than is given to a career.[71]

How could that passage have failed to strike a chord of the author who, in celebrating Coole, had written of 'Marriages, alliances and families, / And every bride's ambition satisfied', or who was to chart the course of a *mésalliance* in *Purgatory*? In sum, Yeats was not converted to eugenics, but rather found in it a scientific diagnosis of modernity that complemented his own intuitive diagnosis. The common had, by weight of numbers, usurped the best, as the assembled kings of *On Baile's Strand* had brought the Hound of Hulin to heel, and the institution that preserved the best, the family, had been stripped of its rights.

Yeats's discovery of eugenics occupied a great part of his attention in the first and only number of *On the Boiler*, a publication Yeats had intended to continue periodically, on the model of *Fors Clavigera*. The main concerns of *On the Boiler* differ not at all from those Yeats had advocated for many years, but eugenics furnished him with a new stick with which to beat opposing doctrines, and he made the most of it, especially in the second essay, 'Tomorrow's Revolution'. Tomorrow's revolution is, of course, the eugenical one. Yeats begins the essay with a mild disclaimer in which he describes himself as being at odds with his era. From the time he had had a violent argument with his father over Ruskin's *Unto This Last*, he had found 'no dominant opinion I could accept', and had consequently 'invented a patter, allowing myself an easy man's insincerity, and for honesty's sake a little malice' to avoid involving himself in constant argument with his contemporaries.[72] 'We who are the opposites of our time should for the most part work at our art and for good manners' sake be silent', he writes, but now the time has come to say what he thinks, no matter how offensive or unwelcome it may be to his hearers. In the essay's second section, he takes as his 'text' a long passage from the *Anatomy of Melancholy* which contrasts the care with which 'an husbandman will sow none but the best and choicest seed upon his land . . . make choice of the best rams for our sheep, rear the neatest kine, and keep the best dogs' to the carelessness in which we propagate our own kind.[73] Burton notes, quoting another author, that in ancient Scotland a bearer of hereditary flaws was 'instantly gelded' if male, and if female 'kept from all company of men; and if by chance . . . she were found to be with child, she with her brood were buried alive'. Burton comments:

A severe doom, you will say, and not to be used among Christians, yet more to be looked into than it is. For now by our too much facility in this kind, in giving way for all to marry that will, too much liberty and indulgence in tolerating all sorts, there is a vast confusion of hereditary diseases, no family secure, no man almost free from some grievous infirmity or other . . . our fathers bad, and we are like to be worse.[74]

So Yeats, first warning the reader that the long-held but never-voiced opinions to follow may well outrage him, then resting on pre-Lockean scientific authority, arrives at the subject of eugenics.

The third section of 'To-morrow's Revolution' summarises the findings of Yeats's researches into eugenics, drawing heavily, but not exclusively, on Cattell. He explains the idea of innate intelligence or 'mother-wit' and how it can be measured 'with great accuracy' by intelligence tests. These tests, he is careful to mention, 'eliminate, or almost eliminate, the child's acquired knowledge'.[75] He then describes the research which proves that innate intelligence is hereditary, that it increases from one level of the social scale to the next, and that in the higher social ranks there is not only greater intelligence, but an increase in 'the size of the body and its freedom from constitutional defects'.[76] (He regrets, in a footnote, that eugenists have as yet not done any research among the leisured classes, since he would like to know 'what happens to the plant when it gets from under the stone'[77] – reminding us again of the image of the bloom in the Cingalese forest.) Then he comes to the crux of the argument: the differential birth rate, and the national degeneration in mind and body the differential birth rate must cause. That degeneration, Yeats notes, following Cattell, is 'already visible in the degeneration of literature, newspapers, amusements', and, going well beyond Cattell into regions uniquely his own, visible as well as 'benefactions like that of Lord Nuffield, a self-made man, to Oxford, which must gradually substitute applied science for ancient wisdom'.[78] Education, the section concludes, will not suffice to halt the slide, since education neither increases nor decreases innate intelligence. The solution to the problem will necessarily be of a harsher sort.

The fourth section of 'To-morrow's Revolution' deals with the future. In the conclusion to his book, Cattell had imagined that the struggle for the acceptance of eugenics would 'be won by men and women fit for the hand-to-hand fighting of committees, with stamina to carry the struggle into the dust and heat of social-welfare work in sordid cities',[79] but Yeats by this time had no such faith in committees or patient labour, and he chooses to make Cattell's martial metaphors literal. Out of either principle (democratic in the United States, Marxist in Russia) or necessity (as in Germany and Italy, where 'dread of attack' led to bounties for large families), governments would refuse to address the imminent biological crisis, which would eventually erupt in a prolonged war between 'the educated classes' and 'the uneducatable masses'.[80] Horrible as this prospect was, the alternative was to Yeats more horrible: 'The danger is that there will be no war, that the skilled will attempt nothing, that the European civilisation, like those older civilisations that saw the triumph of their gangrel stocks, will accept decay.'[81]

Yeats did not, of course, derive his sense of the approaching modern apocalypse from eugenics. Rather, he adapted the ideas of the eugenists to fit an apocalyptic vision that was very much his own. Such was the pattern of his whole interest in the topic, as the fifth and concluding section of the essay shows. This section betrays a certain unsophistication on Yeats's part with eugenics' founding assumptions, or perhaps an unwillingness to let eugenics, however substantial its agreement with certain of his convictions, overrule certain of his other convictions. The published findings of the US Army intelligence tests had included a section analysing the intelligence of foreign-born recruits by country of origin. England, Holland, Denmark, Scotland and Germany, in that order, had produced on the average the brightest recruits. Ireland was some way down the list, just ahead of Turkey, Greece, Russia, Italy and Poland.[82] Yeats did not bring 'To-morrow's Revolution' to a close without noting this fact and entering a few necessary qualifications. The Irish who had emigrated to America were 'unskilled men driven by necessity', they were 'our unemployed', and they were not to be taken as typical, but instead weighed in the balance against 'those that go to posts all over the British Empire as doctors, lawyers, soldiers, civil servants, or drift away drawn to the lights of London'.[83] In naming this group Yeats was most likely thinking of families like the Gregorys, the Anglo-Irish he had once called the 'greatest breed in Europe',[84] but he did not leave the peasant Irish undefended.

Some of the inferiority of our emigrants in the United States and in Scotland may depend upon difference of historical phase. The tests usually employed are appropriate to a civilisation dominated by towns, by their objectivity and curiosity. Some of the tests are rectilinear mazes of increasing difficulty. . . . Probably a city child thinks of neighbouring streets where every turn is a right angle; an Achill child having no such image would probably fail through lack of attention. Other tests consist of fitting certain objects into pictures, but pictures are almost or wholly unknown in our remote districts.[85]

As Yeats had noted earlier in his extraordinarily deft explanation of the eugenists' central claims, these tests were supposed to measure innate intelligence. The results of these tests provided the quantitative evidence – the *only* quantitative evidence – on which the argument about the 'differential birth rate' rested. To argue that the tests in fact measure acquired intelligence or any sort of environmental influence was to pick away at the foundations of the edifice, and the above passage from Yeats, in spite of its reference to 'historical phase', is just such an argument.[86] We cannot say whether Yeats did not realise that such a possibility as he had raised undermined the case he had been making, or whether, having his own priorities thoroughly straight, he did not care. Certainly from this point on the essay departs for familiar Yeatsian territory: 'Then, we Irish are nearer than the English to the Mythic Age', he writes,[87] and goes on to abuse the English on several counts. Yeats was willing to go along with the reasonings and statistics of the eugenists when they proved that modern man was degenerate, but not when they seemed to prove that there remained anywhere a larger residuum of the old heroic stuff than there remained in the Irish aristocrat and the Irish countryman.

'To-morrow's Revolution' is the only section of *On the Boiler* explicitly devoted to eugenics, but the topic appears in some form or other in each of the book's five main prose sections. The revolution referred to in 'Ireland after the Revolution' is again the eugenical revolution, and the Ireland of the future sketched in that section is one that has passed through the 'tragic crisis'[88] predicted in 'To-morrow's Revolution'. Yeats believed Ireland would prosper once it had passed through that crisis, since it had 'as good blood as there is in Europe'.[89] In the introductory essay, 'Preliminaries', Yeats praises the first cabinet of the Irish Free State, then mentions that the families of its ministers 'have already intermarried' and that 'able stocks have begun to appear'.[90] It is on the heels of this remark that Yeats's often-quoted dismissal of contemporary politics occurs.

> I was six years in the Irish Senate; I am not ignorant of politics elsewhere, and on other grounds I have some right to speak. I say to those that shall rule here: 'If ever Ireland again seems as molten wax, reverse the process of revolution. Do not try to pour Ireland into any political system. Think first how many able men with public minds the country has, how many it can hope to have in the near future, and mould your system upon those men. Republics, Kingdoms, Soviets, Corporate states, Parliaments, are trash, as Hugo said of something else, "not worth one blade of grass that God gives for the nest of the linnet". These men, whether six or six thousand, are the core of Ireland, are Ireland itself.'[91]

Some have read this passage as a transcendence of petty political squabbles and an arrival into the upper aether of wise poetic detachment, but Yeats's manifest contempt for all modern political factions should not keep us from seeing that the passage contains a clear and specific political recommendation: Ireland will prosper only if governed by an aristocracy. That aristocracy, the passage's context implies, must be an hereditary aristocracy. If such a government be not attained peacefully it will be attained by force, because of all forms of government it alone has the sanction of nature.

To judge from its parenthetical subtitle, '(Should be skipped by Politicians and Journalists)', the essay titled 'Private Thoughts' is the heart of the book. As is usually the case when Yeats is putting into prose those things that most matter to him, this essay is allusive, elliptical and thickly crowded with ideas. It defies easy summation, but near its centre is the idea of generation. Through generation men tried to conquer the antinomies, the opposites that are 'everywhere face to face, dying each other's life, living each other's death':

> When a man loves a girl it should be because her face and character offer what he lacks; the more profound his nature the more he should realise his lack and the greater be the difference. It is as though he wanted to take his own death into his arms and beget a stronger life upon that death. We should count men and women who pick, as it were, the dam or sire of a Derby winner from between the shafts of a cab, among persons of genius, for this genius makes all other kinds possible.[92]

The meeting of the sexual instinct with the aspiration towards human perfection had produced the civilisation described in Castiglione's *Courtier* as well as that described in Irish legend: Finn had 'stood on the top of a hill and said he would marry the first woman that reached him', Emer had earned the privilege of marrying Cuchulain by 'the strength and volume of her bladder'.[93] In our own age heroism and unity were lost because this genius had been lost, and the best was no longer valued over the mediocre, the small had overwhelmed the great. This inverted order, patently unnatural, would not last. Psychical research, Yeats believed, would restore the old idea of the immortality of the soul, and eugenical research would restore the old ideas of generation and lineage. The world would know again that human kind's highest good was that union of instinct and

aspiration that caused the best to be born of the best, and revere
that union as it had in the birth-scene of Morris's *Sigurd*, a scene
Yeats could not resist evoking, although he does not identify it:

> Eugenical and physical research are the revolutionary movements
> with that element of novelty and sensation which sooner or
> later stir men to action. It may be, or it must be, that the best
> bred of the best shall claim again their ancient omens. And the
> serving women 'shrank in their rejoicing from the eyes of the
> child', and 'the hour was awful to them' as they brought the
> child to its mother.[94]

If science could 'stir men to action' towards this end, more
power to science. Art, of course, had a role to play as well, and
Yeats spells out that role in *On the Boiler*'s concluding prose
section. 'Other Matters' deals mainly with art, particularly with
the vulgarity of much modern art, a vulgarity Yeats attributes to
the tendency of modern artists to represent not an imaginary
ideal, but 'life' in all its blotched imperfection. As he had in *The
King's Threshold* and 'If I were Four-and-Twenty', Yeats defends
ideal art on the eugenic principle that art educates desire, causes
the best to breed with the best, and so slowly brings human kind
towards perfection. Civilisation reached its highest point, as it
had in ancient Greece and Renaissance Italy, when the ideal was
thought of not as impossibly remote, but as the upper limit of the
possible. Aspiration to the ideals set by Pythagoras's inspired
numbers had created Greek perfection:

> There are moments when I am certain that art must once again
> accept those Greek proportions which carry into plastic art the
> Pythagorean numbers, those faces which are divine because all
> there is empty and measured. Europe was not born when
> Greek galleys defeated the Persian hordes at Salamis; but when
> the Doric studios sent out those broad-backed marble statues
> . . . they gave to the sexual instinct of Europe its goal, its fixed
> type.[95]

A work of art that conforms to ideal proportions may seem to lack
'character', as Yeats said in 'The Statues', so long as we see it as
inhuman, unreal or lifeless, but may take on a strange transforming
power if we see it as embodying a distant but perhaps realisable

perfection. Greek and Renaissance art had achieved that transforming power, the effects of which lingered even into our own day; Yeats saw the measurements of Pythagoras on the beaches of the Riviera and 'wherever the lucky or the well-born uncover their sunburnt bodies'.[96] But democracy, which took as its measure the ordinary, had replaced aristocracy, which took as its measure the all but impossible best, and with that change art which imitated the real had replaced art which embodied the ideal – some such chain of association dictated the inclusion of the adjective 'democratic' in the final sentence of Yeats's discussion of classical proportion in art:

> There, too, are doubtless flesh tints that Greek painters loved as have all the greatest since; nowhere upon any beautiful body, whether of man or woman, those red patches whereby our democratic painters prove that they have really studied from the life.[97]

The themes of *On Baile's Strand*, *The King's Threshold* and 'If I were Four-and-Twenty' discussed earlier – the degeneration of man, and his possible regeneration through the right kind of art and the right regard for the best family stocks – thus lie near the centre of Yeats's final blast at the public, *On the Boiler*. They are supported by new evidence from the new science of eugenics and marked by a candour about sexuality that is characteristic only of the older Yeats, but they are recognisably the same. In Yeats's late poetry, because of both the new evidence and the new candour, these themes begin to appear with surprising frequency.

The influence of eugenics – again using that word, with less than perfect accuracy, as shorthand for the interests in generation, degeneration and regeneration that we have been examining – on Yeats's poetry will be more plainly seen if we divide the poems grouped together under the heading 'Last Poems' in the collected and variorum editions into three groups according to the volumes in which they were first published: the poems in *New Poems* (1938), those included in *On the Boiler* (also 1938), and those in *Last Poems and Two Plays* (1939). The poems in *New Poems* and *On the Boiler* dwell particularly on degeneration, with especial bitterness in the latter volume. In *Last Poems and Two Plays* degeneration still figures as a theme, but it is almost jocularly taken for granted, and Yeats pays more attention to the possibility that the aristocratic and heroic sexual instinct or ideal art may in time regenerate human kind.

'The Gyres', which opens *New Poems*, both describes decay ('A greater, a more gracious time is gone') and promises the return of lost greatness and beauty ('all things' shall 'run / On that unfashionable gyre again').[98] As Curtis Bradford has noted, that decay includes physical degeneration.[99] Not only do 'Conduct and work grow coarse, and coarse the soul,' but the 'ancient lineaments are blotted out'; coarsening of the soul is matched by a coarsening of the body as the classical types of human beauty disappear. Yeats describes those who will in time to come bring back what was lost as 'Lovers of horses and of women' – possessors, that is, of aristocratic instincts for mastery and for sexual selection. In 'Are You Content?', the volume's final poem, Yeats wonders if he himself is something less than what his forebears were: 'Have I, that put it into words, / Spoilt what old loins have sent?'[100] Although in old age he has arrived at a wisdom like that of Browning's 'old hunter talking with Gods', his sense of his own worth suffers when he compares himself to

> He that in Sligo at Drumcliffe
> Set up the old stone Cross,
> That red-headed rector in County Down,
> A good man on a horse,
> Sandymount Corbets, that notable man
> Old William Pollexfen,
> The smuggler Middleton, Butlers far back,
> Half legendary men.[101]

Yeats asks his ancestors to 'judge what I have done'. No such judgment issues from them in the poem, but Yeats himself, stirred by their memory, is 'not content'.

Of all the poems in the volume, 'The Old Stone Cross' deals most explicitly with degeneration. In this poem, a 'man in a golden breastplate' / Under the old stone Cross' delivers himself of three attacks on contemporary civilisation. The opinions expressed are certainly Yeats's, but it is worth noting that they are attributed to a voice out of the greater past: the heroic past (the golden breastplate), the national past (the old stone cross is a work of early Irish art) and Yeats's own past (the cross is the one in his great-grandfather's churchyard at Drumcliffe). The man in the golden breastplate begins by denouncing democracy as the plaything of lying politicians and lying journalists and concludes by denouncing 'actors lacking music' who 'shuffle, grunt and groan', but devotes the middle third of his tirade to denouncing the erring sexual instinct of the age and the ruin it has caused:

> Because this age and the next age
> Engender in the ditch,
> No man can know a happy man
> From any passing wretch;
> If Folly link with Elegance
> No man knows which is which,
> *Said the man in the golden breastplate*
> *Under the old stone Cross.*[102]

This stanza, in its juxtaposition of the 'happy man' of sound lineage with the 'passing wretch', suggests that Yeats had already come across the passage from Burton that he took as his 'text' in 'To-morrow's Revolution', the passage in which Burton claimed that owing to our 'giving way for all to marry who will' there was 'no family secure, no man almost free from some grievous infirmity or other'. It suggests also that Yeats was already plotting out the poetic drama *Purgatory*, which concludes *On the Boiler*, and which deals with an aristocratic young woman who so far forgets the responsibilities on which her Elegance depends as to fall in love with a groom, marry him and bear him a son who will carry the curse on to 'the next age' by engendering with a tinker's daughter in a ditch. The essential complaint of the man in the golden breastplate is that the world has come to value the common over the rare. The democratic politician who panders to the majority, the actor who insists on performing naturalistically instead of rounding his scene with 'unearthly stuff', and most crucially the well-born woman who doesn't mind where she marries all have their values upside-down.

The three poems and the play in verse included in *On the Boiler* all touch on degeneration and questions of breeding. The first of these, later titled 'Why should not Old Men be Mad?', occurs in the opening section of the book, as if to explain the splenetic extravagance of what follows. Old men are bound to be mad, the poem argues, because they see in no life 'a finish worthy of the start'. The old man of the poem has seen, for instance, 'A girl that knew all Dante once / Live to bear children to a dunce . . .'.[103] The wrong of this is not only that the girl married a dunce, and so deprived herself of the kind of company she ought to have enjoyed, but also that she bore the dunce's children, and so hastened the decline of human kind.[104]

On the Boiler's second poem, later titled 'Crazy Jane on the Mountain', occurs in the 'Ireland after the Revolution' section. In the first half of this poem, Crazy Jane meditates on the cowardice of King George V, who, Yeats believed, had let himself be dissuaded from helping the Romanoffs because it was feared such help might provoke a revolution in England. In the second half, she recalls a vision she had had the night before, as she lay on the mountain, of Cuchulain and Emer in a chariot. Thinking of the difference between the fiercely independent Cuchulain and the modern king who lacked the will to save his 'beautiful cousins' brings Crazy Jane to tears. Not even kings are what they were, and one reason they are not is hinted at in Crazy Jane's epithet for Emer, 'Great-bladdered'.[105] If the heroic, self-sufficient discipline that ought to go with kingship is not practised in breeding as well as in all else, even a kingly race declines.

The book's third poem, later titled 'The Stateman's Holiday', occurs at the end of the prose part of the book. The poem is spoken by a politician who has abandoned politics in order to become an itinerant minstrel, travelling the south of France with a monkey and a Montenegrin lute. The statesman-minstrel is a latter-day (and, if you will, degenerate) King Goll, the king out of Irish legend who in one of Yeats's earliest poems lost his mind in a battle, gave up his kingdom and took to wandering Ireland with a harp.[106] The statesman has none of King Goll's visionary dignity – his 'secret spirit' holds no 'wild and whirling fire', to quote the earlier poem – but that is only because, as he freely admits in the poem's opening lines, men are not what they were and are daily becoming worse:

> I lived among great houses,
> Riches drove out rank,
> Base drove out the better blood,
> And mind and body shrank.[107]

The statesman does not remember who he was before he gave up politics, although all the possibilities that occur to him are of modern leaders who in one instance or another failed to lead.[108] He gives up the attempt, turns again to his lute, and like Crazy Jane dwells on vanished greatness: '*Tall dames go walking in grass-green Avalon*', runs the poem's refrain.

There is none of the satiric merriment of 'The Statesman's Holiday' in *Purgatory*, which immediately follows it in *On the Boiler*. *Purgatory* dramatises Yeats's idea of what becomes of the dead: they 'suffer remorse and re-create their old lives', as he explained after the first performance of the play.[109] It also dramatises, as has been shown, Yeats's interpretation of the history of Ireland in his lifetime.[110] What is interesting about the play in the light of our topic, though, is that the burden of the play's meaning is made to rest on a question of breeding, as it had been in *On Baile's Strand* and *The King's Threshold*. Yeats made this clear when asked to explain the play:

> In my play a spirit suffers because of its share, when alive, in the destruction of an honoured house; that destruction is taking place all over Ireland today. Sometimes it is a result of poverty, but more often because a new individualistic generation has lost interest in the ancient sanctities. . . . In some few cases a house has been destroyed by mesalliance. I have founded my play on this exceptional case, partly because of my interest in certain problems of eugenics, partly because it enables me to depict more vividly than would otherwise be possible the tragedy of the house.[111]

Yeats's interest in eugenics had served to remind him of the regard paid to sexual choice not only in Irish folklore, but also in the traditions of the landed aristocracy. The crime the ghost of his play must expiate is a mistaken sexual choice. Moved by the groom's handsomeness and unmindful of her genetic responsibility, so to speak, she 'Looked at him and married him', as the Old Man says not once but twice, struck by the awful power of his mother's erring instinct.[112] The Old Man never doubts that his mother did wrong, however. 'Her mother never spoke to her again, / And she did right,' he says at one point,[113] and at another point grants that the groom was handsome but insists that 'She should have known he was not her kind'.[114] He sees the corruption consequent on his mother's mistake both in himself and in his son. Of himself he says that though some who 'Half-loved me for my half of her' gave him the education his father withheld,[115] he is nonetheless unfit to be anything better than a pedlar simply 'Because I am my father's son / Because of what I did or may do'.[116] His son he calls 'A bastard that a pedlar got / Upon a tinker's daughter in a ditch',[117] whose murder he justifies partly because 'He would have struck a woman's fancy, / Begot, and passed pollution on'.[118] Influenced by an 'interest in certain problems of eugenics', Yeats found no more nearly complete way to figure the power of consequence over individuals, families, nations and even the dead than this story of mistaken sexual choice. The woman's error defeats even poetry, since right breeding was, to Yeats, poetry's ancient theme. In the terrible moment after the boy's murder, when the stage has once more darkened, the old man begins to sing, yet stops when he realises his mother's act has emptied the song of meaning:

> 'Hush-a-bye baby, thy father's a knight,
> Thy mother a lady, lovely and bright.'
> No, that is something that I read in a book,
> And if I sing, it must be to my mother,
> And I lack rhyme.[119]

Poetry was once sung, and guided conduct, but now is confined to print, and guides nothing – accordingly, the Old Man gives over his ballad. The literal degeneration on which the play's story turns includes, by this touch, the 'degeneration' of civilisation itself.

   Although the poems of *Last Poems and Two Plays* refer to degeneration almost as frequently as do those of *New Poems* and *On the Boiler*, they counterpose to degeneration two forces that could set it right: Heroic or aristocratic (these categories, in Yeats, overlap) sexual instinct, and ideal, as opposed to realistic, art. In one poem, 'A Bronze Head', no such counterposition occurs. Yeats instead advances degeneration as the last of his many explanations of Madame MacBride's tumultuous career, and leaves it at that. The last stanza of that poem is perhaps the plainest evocation of degeneration anywhere in Yeats's poetry:

> Or else I thought her supernatural;

As though a sterner eye looked through her eye
On this foul world in its decline and fall;
On gangling stocks grown great, great stocks run dry,
Ancestral pearls all pitched into a sty,
Heroic reverie mocked by clown and knave,
And wondered what was left for massacre to save.[120]

Elsewhere in the volume, though, Yeats suggests cures in addition to diagnosing the disease. The cures may strike the reader as unlikely or, alternately, brutal, but they lend the volume much of its often-remarked pungency.

At first glance, the three songs grouped together under the title 'Three Songs to the One Burden' appear to have nothing in common beyond their shared burden, *'From mountain to mountain ride the fierce horsemen'*, but if we look at them from a eugenical viewpoint we notice that they deal in turn with the old heroic sexual instinct, modern degeneration and the regenerative property of ideal art. The first of the three songs is delivered by Mannion, the Roaring Tinker, who claims descent from Manannan Mac Lir, god of the sea in old Irish legend. Mannion admits to being a lesser character than his ancestor, who never 'made an iron red / Nor soldered pot or pan',[121] yet he has retained the ancient heroic wisdom that cherishes the best and scorns the mediocre, particularly in matters generative. Mannion, unembarrassed by more charitable modern tendencies, gleefully carries his convictions into the sphere of direct action:

The Roaring Tinker if you like,
But Mannion is my name,
And I beat up the common sort
And think it is no shame.
The common breeds the common,
A lout begets a lout,
So when I take on half a score
I knock their heads about.[122]

In the second stanza of his song Mannion recalls his ancestor, and in the third dreams of a day when Manannan will return, Crazy Jane regain her youth and the three of them together forcibly reform the nation according to the principles of heroic eugenics:

> Could Crazy Jane put off old age
> And ranting time renew,
> Could that old god rise up again
> We'd drink a can or two,
> And out and lay our leadership
> On country and on town,
> Throw likely couples into bed
> And knock the others down.[123]

The second song is delivered by Henry Middleton, an eccentric cousin of Yeats who lived an extraordinarily retired life in Sligo in a house named Elsinore.[124] Like Mannion, Henry Middleton has an illustrious ancestor: William Middleton, the 'smuggler Middleton' of 'Are You Content?' and the 'old merchant skipper' who leapt into Biscay Bay to retrieve a hat in 'Pardon, old fathers . . .'. Again like Mannion, he carries some tincture of his ancestor, in that his imagination wanders towards images of the sea: his house is set 'On a storm-bitten green', and he ends his song with the lines, 'There's not a pilot on the perch / Knows I have lived so long.'[125] Like Mannion once more, Henry Middleton is not content with the rising generation: 'I pity all the young, / . . . / The wisdom of the people's gone, / How can the young go straight?' Henry Middleton represents a farther falling-off than does Mannion, however, for if Mannion retains some of the old heroic strength of arm, Henry Middleton retains none of the old heroic extravagance. His life consists of housekeeping and Sunday afternoon walks. The extravagance of the young, their likeness to his sea-faring grandfather, is the very thing he dislikes in them: 'Their drink, their pitch-and-toss by day, / Their robbery by night . . .'. Mannion and Henry Middleton are alike ruined versions, the one of heroic age Irishmen and the other of eighteenth-century Irishmen, and in their juxtaposition they suggest the futility of strength without a sense of civilisation, or of a sense of civilisation without strength. Yet Mannion's purposeful brutality has the advantage over Henry Middleton's acquiescence, since the latter has arrived at the point of sterility while the former holds at least a possibility of regeneration.

A less direct but perhaps equally effective way towards regeneration is hinted at in the third song, an actor's song of praise for the Easter Rising. The actor describes the Rising as a play, its leaders as players who consciously chose a high tragic

Grotowski studied all the major actor-training methods of Europe + afar. Most important to him were Dullin's rhythm exercises, Delsartes investigations of extroversive & introversive Reactions, Stanislavsky's work on "Physical Actions", Meyerhold's bio-mechanical training + Vakhtangov's synthesis. Also, particularly stimulating to him were the training techniques of Asian theatre - specifically the Peking Opera, Indian Kathakali & Japanese Noh theatre.

②

role, as an artist might paint impossibly beautiful bodies, that the real might be transformed by the presence of the ideal:

> Some had no thought of victory
> But had gone out to die
> That Ireland's mind be greater,
> Her heart mount up on high; . . .[126]

Although this third song does not allude to questions of breeding, its use of the Easter Rising as an example of art shaping actuality connects it to 'The Statues', in which the example is used again, and in which, as we shall see later, Yeats puts into verse his argument that Greek art created Europe by guiding desire. As degeneration had been connected to realistic or naturalistic art in 'The Old Stone Cross', so it is here, with the difference that here the regenerative nature of ideal art is emphasised. But the actor's song does not promise that art will prove a more peaceable way to regeneration than Mannion's knocking of heads. His song ends:

> And yet who knows what's yet to come?
> For Patrick Pearse had said
> That in every generation
> Must Ireland's blood be shed.

Modern civilisation's deadly torpor – the torpor of Henry Middleton – will be broken only by violence. Accordingly, the horsemen who ride from mountain to mountain at the close of each stanza are 'fierce'. The horsemen belong to a higher race, for they are the horsemen of whom Mary Battle said, 'There is no such race living now, none so finely proportioned',[127] and those whose 'Complexion and form' prove them 'superhuman' in 'Under Ben Bulben'.[128] These horsemen, who throughout *Last Poems* are about to awake, or waking, or already descending, will bring regeneration, but not peace.

Regeneration via the Mannion route – the effort to ensure, as did Cuchulain, Finn and wise aristocratic families, that the best are born of the best – appears in two other of the poems in *Last Poems and Two Plays*, 'News for the Delphic Oracle' and 'Hound Voice'. The first stanza of 'News for the Delphic Oracle' describes the shore that lies beyond birth, death and the body, the second stanza the dolphin-back journey of the dead to that shore. The

third stanza completes the backward movement of the poem by
bringing us again to the world of birth, death and the body,
suggesting by that backward movement the familiar Yeatsian
theme that while we in this world long for the next one, those in
the next world long for this one – 'God possesses the heavens,
but he covets the earth.'[129] For the purposes of our discussion,
what is interesting is that the figuring of the world of birth, death
and the body is accomplished by opposed examples of generation,
the eugenically sound union of Peleus and Thetis and the random
coupling of the nymphs and satyrs. The relish of the last four
lines is so marked that it would be pressing a point to argue that
the poem, in applauding the civic-mindedness of Peleus and
Thetis, utterly deplores the unregulated breeding of the nymphs
and satyrs. Equally marked, though, is the reverential quiet of the
first five lines. The union of Peleus and Thetis will produce a
hero, and it is the lonely, self-sufficient hero that is above all
beloved of the gods (as in 'The Grey Rock'), so this example of
generation serves at least as well as the exuberant riot of the other
example to hint at why the immortal may covet the mortal.
Furthermore, the union of Peleus and Thetis will produce, in
producing Achilles, inexhaustible matter for song and story, will
make poetry possible. Heroic sexual selection, the poem suggests,
is one of the glories of the incarnate world.

Sexual selection appears again as part of heroic or aristocratic
instinct in 'Hound Voice'. This strange and rarely discussed poem
was, according to A. N. Jeffares on information from Mrs Yeats,
'written in a spirit of mockery',[130] but it is difficult to say what is
being mocked. The speaker of the poem identifies himself with
those who 'love bare hills and stunted trees'

> And were the last to choose the settled ground,
> Its boredom of the desk or spade. . . .[131]

This remnant is now dormant, 'slumber-bound', but

> Some few half wake and half renew their choice,
> Give tongue, proclaim their hidden name – 'Hound Voice'.[132]

Hounds play such a large part in Irish legends, particularly that of
Cuchulain, that this remnant's hidden name marks it as a remnant
of the heroic past. That its members 'renew their choice' marks

them as aristocratic: in trying to describe the aristocratic temperament of Lady Gregory, Yeats had written of 'a choice constantly renewed in solitude'.[133] The remnant is marked as aristocratic again in the second stanza, which describes a kind of tragic experience this remnant shares, and calls to mind what Yeats had written of the 'tragedian Parnell', the aristocratic leader who passed 'Through Jonathan Swift's dark grove . . . and there / Plucked bitter wisdom that enriched his blood':

> The women that I picked spoke sweet and low
> And yet gave tongue. 'Hound Voices' were they all.
> We picked each other from afar and knew
> What hour of terror comes to test the soul,
> And in that terror's name obeyed the call,
> And understood, what none have understood,
> Those images that waken in the blood.

'Picked' is a word Yeats sometimes used in writing of sexual choice, as in 'Private Thoughts', where he speaks of 'man-picker' barmaids,[134] and 'News for the Delphic Oracle', where Niamh is also a 'man-picker'. That sexual choice becomes a call obeyed in the name of terror reminds us of 'Private Thoughts' again, particularly the above-quoted passage in which Yeats wrote that a man should seek in the mother of his children what he himself lacks, 'as though he wanted to take his own death into his arms and beget a stronger life upon that death', and that 'the more profound his nature the more should he realise that lack . . .'. Perhaps, then, the call of hound voice to hound voice is the call of one profound, almost instinctive tragic realisation to another, seeking through that call to win back a small victory from life by ensuring that the best will be born of the best. This guiding sexual instinct is bound up with an instinct for violence which the speaker promises will waken from its slumber and (it is implied) regain its old supremacy:

> Some day we shall get up before the dawn
> And find our ancient hounds before the door,
> And wide awake know that the hunt is on;
> Stumbling upon the blood-dark track once more,
> Then stumbling to the kill beside the shore;
> Then cleaning out and bandaging of wounds,
> And chants of victory amid the encircling hounds.

Unless the poem is a mockery of Yeats's own preoccupations in these years, it can only be a mockery of the 'filthy modern tide' and its 'formless spawning fury'.[135] The heroic, aristocratic temper unites the ability to lead, a capacity for violence, and a guiding sexual instinct. The quarry this temper brings to ground in the poem's last stanza may be modernity itself.

However, *Last Poems and Two Plays* dwells most often not on the power of heroic or aristocratic sexual instinct, but on the power of art to transform humanity, in the literal sense. This theme is announced in the volume's first poem, 'Under Ben Bulben', once titled 'His Convictions',[136] which in fact announces many of the volume's themes. The first section introduces the horsemen whose descent from Ben Bulben is imminent, the second establishes the immortality of the soul and the inevitability of reincarnation, the third makes a claim for the necessity of anger and violence. The fourth section, considerably the poem's longest, defends ideal art, in part for its spiritual qualities but no less for its role in the education of desire:

> Poet and sculptor, do the work,
> Nor let the modish painter shirk
> What his great forefathers did,
> Bring the soul of man to God,
> Make him fill the cradles right.[137]

Phidias and Michelangelo serve as the types of artist who have educated desire, made men and women fill the cradles right and gradually improved the kind. This, Yeats points out in one of the poem's more memorable passages, constitutes the profane, as distinct from the sacred, purpose of art:

> Measurement began our might:
> Forms a stark Egyptian thought,
> Forms that gentler Phidias wrought.
> Michael Angelo left a proof
> On the Sistine Chapel roof,
> Where but half-awakened Adam
> Can disturb globe-trotting Madam
> Till her bowels are in heat,
> Proof that there's a purpose set
> Before the secret working mind:
> Profane perfection of mankind.[138]

The poem's fifth section is addressed specifically to Irish artists, and advises them in more particular terms to sing an ideal, the peasantry, the aristocracy, the 'holiness of monks', rather than the present and actual. The unworthiness of the present and actual is graphically rendered as its degeneracy, its eugenical unfitness:

> Irish poets, learn your trade,
> Sing whatever is well-made,
> Scorn the sort now growing up
> All out of shape from toe to top,
> Their unremembering hearts and heads
> Base-born products of base beds.[139]

References in 'Under Ben Bulben' to sculpture and measurement prepare us for 'The Statues', and the reference to Michelangelo prepares us for 'Long-legged Fly'. 'Long-legged Fly' is about the magic of quiet. Caesar needs quiet to plan a victorious campaign, Helen needs quiet to practice her charms that she may break one civilisation and provide the poetic matter of another, and Michelangelo needs quiet for his secret working mind to be about the profane perfection of mankind:

> That girls at puberty may find
> The first Adam in their thought,
> Shut the door of the Pope's chapel,
> Keep those children out.[140]

'The Statues' opposes East and West on the grounds that while the Eastern spiritual ideal was formless, the West by means of Pythagoras's numbers embodied its spiritual ideal in plastic art, and so enabled that ideal to transform the actual. Greek sculptors 'gave women dreams'[141] (or, to quote *On the Boiler*, gave the 'sexual instinct of Europe' its 'fixed type') and so helped along the profane perfection of mankind, ensured the rise of the West. The modern example that matches the Greek statues, as we have mentioned earlier, is the 1916 Rising, which, in its broad, poetic gestures, its sense of the tradition in which it participated and its apparent futility resembled a work of art. There, too, an embodied ideal transformed the actual, accomplished what more realistic and down-to-earth means had been unable to accomplish. The

Irish, Yeats promises in the poem's final lines, would never abandon that idea of the meaning of art born among the Greeks, however much it was forgotten elsewhere in Europe:

> We Irish, born into that ancient sect
> But thrown upon this filthy modern tide
> And by its formless spawning fury wrecked,
> Climb to our proper dark, that we may trace
> The lineaments of a plummet-measured face.[142]

In the short poem 'A Nativity' ideal art – artificial, unrealistic, unmimetic, spiritualised, romantic, 'antithetical' art – attends the most momentous of births, that of the being who will stand to the next age as Christ stood to his and Helen to hers. The poem begins:

> What woman hugs her infant there?
> Another star has shot an ear.[143]

Since this being will usher in an antithetical age, he is naturally surrounded (we might even say, his way has been prepared) by antithetical art: Delacroix's painting has made the drapery glisten, Landor's poetry has sealed the roof, the high tragic acting style of Talma and of Irving has swept away from the scene moth and fly, knave and dolt. The poem ends:

> Why is the woman terror-struck?
> Can there be mercy in that look?

The look is that of the infant, and recalls not only the 'gaze blank and pitiless as the sun' of the beast that slouched towards Bethlehem, but also the look of the infant Sigurd, whose mother's serving-women 'shrank in their rejoicing from the eyes of the child, / so bright and dreadful were they . . .'. The infant's eyes mark him as one of 'the best born of the best' who in the next age 'shall claim their ancient omens', as somehow kin to the horsemen about to descend on Ireland. So antithetical art, by way of its eugenical properties, becomes part of the apocalyptic theme that runs through *Last Poems and Two Plays*.

Yeats's interest in eugenics, to conclude, was more than a final vagary, and was not confined to one section of *On the Boiler*.

Eugenics served as support for long-held convictions of his having to do with modern degeneration and the importance of birth and family, and led him to present those convictions baldly and with unprecedented and uncompromised physicality in his late poems. As always, though, he viewed the findings of scientists from the heights proper to artists. All that is worthy in human kind may well spring from the development of the right genes, but who, finally, was most responsible for the very rightness of those genes? The artist, who by holding to men's eyes things and beings that did not exist brought a pressure to change on things and beings that did exist, who by invoking the intangible transformed the tangible.

Conclusion

Beside a passage of Nietzsche about the 'fewest' who create value, Yeats added a definition: 'Rulers, that is to say the living, or wholly free, wholly self-moving.'[1] As the greatest art comes from the 'antithetical' artist whose imagination carries no burdens but its own, so the best government comes from the 'antithetical' aristocrat who requires and heeds only self-imposed obligations. Since these few individuals defined their own lives, rather than having their lives defined for them, they were the 'living'. They lived the freedom which the artist, in ideal circumstances, enjoyed in his work. The burdens of the artist's imagination, the aristocrat's self-imposed obligations might be enormous – 'whatever whim's most difficult / Among whims not impossible'[2] – but the artist's and the aristocrat's achievement is to carry them effortlessly: the poem that seems a moment's thought, the judgment that seems like intuition, the courtesy of certain women. The gifts that produced the judgment or the courtesy are, as is the poem, economically immeasurable, but they are none the less real for that, and none the less indispensable. Since these gifts are partly innate and partly the result of an education begun in the cradle, they will tend to be the province of a few families; the nation, in its own best interests, will grant these families those privileges which work to preserve the gifts. As the greatest art contains a sense of evil, of human limitation, of the suffering that attends our incarnate condition, so does the aristocratic sensibility. Unlike the Marxist, who is compelled by his doctrine to expect progress toward a perfect society, and unlike the democratic politician or the Nietzschean superman as vulgarly conceived, who achieve their desired selfhood only insofar as and for as long as they are victorious, the aristocrat can affirm both the world's radical imperfectibility and, should it happen, the wreck of his own hopes: 'Bred to a harder thing / Than Triumph',[3] the aristocrat was a tragedian. The greatest ages of our civilisation knew all the above to be true. Since the Renaissance, our conviction of their truth has gradually crumbled, until today we have abolished family privilege, chased after chimeric Utopias, based our governments on the common and general instead of the rare and distinct. The same trouble has overtaken the arts. The 'wholly free, wholly self-moving' imagination is required to duplicate the delusive surface of nature or society, or to illustrate the aspirations of some political party. Since it now refuses to embody reality – which is invisible and immaterial – art has surrendered the transforming, unifying power it once had.

These, in their bare bones, are the principles that underlay Yeats's positions in the various campaigns and controversies we have been examining. They gain immensely in precision – and, if I can say so without necessarily endorsing them, gain somewhat in validity – when we see Yeats forming them and sharpening them by reading or dialectic, acting on them in particular circumstances at particular times. They are not, as I have sometimes been at pains to show, unique to the Yeats of the thirties, but rather ideas he had been meditating on and shaping for many years. I would like to conclude, though, by indicating two important ways in which Yeats's use of these principles in the episodes we have looked at is, indeed, unique to the Yeats of the 1930s.

The first has to do with Yeats's solitude. Yeats had always, in certain ways, had to stand alone. An Irish nationalist, yet not by birth what every Irishman would call Irish, he and his nationalism were marked by what he called 'the Anglo-Irish solitude'.[4] In addition to that, his assumptions about poetic and dramatic art, about the natural and supernatural worlds, were such as could be shared by few. In an occasional aside in the prose one gets a glimpse of how hard a time Yeats had with his contemporaries, as in the opening of *Per Amica Silentia Lunae*: 'When I come home after meeting men who are strange to me, and sometimes even after talking to women, I go over all I have said in gloom and disappointment. Perhaps I have over-stated everything from a desire to vex or startle, from hostility that is but fear; or all my natural thoughts have been drowned by an undisciplined sympathy.'[5] In the 1930s, his solitude increased. The ascendancy of de Valera made the Anglo-Irish tradition of independent nationalism a virtually untenable faith. Most of those with whom Yeats had at one time or another made common cause – John O'Leary, John Synge, Lady Gregory, Kevin O'Higgins, George Russell – were dead. In 'The Municipal Gallery Revisited', surrounded by their portraits, he realises that the turbulent, angry Ireland whose events had determined much of his own career was now distant enough to become myth:

> 'This is not,' I say,
> 'The dead Ireland of my youth, but an Ireland
> The poets have imagined, terrible and gay.'[6]

A triumph for poetry, certainly, even a triumph for Yeats himself, who had done so much to make myths of these people and events, but a triumph that makes of Yeats a man who has outlived his age. 'I am old, I belong to mythology,' says the Old Man who introduces *The Death of Cuchulain*.[7] The newer Irish writers, many of whom he befriended and whose works he often admired, seemed to him to be in pursuit of an art wholly unlike his and that of his old co-workers. 'Like Balzac I know no one who shares the premises from which I work,' he told a 1937 correspondent.[8] *On the Boiler*, like *Per Amica Silentia Lunae*, a work in which Yeats made considerable effort to say just what he really believed, like the earlier essay, contains an admission of how utterly at odds what he believes is with what daily encounters tell him his age believes:

> There was no dominant opinion I could accept. Then finding out that I (having no clear case – my opponent's case had been clarifying itself for centuries) had become both boor and bore, I invented a patter, allowing myself an easy man's insincerity, and for honesty's sake a little malice, and now it seems that I can talk nothing else. But I think I have succeeded, and that none of my friends know that I am a fanatic.[9]

What he called his fanaticism – his solitude in his convictions – consisted in his being one of those 'who are the opposites of our time'. He found what companions he could in the past – ancient Greece, medieval Byzantium, Renaissance Italy, Georgian Ireland – and, increasingly in the thirties, in the future: 'I am a forerunner of that horde that will some day come down the mountains.'[10]

As this solitude grew greater, he grew less apologetic about it, more inclined to insist upon it and glory in it. *On the Boiler* is the obvious example, but one could cite as well *Wheels and Butterflies*, the commentaries in *The King of the Great Clock Tower*, the introduction to *The Oxford Book of Modern Verse*, 'Parnell's Funeral',

'Lapis Lazuli', 'The Old Stone Cross', 'Why should not Old Men be Mad?' and 'Under Ben Bulben'. Yeats had always, of course, been willing 'to vex or startle', and of course even in the thirties sometimes had recourse to some subterfuge or other, such as pronouncing his own theories about history in Balzac's voice, or postulating a new school of poets that he might attribute to them the belief, more his than their's that 'what we call the solid earth was manufactured by the human mind from unknown raw material'.[11] Peculiarly typical of the Yeats of the 1930s, though, is a willingness to dispense with indirection, a desire to outrage. So he defined the task he set himself in deciding to write *On the Boiler*: 'I must lay aside the pleasant paths I have built up for years and seek the brutality, the ill-breeding, the barbarism of truth.'[12]

Yeats's unrepentant solitude and the freedom he found in assuming the part of a 'fanatic' bind together all the episodes we have been considering: his setting himself against the most popular Irish politician of the day, his brief embracing of the Blueshirts' cause, his jabbing at left-leaning writers, his praise of Balzac as a political thinker, his dabbling in eugenics. In all of them we see his wish to appear, in his own famous words, 'A foolish, passionate man',[13] as if appearing foolish were in our time the only reliable sign that one was approaching the truth. To be 'a wise old man / That can be praised of all', to be a revered white-haired poet, was a living death. Yeats wished to be unassimilable, to defeat the expectations that would have locked him into the sterile earnestness that marks so much of the writing of the decade, or have made of him a well-loved nullity.

In a way, despite the massive respect accorded him, he has continued to defeat those expectations up to our own day. It was said of McCoy, the demented Sligo orator who inspired the title of *On the Boiler*, that 'he was a mad ship's carpenter, very good at his trade if he would stick to it, but he went to bed from autumn to spring and during his working months broke off from time to time to read the Scriptures and denounce his neighbours'.[14] Yeats too, it is sometimes intimated, was very good at his trade, but broke off from time to time for such deplorable ventures as *A Vision* and *On the Boiler*. Even when Yeats is sticking to his trade in the final poetry, he manages to upset expectations. That poetry has many admirers, but sometimes even in the full flow of the paean one hears a cough of unease. Thomas Parkinson, in *The Later Poetry*, mentions 'the tendency toward a destructive resolution of problems' and 'the espousal of attitudes that deny the efficacy of rational and humane measures'.[15] Stanley Sultan, in *Yeats at his Last*, thought that 'the poet's iambic and tropologic control of his invective almost legitimized their meaning, but perhaps not quite'.[16] Denis Donoghue, after bringing in the adjectives 'shrill' and 'tiresome', comments:

> I speak harshly of this element in the last Yeats because it seems to me to humiliate the magnanimity of his greatest work, the 'reality and justice' of his central poems. 'My temptation is quiet,' he writes in 'An Acre of Grass', and we know he speaks as a Nietzschean, but we wish he had yielded to it sometimes.[17]

Does it indicate anything that the two poems that come closest to the wise resignation we ordinarily want from an aged poet, 'The Circus Animals' Desertion' and 'Cuchulain Comforted', are the most universally admired? Both are great poems, but can we say what makes them greater than 'Hound Voice' or 'The Black Tower' or 'Under Ben Bulben' or even, to name a personal favourite, 'The Statesman's Holiday', without giving away that what bothers us most is not 'insistent rhymes' or 'blatancy of rhythm' but Yeats's having succeeded so thoroughly in appearing foolish, 'horrible' (to quote 'The Spur'), unbecoming?

In *On the Boiler* Yeats complained of a movement in history that has substituted 'for the old humanity with its unique irreplaceable individuals something that can be chopped and measured like a piece of cheese'.[18] Since universities are often obliged, unfortunately, to chop, measure, and attractively package our few certifiably great poets, it may be all to the good that there is something in Yeats that simply won't be forced through the grater. It is all to the good, as well, that he tried so hard to live up to so complete a definition of the poet's vocation. Finally, we have perhaps as much to learn from those places he chafes us as we do from those places he contents us.

Notes

See pp. ix–x for an explanation of the abbreviations used for Yeats's work.

Notes to the Introduction

1. *E.&I.*, p. 448.
2. *Letters*, pp. 813–15.
3. *E.&I.*, pp. 468–9.
4. *Var. Poems*, p. 610.
5. *Exp.*, pp. 397–8.
6. 'Those Images', *Var. Poems*, pp. 600–1.
7. 'Politics', ibid., p. 631.
8. *Exp.*, p. 463.
9. *Var. Poems*, p. 138.
10. *E.&I.*, p. 208.
11. *Mythologies*, p. 1.
12. For example, Frank Kermode, *The Sense of an Ending: Studies in the Theory of Fiction* (New York: Oxford University Press, 1967) p. 108; Stephen Spender, *The Thirties and After* (London: Macmillan, 1978) pp. 198–9; Denis Donoghue, *William Butler Yeats* (New York: Viking Press, 1971) p. 131.
13. Cairns Craig, *Yeats, Eliot, Pound and the Politics of Poetry: Richest to the Richest* (London and Canberra: Croom Helm, 1982) p. 11.
14. *Var. Poems*, p. 411.
15. *Memoirs*, p. 166.
16. *Uncol. Prose*, I, 104.
17. *Exp.*, p. 369.
18. Grattan Freyer, *W. B. Yeats and the Anti-Democratic Tradition* (Dublin: Gill & Macmillan, 1981) p. 194.
19. *Var. Plays*, p. 306.

Notes to Chapter 1: Yeats and de Valera

1. Sean O'Casey, *Collected Plays* (London: Macmillan, 1951) III, 71–2; Sean O'Casey, *Autobiographies* (London: Macmillan, 1981) II, 155.
2. Oliver St John Gogarty, *Going Native* (New York: Duell, Sloan & Pearce, 1940) p. 6.
3. Richard J. Finneran, George Mills Harper and William M. Murphy (eds), *Letters to W. B. Yeats* (London: Macmillan, 1977) II, 532.

4. Frank O'Connor, *My Father's Son* (London: Macmillan, 1968) p. 115.

5. *Exp.*, p. 372.

6. *Letters*, p. 801. During his 1932–3 American lecture tour, Yeats attacked the Irish censorship at every opportunity. Karin Strand, 'W. B. Yeats's American Lecture Tours', dissertation, Northwestern University (1978) pp. 207–9, 328–37.

7. O'Casey, *Autobiographies*, II, 4.

8. Gogarty, *As I Was Going Down Sackville Street* (New York: Reynal & Hitchcock, 1937) p. 101.

9. O'Connor, *My Father's Son*, p. 113. De Valera attended Russell's funeral in 1935, and his presence on that occasion bothered Yeats (see O'Connor, *My Father's Son*, p. 117) much as the presence of Synge's attackers at Synge's funeral had years before (*Auto.*, pp. 508–9).

10. James Joyce, *Finnegans Wake* (New York: Viking Press, 1939) pp. 342, 473; Richard Ellmann, *James Joyce* (New York: Oxford University Press, 1959) p. 635.

11. Sean O'Faolain, *De Valera* (Harmondsworth: Penguin, 1939) pp. 52–3.

12. *Uncol. Prose*, II, 438.

13. Terence de Vere White, 'Social Life in Ireland 1927–1937', in Francis MacManus (ed.), *The Years of the Great Test* (Cork: Mercier Press, 1967) p. 24.

14. O'Faolain, *De Valera*, p. 68.

15. F. S. L. Lyons, *Ireland Since the Famine* (London: Weidenfeld & Nicolson, 1971) p. 493.

16. Quoted in Earl of Longford and Thomas P. O'Neill, *Eamon de Valera* (London: Hutchinson, 1970) p. 176.

17. Ibid., p. 176.

18. O'Connor, *My Father's Son*, p. 199.

19. Quoted in Donald T. Torchiana, *W. B. Yeats and Georgian Ireland* (Evanston, Ill.: Northwestern University Press, 1966) p. 161.

20. *Exp.*, p. 451.

21. M. J. MacManus, *Eamon de Valera*, new edn with additional matter (Dublin: Talbot Press, 1957) pp. 341–2.

22. *Exp.*, p. 335; prefatory poem to *Responsibilities*, *Var. Poems*, p. 270.

23. See *Exp.*, pp. 123, 276.

24. *Var. Poems*, p. 590.

25. Ibid., p. 543.

26. Quoted in Joseph Hone, *W. B. Yeats: 1865–1939* (London: Macmillan, 1942) p. 323.

27. *Letters*, p. 678. On Yeats and the Oath, see Torchiana, *W. B. Yeats and Georgian Ireland*, pp. 206–9.

28. See *Senate Speeches*, pp. 33–4, 54, 60. Yeats's independence as a senator has been amply demonstrated by Bernard G. Krimm, *W. B. Yeats and the Emergence of the Irish Free State 1918–1939: Living in the Explosion* (Troy, New York: Whitston, 1981) pp. 71–6.

29. As well as endangering his life, Yeats's public support of these measures strained his relations with some close to him, including Lady Gregory (*Lady Gregory's Journals: 1916–1930*, ed. Lennox

Robinson (London: Putnam, 1946) pp. 190–2), and his brother Jack, a firm Republican (Terence de Vere White, 'The Personality of Jack B. Yeats' in Roger McHugh (ed.), *Jack B. Yeats: A Centenary Gathering*, Tower Series of Anglo-Irish Studies 3 (Dublin: Dolmen Press, 1971) p. 33).

30. *Var. Poems*, p. 831.
31. *Uncol. Prose*, II, 486.
32. Ibid., II, 487.
33. Yeats might have chosen not to mention the censorship because, as he had written earlier, he did not blame that piece of legislation on the Cosgrave government, blaming instead Catholic mass opinion (ibid., II, 480).
34. Ibid., II, 488.
35. Longford and O'Neill, *Eamon de Valera*, pp. 245–6.
36. See J. H. Whyte, *Church and State in Modern Ireland 1923–1970* (Dublin: Gill & Macmillan, 1971) pp. 40–9.
37. *Uncol. Prose*, II, 487.
38. de Vere White, 'Social Life in Ireland 1927–1937', p. 24.
39. O'Faolain, *De Valera*, p. 140.
40. M. J. MacManus, *Eamon de Valera* (Chicago: Ziff-Davis, 1946) p. 275.
41. de Vere White, 'Social Life in Ireland 1927–1937', p. 24.
42. Gogarty, *As I Was Going Down Sackville Street*, p. 111.
43. *Letters*, p. 796.
44. *Moore*, p. 177.
45. *Var. Poems*, p. 855.
46. 'Modern Ireland: an Address to American Audiences 1932–1933', ed. Curtis Bradford, *Massachusetts Review*, v (1964) p. 256.
47. Ibid., p. 267.
48. Ibid., p. 258.
49. Ibid., p. 259.
50. Ibid., p. 261. O'Leary was not, to be sure, a Protestant. He was born of Catholic parents and died, after nearly lifelong alienation from the church because of his Fenianism, a Catholic. However, he was educated in Protestant schools, 'often seemed to live in the eighteenth century, to acknowledge its canons alone in literature and in the arts' (*Exp.*, p. 344), and in his old age won the respect 'perhaps particularly of the Protestants and Unionists' (Hone, *W. B. Yeats: 1865–1939*, p. 52). O'Leary's case is such that one respected Irish historian simply assumed he was Protestant (P. S. O'Hegarty, *A History of Ireland under the Union* (London: Methuen, 1952) p. 435). More important than the question of O'Leary's religion, though, is noting that while Yeats associated the public virtues he admired with a particular class, he admired them as unreservedly when they occurred in men born out of that class, such as O'Leary and Kevin O'Higgins.
51. Ibid., pp. 264–7.
52. Ibid., p. 259.
53. Ibid., p. 262. Bradford adds in a note a cancelled passage which immediately followed in the MS: 'In my later poems I have called it Byzantium, that city where the saints showed their wasted forms

upon a background of gold mosaic, and an artificial bird sang upon a tree of gold in the presence of the emperor; and in one poem I have pictured the ghosts swimming, mounted upon dolphins, through the sensual seas, that they may dance upon its pavements.' To find John O'Leary in the background of 'Byzantium' is astonishing, but indicates how inextricable Yeats's political interests were from his artistic ones.

54. Ibid., p. 263.
55. Ibid., p. 268.
56. S. J. Woolf, 'Yeats Foresees an Ireland of Reality', *New York Times Magazine*, 13 Nov. 1932, p. 7.
57. *Letters*, p. 806.
58. *Moore*, p. 46.
59. Elizabeth Cullingford, *Yeats, Ireland and Fascism* (New York and London: New York University Press, 1981) p. 200.
60. *Letters*, p. 805.
61. Ibid., p. 806.
62. Ibid., p. 808.
63. Ibid., p. 812.
64. Conor Cruise O'Brien, 'Passion and Cunning: an Essay on the Politics of W. B. Yeats', in A. Norman Jeffares and K. G. W. Cross (eds), *In Excited Reverie: A Centenary Tribute to William Butler Yeats 1865–1939* (New York: St Martin's Press, 1965) p. 256.
65. *Var. Poems*, p. 837.
66. Ibid., p. 546.
67. Ibid., pp. 548–9.
68. Ibid., p. 836.
69. Ibid., p. 837.
70. Ibid., p. 554.
71. Ibid., p. 855.
72. Ibid., p. 542.
73. Ibid., p. 835. Yeats may have intended not 'proceeding' but 'preceding'.
74. Ibid., p. 834.
75. F. A. C. Wilson, *W. B. Yeats and Tradition* (London: Gollancz, 1958) pp. 53–94.
76. *Var. Poems*, p. 542.
77. *Auto.*, p. 14.
78. Ibid., p. 410.
79. *Exp.*, p. 82.
80. *Uncol. Prose*, ii, 349.
81. *Exp.*, p. 193.
82. *Auto.*, p. 206.
83. Ibid., p. 504.
84. Ibid., p. 472.
85. *E.&I.*, pp. 314–15.
86. *Exp.*, p. 149.
87. Ibid., p. 168.
88. Ibid., pp. 161–2.
89. *Var. Poems*, p. 425.

90. *Auto.*, p. 488.
91. *Exp.*, p. 72.
92. This essay is one of the unpublished Yeats pieces transcribed by the late Curtis Bradford, which transcriptions are now held in Burling Library, Grinnell College, Grinnell, Iowa, USA. It is discussed in greater detail in the present author's dissertation 'W. B. Yeats and Politics in the 1930s', Dissertation, Northwestern University 1984, pp. 57–9.
93. *E.&I.*, p. 251.
94. Ibid., p. 260.
95. On 'recklessness', see especially 'Poetry and Tradition', ibid., pp. 246–60; on 'innocence', the famous lines from 'A Prayer for my Daughter' and 'The Second Coming'.
96. Michael Adams, *Censorship: The Irish Experience* (Dublin: Sceptre Books, 1968) p. 243.
97. O'Connor, *My Father's Son*, pp. 224–5. According to O'Connor, the resisted nominee was 'a notorious and unscrupulous politician named Magennis' (p. 177).
98. Peter Kavanagh, *The Story of the Abbey Theatre: From the Origins in 1899 to the Present* (New York: Devin-Adair, 1950) p. 161.
99. Quoted ibid., p. 161.
100. Hone, *W. B. Yeats: 1865–1939*, pp. 425–6.
101. *Uncol. Prose*, ii, 500; Krimm, *W. B. Yeats and the Emergence of the Irish Free State*, pp. 128–30.
102. 'De Valera as Play Censor', in E. H. Mikhail, *W. B. Yeats: Interviews and Recollections* (London: Macmillan, 1977) ii, 225. De Valera may never have seen an official Abbey production, but according to Longford and O'Neill he did once set foot inside the premises to play a small part in an amateur production, written by a friend of his and titled 'A Christmas Hamper', in 1905 (*Eamon de Valera*, p. 12).
103. *Var. Poems*, p. 836.
104. *Exp.*, p. 395.
105. Ibid., p. 357.
106. Ibid., p. 357.
107. Ibid., p. 375.
108. Ibid., p. 376.
109. Ibid., p. 397.
110. Ibid., p. 398.
111. William Rothenstein, *Since Fifty: Men and Memories, 1922–1938* (New York: Macmillan, 1940) p. 230; Mikhail, *W. B. Yeats: Interviews and Recollections*, p. 268.
112. Torchiana, *W. B. Yeats and Georgian Ireland*, pp. 354–6.
113. T. R. Henn, 'Yeats and the Poetry of War', in *Last Essays* (Gerrards Cross: Colin Smythe, 1976) p. 95.
114. *Var. Poems*, p. 635.
115. 'Michael Robartes: Two Occult Manuscripts', ed. Walter Kelly Hood, in George Mills Harper (ed.), *Yeats and the Occult* (Toronto: Macmillan of Canada, 1975) p. 219.
116. *E.&I.*, p. 526.

117. *Exp.*, p. 438.
118. See Stanley Sultan, *Yeats at his Last*, New Yeats Papers XI (Dublin: Dolmen Press, 1975) pp. 29–30.
119. *Letters*, p. 873.
120. *Var. Poems*, p. 635. The first line of the refrain alters as the poem progresses, from 'There in the tomb stand the dead upright' to 'There in the tomb drops the faint moonlight' to 'There in the tomb the dark grows blacker'. Since the dark of the moon symbolised for Yeats the complete and final phase of a 'primary' gyre, this very darkness presages the imminent reawakening of the warriors' bones, and gives weight to the 'but' that begins the refrain's second line. If the wind here symbolises social levelling, as it does in several Yeats poems, that is further reason for supposing de Valera and Fianna Fail a part of the company of besiegers (Torchiana, *W. B. Yeats and Georgian Ireland*, pp. 329–30).

Notes to Chapter 2: The Blueshirt Episode and its Background

1. 'Prayer for Old Age', *Var. Poems*, p. 553. 'In some ways the Steinach operation for sexual rejuvenation he underwent in 1934 is the physiological equivalent of his excited, furtive fascination with Fascist politics', Douglas Archibald has recently written in his *Yeats* (New York: Syracuse University Press, 1983) p. 147.
2. Earnán de Blaghd, 'The Yeats I Knew', in E. H. Mikhail (ed.), *W. B. Yeats: Interviews and Recollections*, II, 393.
3. John Murphy, *Ireland in the Twentieth Century*, Gill History of Ireland 11 (Dublin: Gill & Macmillan, 1975) p. 82.
4. *Var. Poems*, p. 837.
5. Ibid., p. 543.
6. See, for instance, the third section of 'The Death of Synge', *Auto.*, p. 500.
7. 'Upon a House shaken by the Land Agitation' (*Var. Poems*, p. 264), 'Coole Park, 1929' (ibid., p. 488), and 'Coole Park and Ballylee, 1931' (ibid., p. 490).
8. *E.&I.*, p. 260.
9. On the damage Yeats thought English plays had done to Irish taste, see his opinions on *Mice and Men* and *Caste*, *Exp.*, pp. 112–13, 188–9.
10. So he argued in 1903 in 'The Irish National Theatre and Three Sorts of Ignorance', *Uncol. Prose*, II, 306–8.
11. *Exp.*, pp. 140, 204.
12. *Auto.*, p. 469.
13. Ibid., p. 489.
14. *Uncol. Prose*, II, 459.
15. Herbert Davis (ed.), *The Prose Works of Jonathan Swift* (Oxford: Shakespeare Head Press, 1939) I, 225. For Yeats's discovery of the passage, see *Exp.*, pp. 292–3.

16. An unidentified clipping on the fifth page of a book of clippings in the possession of the National Library of Ireland, MS no. 12, 146.
17. *E.&I.*, p. 344. Yeats's admiration for Lady Gregory's nephews has been carefully examined in Torchiana, *W. B. Yeats and Georgian Ireland*, pp. 44–64.
18. *Var. Poems*, p. 489.
19. *E.&I.*, p. 343.
20. *Exp.*, p. 351.
21. Ibid., p. 357.
22. Ibid., p. 168.
23. *E.&I.*, p. 260.
24. *Var. Poems*, p. 328.
25. *Auto.*, p. 395.
26. Ibid., p. 471.
27. *Var, Poems*, p. 417.
28. *Exp.*, p. 358.
29. *Auto.*, p. 381.
30. 'Major Cooper's Candidature', *Irish Times*, 25 August 1923, p. 7.
31. *Exp.*, p. 123.
32. *E.&I.*, p. 488. Yeats recalled some Irish examples of the hypocrisy into which democratic politicians may drift in 'The Stirring of the Bones' (*Auto.*, p. 359).
33. *Exp.*, p. 410.
34. *E.&I.*, p. 249.
35. Ibid., p. 400.
36. *Auto.*, p. 209. Yeats had previously paid tribute to O'Leary's independence in an 1897 review of O'Leary's memoirs by quoting one of the young men who found O'Leary 'magnetic': 'Our public men, with the exception of Mr. John O'Leary, have been afraid to differ from the people in anything, and now we haven't got a pinsworth of respect for anybody but Mr. John O'Leary' (*Uncol. Prose*, II, 36).
37. Yeats was tremendously impressed by a remark O'Higgins once made to him, 'Nobody can expect to live who has done what I have' (*Letters*, p. 809).
38. *Auto.*, pp. 473–4.
39. *Exp.*, p. 236.
40. *E.&I.*, p. 253.
41. *Exp.*, p. 305.
42. *Vision*, p. 73.
43. Ibid., p. 104.
44. Ibid., p. 263. Yeats may have intended not 'imminent' but 'immanent'.
45. *Var. Poems*, p. 426.
46. Ibid., p. 418. This line ended with exclamation points, not question marks, in all the poem's publications preceding that in *The Poems of W. B. Yeats* (London: Macmillan, 1949).
47. *Exp.*, p. 312.
48. Perhaps Lady Gregory's religious devotion or philanthropic efforts led Yeats to assign her to a primary phase for all his other accounts of

her dwell on her 'solitude', her 'isolation', her 'self-possession', her holding herself aloof from 'all contagious opinions of poorer minds' (*Auto.*, pp. 395, 473). He does say of Phase 24, Lady Gregory's phase, that it allows for 'the nearest the natural self can come to the self-expressing mastery of Phase 10' – Parnell's phase – and writes of the 'self-surrender' that becomes its 'pride' (*Vision*, pp. 169–70). George Mills Harper and Walter Kelly Hood, editors of *A Critical Edition of Yeats's 'A Vision' (1925)* (London: Macmillan, 1978) note of this passage: 'One of the most extensively revised Phases, its original opening may have been an indirect tribute to Lady Gregory: "The most obviously impressive of all the phases when true to phase"' (p. 27 of the 'Notes').

49. 'Modern Ireland', p. 259.
50. On Yeats's dislike of these two influences on Irish opinion, see 'The Theatre, the Pulpit, and the Newspapers', *Exp.*, pp. 119–23.
51. 'The Tower', *Var. Poems*, p. 414.
52. 'Modern Ireland', p. 267.
53. *Auto.*, p. 353.
54. W. B. Yeats, *Tribute to Thomas Davis* (Oxford: Basil Blackwell for Cork University Press, 1947) p. 15.
55. Ibid., p. 15.
56. *Vision*, p. 122.
57. *Auto.*, p. 232.
58. 'Modern Ireland', p. 258; *Var. Poems*, p. 835.
59. Yeats tells of the torn hands in 'A Commentary on a Parnellite at Parnell's Funeral' (*Var. Poems*, p. 835), 'Ireland after Parnell' (*Auto.*, p. 232), and *A Vision*, p. 124. The peculiar importance Parnell assumed for some Irish writers is discussed by Malcolm Brown in 'Literary Parnellism', a chapter of *The Politics of Irish Literature* (London: George Allen & Unwin, 1972) pp. 371–90.
60. *Vision*, pp. 123–4. According to Harper and Kelly, Yeats here refers to Odin (*A Critical Edition of Yeats's 'A Vision' (1925)* p. 18 of the 'Notes').
61. 'Logic is a machine . . .' (*Auto.*, p. 461); 'So much of the world as is dominated by the contest of interests is a machine. The newspaper is the roar of the machine' (ibid., p. 463). On 'mechanist' philosophers and matter, see *E.&I.*, p. 461.
62. *Exp.*, p. 336.
63. *Memoirs*, p. 213. Yeats did not include this entry among those he later published in *Autobiographies*.
64. *Auto.*, p. 195.
65. *Var. Poems*, p. 835.
66. *Auto.*, pp. 362–3.
67. *Exp.*, p. 227.
68. Ibid., pp. 279–80.
69. *Moore*, p. 46.
70. *Letters*, pp. 681–2.
71. Ibid., p. 690.

72. Daniel J. Murphy (ed.), *Lady Gregory's Journals* (New York: Oxford University Press, 1978) p. 334.
73. *Letters*, p. 693.
74. Stanfield, 'W. B. Yeats and Politics in the 1930s', p. 118; Joseph Hone, 'Yeats as a Political Philosopher', *London Mercury*, 39 (1939) 493.
75. *Uncol. Prose*, II, 435, 433.
76. *Letters*, p. 694.
77. *Senate Speeches*, p. 33.
78. Cullingford, *Yeats, Ireland and Fascism*, p. 169.
79. *Vision*, p. 26.
80. 'Modern Ireland', p. 258.
81. *Vision*, p. 27.
82. *Senate Speeches*, pp. 151–2.
83. *Exp.*, pp. 412–13.
84. *Letters*, p. 693.
85. *Uncol. Prose*, II, 435.
86. Quoted in Hone, *W. B. Yeats: 1865–1939*, p. 365.
87. *Senate Speeches*, pp. 110–11; *Uncol. Prose*, II, 459.
88. Ezra Pound, *Jefferson and/or Mussolini* (first published 1935; reprinted New York: Boni & Liveright, 1970) p. 110.
89. James Strachey Barnes, *The Universal Aspects of Fascism* (London: Williams & Northgate, 1928; 2nd edn, 1929) p. 26. Yeats owned a copy of this book.
90. For instance: 'He knows its [his race's] mind better than it does itself, and has used force to compel it to accept a regime that is merely the political expression of its own soul' (Stanley B. James, 'Some Mussolini Paradoxes', *Irish Monthly*, LXI (1933) 24). Similar conclusions can be found in Rev. T. O'Herlihy, 'Fascist Italy', *Irish Ecclesiastical Record*, 31 (1928) 506–16; and in Virginia Crawford, 'The Rise of Fascism and what it Stands for', *Studies*, XII (1923) 539–52.
91. 'Nineteen Hundred and Nineteen', *Var. Poems*, p. 429.
92. *Exp.*, p. 293.
93. Ibid., p. 354. Barnes mentions Vico's possible influence on Fascism (via Croce and Gentile) in a note on p. 4 of *The Universal Aspects of Fascism*.
94. *Letters*, p. 813.
95. The following account of the Blueshirts draws on those in Maurice Manning, *The Blueshirts* (Toronto: University of Toronto Press, 1971); F. S. L. Lyons, *Ireland Since the Famine* (London: Weidenfeld & Nicolson, 1971); Donal O'Sullivan, *The Irish Free State and its Senate: A Study in Contemporary Politics* (London: Faber & Faber, 1940); John A. Murphy, *Ireland in the Twentieth Century*, Gill History of Ireland, 11 (Dublin: Gill & Macmillan, 1975); and David Thornley, 'The Blueshirts', in Francis MacManus (ed.), *The Years of the Great Test* (Cork: Mercier Press, 1967).
96. *United Irishman*, 10 Oct. 1932, pp. 5, 7.
97. Ibid., 11 Feb. 1933, p. 5.

98. Ibid., 18 Mar. 1933, p. 3.
99. *Letters*, p. 808. Krimm suggests that the 'philosopher' might have been Michael Tierney, a scholar much interested in the corporate state, who was acquainted with Yeats and later associated with Fine Gael.
100. In 'Four Years: 1887–1891' Yeats recalled discussing the idea of 'Unity of Being' with his father: 'When I began, however, to apply this thought to the state and to argue for a law-made balance among trades and occupations my father displayed at once the violent free trader and propagandist of liberty' (*Auto.*, p. 190).
101. *United Irishman*, 15 April 1933, p. 5.
102. Ibid., 10 June 1933, p. 7.
103. Ibid., 17 June 1933, p. 7.
104. Ibid., 1 July 1933, p. 7.
105. *The Blueshirt*, 12 August 1933, p. 1.
106. Ibid., 12 August 1933, p. 4.
107. *Letters*, pp. 811–12.
108. Ibid., p. 812.
109. Ibid., p. 814.
110. Ibid., p. 815.
111. T. Desmond Williams, 'De Valera in Power', in MacManus (ed.), *The Years of the Great Test*, p. 36.
112. *Letters*, p. 813.
113. W. B. Yeats and Margot Ruddock, *Ah, Sweet Dancer*, a correspondence edited by Roger McHugh (New York: Macmillan, 1971) p. 32.
114. *Letters*, p. 812.
115. Quoted in Torchiana, *W. B. Yeats and Georgian Ireland*, p. 161.
116. Cullingford, *Yeats, Ireland and Fascism*, p. 205.
117. *Letters*, p. 813.
118. Ibid., p. 814.
119. Lyons, *Ireland since the Famine*, p. 525.
120. *Letters*, p. 815.
121. Ibid., p. 820.
122. Ibid., p. 812.
123. *Var. Poems*, pp. 543–4.
124. Ibid., p. 543.
125. Conor Cruise O'Brien, 'Passion and Cunning: an Essay on the Politics of W. B. Yeats', in A. Norman Jeffares and K. G. W. Cross (eds), *In Excited Reverie*, p. 257.
126. T. R. Henn, *The Lonely Tower* (London: Methuen, 1950; 2nd edn, 1965) p. 344. See also D. E. S. Maxwell, 'Swift's Dark Grove: Yeats and the Anglo-Irish Tradition', in D. E. S. Maxwell and S. B. Bushrui (eds), *Centenary Essays on the Art of W. B. Yeats* (Nigeria: University of Ibadan Press, 1965) p. 20; Mary Carden, 'The Few and the Many: an Examination of W. B. Yeats's Politics', *Studies*, LVIII (1969) 61; Cullingford, *Yeats, Ireland and Fascism*, p. 212.
127. Freyer, *Yeats and the Anti-Democratic Tradition*, p. 78.
128. Hone, *W. B. Yeats: 1865–1939*, p. 459. I have taken liberties with Hone's punctuation. His version reads: 'Conflict, more conflict'.

129. *Var. Poems*, pp. 545, 616, 638.
130. *Exp.*, p. 425.
131. Ibid., p. 441.
132. Ibid., pp. 338–9.
133. *Uncol. Prose*, II, 487.
134. E. M. Forster, 'What I Believe', in *Two Cheers for Democracy* (London: Edward Arnold, 1951) pp. 80–1.
135. Stephen Spender, *World Within World* (Berkeley, Calif.: University of California Press, 1966) p. 147.
136. Edward Mendelson (ed.), *The English Auden* (London: Faber & Faber, 1977) p. 425.
137. Sonia Orwell and Ian Angus (eds), *The Collected Essays, Journalism and Letters of George Orwell* (London: Secker & Warburg, 1968) II, 516.
138. Ibid., I, 296.
139. George Watson, *Politics and Literature in Modern Britain* (Totowa, N.J.: Rowman & Littlefield, 1977) pp. 46–70.
140. *United Irishman*, 20 May 1933, p. 7.
141. *Letters*, p. 812.
142. *Var. Poems*, p. 837.
143. Grattan Freyer, 'The Politics of W. B. Yeats', *Politics and Letters*, 1 (1947) 18.
144. Torchiana, *W. B. Yeats and Georgian Ireland*, p. 159.
145. Freyer, *Yeats and the Anti-Democratic Tradition*, pp. 127–8.
146. Watson, *Politics and Literature in Modern Britain*, p. 78.
147. These notes are included in Curtis Bradford's transcriptions of Yeats's unpublished prose (see Notes to Chapter 1, note 92). They are discussed in Stanfield, 'W. B. Yeats and Politics in the 1930s', pp. 145–9.
148. Yeats could have acquired from Barnes's *Universal Aspects of Fascism* the idea that Fascist philosophy, founded on Croce and Gentile, was a refutation or radical revision of Hegel. Yeats read Croce's *Hegel* and his *Philosophy of Vico*, either of which could have persuaded him that the Fascist interpretation of history was a significant departure from the Marxist interpretation (Hone, *W. B. Yeats*, p. 368).
149. *Vision*, pp. 81–2. Yeats considered Blake, as well as Vico, his ally in the argument against Hegel's and Marx's too linear, too progressive idea of history. He wrote in 1934: '. . . the spring vegetables may be over, they have not been refuted. I am Blake's disciple, not Hegel's: "contraries are positive. A negation is not a contrary" ' (*Var. Poems*, p. 835).
150. Contained in an appendix to A. N. Jeffares, *W. B. Yeats: Man and Poet* (New Haven, Conn.: Yale University Press, 1949) pp. 351–2.
151. *Letters*, p. 813.
152. Ibid., p. 885.
153. *Var. Poems*, p. 836.
154. *Exp.*, p. 375.
155. *E.&I.*, pp. 371–2.
156. *Letters on Poetry*, p. 8.

157. Walter Kelly Hood (ed.), 'Michael Robartes: Two Occult Manuscripts', in George Mills Harper (ed.), *Yeats and the Occult* (Toronto: Macmillan of Canada, 1975) p. 222.

158. Cullingford, *Yeats, Ireland and Fascism*, p. 219.

159. *Vision*, pp. 301–2.

160. *Exp.*, p. 414.

161. Ibid., p. 437.

Notes to Chapter 3: Yeats, Socialism and Tragedy

1. George Watson, *Politics and Literature in Modern Britain*, p. 88. The Orwell quotation is from 'The Lion and the Unicorn', in Sonia Orwell and Ian Angus (eds), *The Collected Essays, Journalism, and Letters of George Orwell*, II, 74.

2. *Exp.*, p. 275.

3. *Auto.*, p. 146.

4. *Letters*, p. 42.

5. *Auto.*, p. 149.

6. *E.&I.*, p. 61.

7. *Exp.*, p. 275.

8. *Auto.*, p. 142.

9. *Exp.*, p. 276.

10. Ibid., pp. 268, 269.

11. *Auto.*, p. 192.

12. *Letters*, p. 680.

13. *Mythologies*, p. 332.

14. 'Had not Dante and Villon understood that their fate wrecked what life could not rebuild, had they lacked their Vision of Evil, had they cherished any species of optimism, they could but have found a false beauty, or some momentary instinctive beauty . . .' wrote Yeats in 'Hodos Chameliontos', one of the sections of *The Trembling of the Veil* (*Auto.*, p. 273). The 'Vision of Evil' often enters into Yeats's discussion of his friends of the 1890s, whom he calls (significantly, so far as the present argument is concerned) the 'Tragic Generation'.

15. *Var. Poems*, p. 428. This poem was written not in 1919, but in 1921. Accordingly, the title signifies not simply 'the present', but the year in which European civilisation apparently changed course.

16. *Letters*, p. 668.

17. *Var. Poems*, p. 428.

18. 'My Table', ibid., p. 421.

19. Quoted in Hone, *W. B. Yeats*, p. 365.

20. *Exp.*, p. 355.

21. 'The Tower,' *Var. Poems*, p. 415.

22. Harold J. Laski, *Communism* (New York: Henry Holt; London: Thornton, Butterworth, 1927) p. 61.

23. *O. B. M. V.*, p. xxxvii.

24. *E.&I.*, pp. 62–3.

25. *Letters*, p. 656.
26. David Krause (ed.), *The Letters of Sean O'Casey* (London: Macmillan, 1975) I, 102–3.
27. The best account of the controversy is that in Robert Hogan, *The Experiments of Sean O'Casey* (New York: St Martin's Press, 1960) pp. 184–206. There is also an extended account, somewhat weighted in O'Casey's favour, in David Krause, *Sean O'Casey: The Man and his Work* (New York: Macmillan, rev. edn, 1975) pp. 99–109. The important documents of the controversy, from both sides, are collected in the first volume of *The Letters of Sean O'Casey*, pp. 226–316.
28. *Letters*, p. 741.
29. Ibid., p. 743.
30. Krause (ed.), *The Letters of Sean O'Casey*, I, 270, 288–9, 320. When O'Casey wrote about the episode years later in his autobiography, he still seemed to believe it was his abandonment of his former naturalistic style that had caused the rejection. See his *Autobiographies*, II, 277, 338.
31. *Letters*, p. 741.
32. O'Casey, *Autobiographies*, II, 270.
33. *O. B. M. V.*, pp. xxxiv–xxxv; *E.&I.*, p. 523.
34. Thomas Common (compiler), *Nietzsche as Critic, Philosopher, Poet and Prophet: Choice Selections from his Works* (London: Grant Richards, 1901) p. 142. Yeats owned a copy of this book, and apparently read it attentively. He never, when writing on tragedy, mentions Nietzsche by name, but critics have noticed a striking congruity between the poet's and the philosopher's ideas on tragedy. See David Thatcher, *Nietzsche in England 1890–1914: The Growth of a Reputation* (Toronto: University of Toronto Press, 1970) p. 172; and Otto Bohlmann, *Yeats and Nietzsche* (Totowa, N.J.: Barnes & Noble, 1982).
35. For example, an internal fire accomplishes Goll's translation from warrior-king to wandering minstrel: 'In my most secret spirit grew/A whirling and a wandering fire . . .' (*Var. Poems*, p. 83). The medieval poet of 'Sailing to Byzantium' is gathered into the artifice of eternity only after the sages standing in 'God's holy fire' have consumed his heart away (ibid., p. 408). In *Per Amica Silentia Lunae*, Yeats opposes the condition of fire to our incarnate, necessarily evil condition: 'There are two realities, the terrestrial and the condition of fire. All power is from the terrestrial condition, for there all opposites meet and there only is the extreme of choice possible, full freedom. And there the heterogeneous is, and evil, for evil is the strain one upon another of opposites; but in the condition of fire is all music and all rest.' Yeats adds in a 1924 note that for the anti-self, or 'Daimon', the self's terrestrial condition serves as the condition of fire. It may be the tragic hero's anti-self, his Daimon, that asserts itself when the hero elects to affirm his condition, to treat his evil circumstances as a place of 'music and rest', to achieve the Yeatsian paradox of tragic joy (see *Mythologies*, pp. 356–7).
36. Yeats tried to bring something of the kind about in one of his own

plays, *Where There is Nothing*. At one point the hero, Paul Ruttledge, explains, 'I am led by hands that are colder than ice and harder than diamonds. They will lead me where there will be hard thoughts of me in the hearts of all that love me, and there will be a fire in my heart that will make it as bare as the wilderness' (*Var. Plays*, p. 1141). Later, when tempted to lead an uprising, he says, 'I was forgetting, we cannot destroy the world with armies, it is inside our minds that it must be destroyed, it must be consumed in a moment inside our minds' (p. 1158). At play's end, his final words before being beaten almost to death by a mob are 'I go to the invisible heart of flame!' (p. 1162). This play, much revised, became *The Unicorn from the Stars*, Paul Ruttledge became Martin Hearne, and the fire became literal: driven by a half-understood vision, Martin leads a peasant uprising in which the local Big House is burnt down. Afterwards, coming to a fuller understanding of his vision, he reaches a conclusion much like Paul Ruttledge's. 'The battle we have to fight is fought out in our own mind. There is a fiery moment, perhaps once in a lifetime, and in that moment we see the only thing that matters. It is in that moment that great battles are lost and won, for in that moment we are a part of the host of Heaven' (p. 705).

37. *Exp.*, p. 449.
38. O'Casey, *Collected Plays* (London: Macmillan, 1949) II, 102.
39. *Letters*, p. 741.
40. *Exp.*, p. 245.
41. *Letters*, p. 741.
42. Ibid., p. 742.
43. Krause (ed.), *The Letters of Sean O'Casey*, I, 238.
44. *Exp.*, pp. 333–4. On the influence of Berkeley on Yeats's aesthetic, political and philosophical ideas, see Torchiana, *W. B. Yeats and Georgian Ireland*, pp. 222–65.
45. *Exp.*, p. 333. Somewhat conveniently for Yeats's analysis, O'Casey wrote most of the *Tassie* in London.
46. Ibid., pp. 339–40.
47. *E.&I.*, p. 401.
48. *Exp.*, p. 428.
49. *Vision*, p. 263.
50. Common (compiler), *Nietzsche as Critic, Philosopher, Poet and Prophet*, p. 114.
51. Ibid., p. 100.
52. Ibid., pp. 100–1.
53. *E.&I.*, p. 523. Earlier Yeats had written, 'Realism is created for the common people and was always their peculiar delight, and it is the delight to-day of all those whose minds, educated alone by schoolmasters and newspapers, are without memory of beauty and emotional subtlety.' On the other hand, the 'great speeches' of Elizabethan tragedy 'were written by poets who remembered their patrons in the covered galleries' (ibid., p. 227).
54. *Var. Poems*, p. 835.

55. Wilfred Owen, *Collected Letters*, ed. Harold Owen and John Bell (London: Oxford University Press, 1967) p. 131.

56. *Letters on Poetry*, p. 124.

57. See Cecil Day-Lewis, *A Hope for Poetry* (first published 1934; 8th edn, Oxford: Basil Blackwell, 1947) pp. 3, 15; Stephen Spender, *The Destructive Element* (first published 1935; paperback edn, Philadelphia: Albert Saifer, 1953) pp. 130–1.

58. Rickwood's opinion is quoted in D. E. Savage's article, 'Two Prophetic Poems', *Adelphi*, 22, no. 1 (1945) p. 32. Day-Lewis made a similar point in *A Hope for Poetry*, p. 17.

59. Orwell discusses this trend with special reference to the way the temper of the left changed with the outbreak of the Spanish Civil War (Sonia Orwell and Ian Angus (eds), *The Collected Essays, Journalism and Letters of George Orwell*, II, 251); see also Samuel Hynes, *The Auden Generation: Literature and Politics in England in the 1930s* (London: Bodley Head, 1976) pp. 194–6.

60. Robert Wohl, 'England: Lost Legions of Youth', in *The Generation of 1914* (Cambridge, Mass: Harvard University Press, 1979) pp. 85–121; Martin Green, *Children of the Sun* (New York: Basic Books, 1976) pp. 42–8. Yeats was unsympathetic toward the anti-war feeling that began to prevail in Great War memoirs and novels at this time, to judge from the snort of impatience discernible in the following: 'It was in Eliot that certain revolutionary War poets, young men who felt they had been dragged away from their studies, from their pleasant life, by the blundering frenzy of old men, found the greater part of their style' (*E.&I.*, pp. 499–500).

61. Edward O'Shea, *Yeats as Editor*, New Yeats Papers XII (Dublin: Dolmen Press, 1975) p. 71.

62. *Letters on Poetry*, pp. 124–5.

63. *O. B. M. V.*, p. xxxiv.

64. See, for example, D. E. Savage's above-cited article, 'Two Prophetic Poems', and Jon Silkin's introduction to *The Penguin Book of First World War Poetry* (Harmondsworth: Penguin, 1979) esp. pp. 31–2, 43–4.

65. *Letters*, p. 58.

66. Ibid., p. 82.

67. *Vision*, p. 81.

68. Ibid., p. 183.

69. *O. B. M. V.*, p. xxvii.

70. For instance, *E.&I.*, p. 446; *Exp.*, 333, 373.

71. *O. B. M. V.*, pp. xxvii–xxviii. Yeats might have excepted from this general judgment on modern fiction a novel of Frederick Rolfe, *Hadrian the Seventh*. He described it to Olivia Shakespear as 'nearly a great book, my sort of book, the love of the ruling mind, the ruling race. An imaginary Pope is the theme, with enough evil to be a great man. I hate the pale victims of modern fiction – that suffer that they may have minds like photographic plates' (*Letters*, p. 827).

72. *O. B. M. V.*, p.xxxiv–xxxv.

73. Ibid., p. xxxiii.
74. Edmund Blunden, 'Memoir', in *The Poems of Wilfred Owen* (London: Chatto & Windus, 1931) p. 25.
75. Ibid., p. 29.
76. Ibid., p. 38. Yeats probably looked at this memoir, for he refers to this sentence in his introduction to the *Oxford Book*, writing that the war poets 'felt bound, in the words of the best known, to plead the suffering of their men' (p. xxxiv). If he did read it, its insistence on Owen's self-abnegation may have predisposed him against Owen. Also, as it happens, the first poem in Blunden's edition, 'From my Diary, July 1914', was a poem Yeats particularly disliked (see *Letters on Poetry*, p. 124).
77. Blunden, 'Memoir', in *The Poems of Wilfred Owen*, p. 40.
78. Savage, 'Two Prophetic Poems', p. 29.
79. *Letters on Poetry*, p. 126.
80. George Mills Harper and Walter Kelly Hood (eds), *A Critical Edition of Yeats's 'A Vision' (1925)* pp. 186–7.
81. *Vision*, p. 275.
82. *Letters on Poetry*, p. 124.
83. *O. B. M. V.*, pp. 292, 347, 332.
84. Joseph Cohen, 'In Memory of W. B. Yeats – and Wilfred Owen', *Journal of English and Germanic Philology*, 58 (Oct. 1959) 643.
85. *O. B. M. V.*, p. 359.
86. *Var. Poems*, pp. 423–4. T. R. Henn has best expressed the connection Yeats drew between soldierly heroism and tragic heroism: 'War as a subject for poetry was valid only in so far as circumstances allowed him to celebrate the response to its challenge of the individual or of a small heroic group, and to return to his favourite concept of tragedy; the confrontation of the utmost obstacles to the hero's will, the resolution of conflict in the central paradox of "tragic joy"' ('Yeats and the Poetry of War', p. 82).
87. *Auto.*, p. 469.
88. Ibid., p. 477.
89. *Mythologies*, p. 333.
90. See Torchiana, *W. B. Yeats and Georgian Ireland*, pp. 292–4.
91. *Vision*, p. 136.
92. *Var. Poems*, p. 375.
93. Ibid., p. 388.
94. Ibid., p. 327.
95. 'Vacillation', ibid., p. 501. Also relevant here is a passage from the 1930 diary: 'History is necessity until it takes fire in someone's head and becomes freedom or virtue. Berkeley's Salamis was such a conflagration, another is about us now' (*Exp.*, p. 336).
96. *Vision*, pp. 136–7.
97. See also *E.&I.*, pp. 361, 409, 510–11.
98. Friedrich Nietzsche, *Thus Spake Zarathustra*, trans. Thomas Common, in Willard Huntington Wright (ed.), *The Philosophy of Nietzsche* (New York: Modern Library, n.d.) p. 153.
99. *Auto.*, p. 189.

100. *Letters*, p. 833.
101. *E.&I.*, p. 499.
102. *Exp.*, p. 373. Yeats made a similar comment on Pound in his essay on Berkeley (*E.&I.*, p. 405).
103. *O. B. M. V.*, pp. xxvi, xxxvii.
104. Ibid., pp. xxxvii–xxxviii.
105. In December 1930, two years into the First Five Year Plan, Stalin conferred with a group of Russian philosophers to warn them against 'both bourgeois "idealist" philosophies and the Trotskyite and Bukharinite perversions of Marxism' (Adam B. Ulam, *Stalin: The Man and his Era* (New York: Viking Press, 1973) p. 339). Stalin wished to make clear, among other things, that bourgeois notions of what was practical or feasible did not hold for Marxist societies in general or for the Five Year Plan in particular; hence Yeats's statement that Stalin had 'silenced' the 'Mechanists'. Stalin's stance on this point later contributed to the unusual career of Trofim Lysenko, who 'cleverly exploited Stalin's predilection for scientists who refused to be intimidated by alleged scientific laws and who, if higher production was at stake, overcame those laws in the spirit of "There is no fortress we Bolsheviks cannot take"' (ibid., p. 444).
106. *O. B. M. V.*, pp. xxxv–xxxvi.
107. Ibid., pp. xxxvi, xxxvii.
108. *Vision*, p. 104.
109. Ibid., p. 164.
110. Ibid., p. 179.
111. Ibid., p. 183.
112. *O. B. M. V.*, p. xxxviii.
113. *Letters on Poetry*, p. 8. As the reference to Major Douglas shows, Yeats habitually thought of Pound, the poetical polemicist for Social Credit, as temperamentally akin to Auden, Spender and Day-Lewis, the poetical polemicists for Marxism.
114. Samuel Hynes, *The Auden Generation*, pp. 86–97, 122–3.
115. Robin Skelton (ed.), *Poetry of the Thirties* (Harmondsworth: Penguin, 1964) pp. 30–1.
116. Humphrey Carpenter, *W. H. Auden: A Biography* (London: George Allen & Unwin, 1981) p. 113.
117. Spender, *World Within World*, pp. 119, 137. See also Day-Lewis, *A Hope For Poetry*, p. 47.
118. See Green, *Children of the Sun*, p. 273. In this connection, one thinks also of the attitude of the partyman Percy Hardcaster towards the communists of London Bohemia in Wyndham Lewis's *Revenge For Love*, and of the attitude taken by George Orwell towards Auden and Spender in the second section of 'Inside the Whale'.
119. *O. B. M. V.*, p. xxxviii.
120. *Letters on Poetry*, p. 8.
121. *E.&I.*, p. 523.
122. 'Vacillation', *Var. Poems*, pp. 500–1.
123. Skelton (ed.) *Poetry of the Thirties*, pp. 28–30; Green, *Children of the Sun*, p. 299.

124. *E.&I.*, p. 503. This idea was, perhaps, more Yeats's own than it was that of the poets discussed.
125. *O. B. M. V.*, p. xxviii.
126. Ibid., p. xxviii.
127. Ibid., p. xxix.
128. Ibid., p. xxix.
129. Ibid., pp. xxvii–xxix.
130. Ibid., pp. xxxi–xxxii, xxxii–xxxiii.
131. Ibid., p. xv.
132. Ibid., p. xv. Yeats also wrote of Gogarty's 'brave song' (*Letters on Poetry*, p. 128).
133. *Letters on Poetry*, p. 8.
134. Ibid., pp. 40, 64.
135. *E.&I.*, p. 503.
136. *Exp.*, p. 428.
137. *O. B. M. V.*, p. xi. Yeats had made rhetorical use of these women as long ago as 1908 in order to upbraid militant Irish nationalists in the *Samhain*, there too calling up the image of Nero (*Exp.*, p. 239). One wonders if Henry James met one or several of these very women, for in *The Princess Casamassima* the Princess takes the identical line with the bookbinder Hyacinth Robinson (New York: Charles Scriber's Sons, 1908) vi, 259.
138. Samuel Hynes, 'Yeats and the Poets of the Thirties', in Raymond J. Porter and James D. Brophy (eds), *Modern Irish Literature: Essays in Honor of William York Tindall* (New York: Iona College Press and Twayne Publishers, 1972) p. 12.
139. *Var. Poems*, p. 566.
140. Ibid., p. 479.
141. *Letters on Poetry*, p. 9.
142. *Var. Poems*, p. 291.

Notes to Chapter 4: Yeats and Balzac

1. *E.&I.*, p. 447.
2. *Auto.*, p. 48.
3. *Exp.*, p. 269.
4. Quoted in Hone, *W. B. Yeats: 1865–1939*, pp. 424–5.
5. *Letters*, pp. 791, 805.
6. *E.&I.*, p. 425.
7. *Letters*, p. 513.
8. Ibid., p. 886.
9. See, for instance, V. S. Pritchett, *Balzac* (London: Chatto & Windus, 1973) pp. 149, 119; and Félicien Marceau, *Balzac et son monde* (Paris: Gallimard, 1955) pp. 329, 414.
10. See Lee Baxandall and Stefan Morawski (eds), *Karl Marx and Frederick Engels on Literature and Art: A Selection of Writings* (New York: International General, 1974) pp. 116–17; Georg Lukács, *Balzac et le*

réalisme français, trans. Paul Laveau (Paris: François Maspero, 1967) pp. 16–17; Fredric Jameson, *The Political Unconscious: Narrative as Socially Symbolic Act* (Ithaca, N.Y.: Cornell University Press, 1981) pp. 151–84.

11. André Wurmser, 'Preface' to *César Birotteau,* by Honoré de Balzac (Paris: Gallimard, 1975) pp. 26–7.
12. *Uncol. Prose,* II, 356, 450–1, 482.
13. *Letters,* p. 656.
14. *Exp.,* p. 269.
15. Ibid., p. 269.
16. Ibid., p. 270.
17. Ibid., p. 270.
18. Ibid., p. 270–1.
19. Lawrence Stone, *The Family, Sex and Marriage in England 1500–1800,* abridged edn (New York: Harper Colophon Books, 1979) p. 69.
20. Balzac, *The Touraine Edition of the Comédie humaine,* trans. Ellen Marriage, James Waring and others; prefaces by George Saintsbury (Philadelphia: Gebbie, 1899) I, xlviii. This edition contains the same translations (not, by reputation, reliable ones) used in Yeats's edition. Throughout the chapter I have followed Yeats's own practice of quoting from the works in English, yet giving their titles in French.
21. *The Works of Honoré de Balzac,* University Edition (Philadelphia: Avil Publishing, 1901) VI, 72. This edition (hereafter *Works*) also contains the translations Yeats would have read. The quotation from *La Cousine Bette* ('*Cousin Betty*') is taken from the Touraine Edition, p. 117.
22. Balzac, *Works,* V, 184–5.
23. *Exp.,* p. 271.
24. *Auto.,* p. 546. Some years later Yeats expressed a very different idea of the part old age could assume in government: 'The art and politics of the antithetical age expressed a long maturing tradition and were best practiced by old men' ('Michael Robartes: Two Occult Manuscripts', p. 222).
25. Thomas Common (compiler), *Nietzsche as Critic, Philosopher, Poet and Prophet: Choice Selections from his Works,* pp. 136–7.
26. Balzac, *Works,* II, 8, 10, 192.
27. *Exp.,* p. 277. The Balzacian idea of Protestantism perhaps plays a part in the apparently thoroughly Irish 'The Curse of Cromwell', since in that poem Yeats equates Calvinism with political levelling. In a letter to Dorothy Wellesley, Yeats wrote that Cromwell was 'the Lennin [sic] of his day' (*Letters on Poetry,* p. 131), and in the already-quoted letter in which he compared his own ideas and situation to Balzac's, he continued, 'What can I do but cry out, lately in simple peasant songs that hide me from the curious?' and quoted the first two lines of the then-unpublished poem (*Letters,* p. 886).
28. Hugh Kingsmill, 'Meeting with Yeats', in E. H. Mikhail (ed.), *W. B. Yeats: Interviews and Recollections,* II, 296.
29. *Exp.,* p. 274. The quotation is from Thomas Davis's 'Lament for Owen Rua O'Neill'.

30. Among the pieces transcribed by Curtis Bradford. (See Notes to Chapter 1, note 92.) For a fuller discussion, see Stanfield, 'W. B. Yeats and Politics in the 1930s', pp. 258–60.
31. *Exp.*, p. 435.
32. Ibid., p. 279.
33. Ibid., p. 312.
34. Ibid., p. 335.
35. A passage from *A Vision* sheds some light on Yeats's use of the cathedral as a political metaphor: 'I do not see in Gothic architecture, which is a character of the next gyre, that of Phases 5, 6 and 7, as did the nineteenth-century historians, ever looking for the image of their own age, the creation of a new communal freedom, but a creation of authority, a suppression of that freedom though with its consent, and certainly St Bernard when he denounced the extravagance of Romanesque saw it in that light' (*Vision*, p. 287).
36. Hone, *W. B. Yeats: 1865–1939*, pp. 424–5.
37. See, for instance, Balzac, *Works*, II, 66.
38. 'Genealogical Tree of Revolution', p. 351.
39. Ibid., p. 352.
40. *Exp.*, p. 271. Yeats once believed Fascist Italy put into practice a similar conviction, believing that 'class war though it may be regulated must never end' (*Vision*, p. 82).
41. *Exp.*, p. 269.
42. Ibid., p. 393.
43. Balzac, *The Touraine Edition of the Comédie humaine*, I, 47–8.
44. *E.&I.*, p. 468.
45. Balzac, *Works*, II, 44.
46. Ibid., II, 9.
47. *Vision*, p. 296.
48. Common (compiler), *Nietzsche as Critic, Philosopher, Poet and Prophet*, pp. 128–9. In Yeats's copy of this book, now held in the Special Collections Room of the Northwestern University Library, the words 'German and English' have been underlined.
49. *E.&I.*, pp. 466–7. Five years previously Yeats had been more willing to agree with Hegel: 'Hegel set free the human soul when he declared ("the thing is itself", this theological echo had just been proved unnecessary) that "there is nothing that is not accessible to intellect". One must qualify this sentence but it still keeps sufficient truth' (*Moore*, p. 146). Yeats wrote in *On the Boiler* that Hegel's historical ideas were 'false', yet thought that 'in his more popular writings' Hegel 'seems to misrepresent his own thought' (*Exp.*, pp. 429–30).
50. *E.&I.*, pp. 467–8.
51. Ibid., pp. 468–9.
52. *Vision*, p. 301.
53. Balzac, *The Touraine Edition of the Comédie humaine*, XV, 343. This is certainly the passage Yeats had in mind, for he follows it closely in the introduction to *The Holy Mountain*. One wonders, though, why he refers to it here as an 'open letter' and in *On the Boiler* as a 'letter'. On the story's first page, the text is immediately preceded by the

dedicatory 'To Madame la Duchesse de Castries', but what follows seems not at all like a letter, even an open letter. Possibly Yeats, realising that 'L'Illustre Gaudissart' did not sound like the title of a prophetic work, chose to be obscure.

54. *Exp.*, p. 245; *Letters on Poetry*, p. 196.
55. 'Michael Robartes: Two Occult Manuscripts', p. 222.
56. Ibid., p. 223.
57. Ibid., p. 224.
58. *Vision*, pp. 52–3. Yeats used this passage again in *On the Boiler*, *Exp.*, p. 425.
59. *Exp.*, pp. 433–4.
60. Yeats discusses Balzac as an historian in *Wheels and Butterflies*, the 'Introduction' to *The Holy Mountain*, *A Vision* and *On the Boiler*, in each instance naming one, two or all three of the works we have been discussing.
61. *E.&I.*, p. 443.
62. *Vision*, pp. 298–9.
63. *O. B. M. V.*, p. xxvii.
64. *E.&I.*, p. 446.
65. Louise Morgan, 'W. B. Yeats,' in Mikhail, *W. B. Yeats: Interviews and Recollections*, II, 202.
66. *Exp.*, p. 373.
67. *Vision*, p. 160.
68. Ibid., p. 163.
69. *Exp.*, p. 373.
70. Ibid., pp. 240–1.
71. Ibid., p. 238.
72. Ibid., pp. 238, 239.
73. *Auto.*, p. 466.
74. Ibid., p. 104. Yeats used this biographical detail again in the *Holy Mountain* introduction (*E.&I.*, p. 468).
75. *E.&I.*, p. 442.
76. *Mythologies*, pp. 344–5.
77. *Exp.*, p. 271; *Vision*, p. 162.
78. *E.&I.*, p. 404.
79. *Moore*, pp. 63, 68, 80, 131.
80. *O. B. M. V.*, p. xxvii.
81. *E.&I.*, p. 405.
82. *Exp.*, p. 375.
83. *E.&I.*, p. 424.
84. George Bornstein, *Yeats and Shelley* (Chicago and London: University of Chicago Press, 1970).
85. *Letters*, p. 402.
86. *E.&I.*, p. 296.
87. *Exp.*, p. 277; *Auto.*, p. 326.
88. *Vision*, p. 144.
89. Harold Bloom, *Yeats* (New York: Oxford University Press, 1970) p. 62.
90. *E.&I.*, p. 425.

91. Ibid., p. 420.
92. Ibid., p. 422.
93. *Vision*, p. 144; *E.&I.*, pp. 421, 425.
94. *Vision*, p. 144.
95. *E.&I.*, p. 425.
96. *Exp.*, p. 270.
97. The figure employed here is, indirectly, Yeats's own. In 'Bishop Berkeley' he wrote, 'And why should I, whose ancestors never accepted the anarchic subjectivity of the nineteenth century, accept its recoil; why should men's heads ache that never drank?' (*E.&I.*, p. 407).
98. *Vision.*, p. 151.
99. *E.&I.*, p. 440; *Letters*, p. 805.
100. Ibid., pp. 443–4.
101. Ibid., p. 445.
102. Hone, *W. B. Yeats: 1865–1939*, p. 425.
103. Richard Ellmann (ed.), *The Artist as Critic: Critical Writings of Oscar Wilde* (New York: Random House, 1969) p. 309.
104. Baxandall and Morawski (eds), *Karl Marx and Frederic Engels on Literature and Art: A Selection of Writings*, p. 116.
105. *E.&I.*, p. 443.
106. Ibid., p. 445.
107. Ibid., p. 448.
108. 'The Statues', *Var. Poems*, p. 610.
109. Although T. R. Henn (*The Lonely Tower*, p. 214) and Harold Bloom (*Yeats*, p. vii) have both suggested that Balzac's influence was important to Yeats, only two writers have considered the question in much detail: Carl Benson, in 'Yeats and Balzac's *Louis Lambert*', *Modern Philology*, 49 (1952), 242–7, and Daphne Fullwood, in 'Balzac and Yeats', *Southern Review*, 5 (1969), 935–49. The quoted passage from Benson is on p. 247.
110. *Var. Poems*, p. 502.
111. *Exp.*, p. 272.
112. Ibid., p. 271.
113. *E.&I.*, p. 102.
114. Ibid., p. 445.
115. *Letters*, p. 807.
116. *Exp.*, p. 275.
117. *E.&I.*, p. 425.
118. Ibid., p. 447.
119. *Essays 1931–1936*, p. 73. In *E.&I.*, the phrase 'where the French kings lie buried' is dropped.
120. *O. B. M. V.*, p. xxxviii.

Notes to Chapter 5: Yeats and Eugenics

1. Hone, *W. B. Yeats: 1865–1939*, p. 400. While Antheil was writing

music for a production of Yeats's *Fighting the Waves*, Yeats wrote to Lady Gregory, 'There will be masks and all singing within the range of the speaking voice – for my old theories are dogmas it seems of the new school' (*Letters*, p. 760).

2. Torchiana, W. B. *Yeats and Georgian Ireland*, p. 347.
3. 'A Bronze Head', *Var. Poems*, p. 619.
4. 'Three Songs to the One Burden', ibid., p. 606.
5. *Letters*, p. 379.
6. F. S. L. Lyons, *Ireland Since the Famine* (London: Weidenfeld & Nicolson, 1971) p. 241.
7. *Exp.*, p. 131.
8. *Memoirs*, p. 145.
9. *Var. Plays*, pp. 1119–20.
10. Ibid., p. 481. Neither this passage nor any of the other passages referring to degeneration appeared in the first published version of the play, that of 1903. The play was heavily revised, and the idea of degeneration introduced, sometime prior to the publication of the play in *Poems, 1899–1905*, in 1906. Since Yeats eventually dated the play '1904', I take that to be the year he decided the play should have the form it had ever after, which form included the play's concern over heredity. The only version of the play actually published in 1904 was nearly identical to that of 1903.
11. *Var. Plays*, p. 483.
12. Ibid., pp. 483, 485.
13. Ibid., p. 487.
14. Ibid., p. 487.
15. Ibid., p. 521.
16. Ibid., p. 503.
17. Ibid., p. 505.
18. Ibid., p. 507.
19. Ibid., p. 507.
20. Ibid., p. 510.
21. Ibid., p. 514.
22. Ibid., pp. 264–5.
23. Ibid., p. 266.
24. Ibid., p. 294.
25. Ibid., p. 299.
26. Ibid., p. 301.
27. 'Eugenics is the study of human improvement in all aspects by genetic means. . . . A companion science, euthenics, is also concerned with the improvement of mankind, but by adjustment of the environment. Obviously both concerns are essential to the well-being of man, and since neither science can stand alone, the term "humanics" has been suggested to embrace both aspects of human improvement' (Frederick Henry Osborn, 'Eugenics', *Encyclopaedia Britannica: Macropaedia*, 1980 edn, vol. 6, p. 1023).
28. *Exp.*, p. 263.
29. Ibid., p. 272.
30. Ibid., p. 269.

31. Ibid., p. 270.
32. Ibid., p. 270.
33. Ibid., pp. 269–70.
34. Ibid., p. 272.
35. Ibid., p. 268.
36. Ibid., p. 273. See Vladimir Solovyof, *The Justification of the Good: An Essay on Moral Philosophy*, trans. Nathalie Duddington (New York: Macmillan, 1918) pp. 357, 419.
37. *Exp.*, p. 273.
38. Ibid., p. 274.
39. Ibid., pp. 279–80.
40. Stanfield, 'W. B. Yeats and Politics in the 1930s', pp. 317–18.
41. *Auto.*, p. 547. Yeats had previously mentioned the artistic 'dynasties' of old Japan in 'Certain Noble Plays of Japan', *E.&I.*, pp. 229–30.
42. *Exp.*, pp. 274–5.
43. 'Genealogical Tree of Revolution', p. 351.
44. Ibid., p. 352.
45. Ibid., p. 351.
46. Ibid., p. 352.
47. *Exp.*, p. 270.
48. *Auto.*, p. 547.
49. *Exp.*, p. 312.
50. *E.&I.*, p. 526.
51. *Letters*, p. 816.
52. William Morris, *The Story of Sigurd the Volsung and the Fall of the Niblungs* (London: Longman, Green, 1898) p. 71.
53. *Exp.*, p. 376.
54. Ibid., p. 376.
55. G. R. Searle, *Eugenics and Politics in Britain 1900–1914*, Science in History no. 3 (Leyden, The Netherlands: Noordhoff International Publishing, 1976) pp. 12–13. The whole of my discussion of the eugenical movement is greatly indebted to this book and to Stephen Jay Gould's *The Mismeasure of Man* (New York: W. W. Norton, 1981).
56. The published results of these tests had an impact which was felt as far away as Ireland, and of which Yeats himself was aware. The tests had determined that the average 'mental age' of the male American negro was 10.41 years (well within the 'moron' range) and controversy arose over what ought to be done (Gould, *The Mismeasure of Man*, p. 197). Yeats made a light reference to the controversy in a 1922 letter to Olivia Shakespear: 'I interrupt my letter at intervals and watch my canaries in their big cage where there are two nests; one, which disturbs George, is the nest of a half-caste, a bird that looks half sparrow and it threatens to abound in young. It is the American negro question and all the more because George's English mind has conceived a project of selling canaries through the newspapers. Who will want half-castes? Will even our friends accept them as presents? The other nest however is above reproach' (see *Letters*, pp. 685–6).
57. Mark Haller, *Eugenics: Hereditarian Attitudes in American Thought* (New Brunswick, N.J.: Rutgers University Press, 1963) p. 137.

58. Ibid., pp. 139–40.
59. *Exp.*, p. 340.
60. Yeats recommended this book to the readers of *On the Boiler*, adding, 'I have taken most of the facts in this section, and some of the arguments and metaphors that follow, from this book' (*Exp.*, p. 423).
61. *E.&I.*, p. 110.
62. *Exp.*, p. 140.
63. Raymond B. Cattell, *The Fight for our National Intelligence* (London: P. S. King, 1937) p. 54.
64. Ibid., p. 54.
65. Ibid., p. 90.
66. Ibid., pp. 60–1.
67. Ibid., p. 66.
68. 'Genealogical Tree of Revolution', p. 352.
69. Cattell, *The Fight for our National Intelligence*, p. 93.
70. Ibid., pp. 1–2.
71. Ibid., p. 135.
72. *Exp.*, p. 417.
73. Quoted ibid., pp. 418–19.
74. Quoted ibid., pp. 419–20.
75. Ibid., p. 420.
76. Ibid., p. 422.
77. Ibid., p. 421.
78. Ibid., p. 423.
79. Cattell, *The Fight for our National Intelligence*, p. 164.
80. *Exp.*, pp. 424–5.
81. Ibid., p. 425.
82. Robert M. Yerkes, *Psychological Examining in the United States Army*, Memoirs of the National Academy of Sciences xv (Washington: Government Printing Office, 1921) p. 697.
83. *Exp.*, p. 426.
84. Oliver St John Gogarty, *As I Was Going Down Sackville Street*, p. 34.
85. *Exp.*, pp. 426–7.
86. Cattell, well aware that to admit the influence of environment was to undo his argument, accounted for the difference between urban and rural scores another way: 'All considerations indicate that the rural poverty of intelligence is due to a greater readiness of the more intelligent families to migrate to the towns', where there were more opportunities (p. 14). Yeats must have found this explanation unsatisfactory.
87. *Exp.*, p. 427.
88. Ibid., p. 438.
89. Ibid., p. 442.
90. Ibid., p. 413.
91. Ibid., p. 414.
92. Ibid., p. 430.
93. Ibid., p. 433.
94. Ibid., p. 437.
95. Ibid., p. 451.

96. Ibid., p. 451.
97. Ibid., p. 451. In *Reveries Over Childhood and Youth* Yeats recalled that 'a picture at the Hibernian Academy of cocottes with yellow faces sitting before a cafe by some follower of Manet's made me miserable for days' during his time as an art student (*Auto.*, p. 82).
98. *Var. Poems*, p. 564.
99. Curtis Bradford, *Yeats at Work* (Carbondale, Ill.: Southern Illinois University Press, 1965) p. 150: 'And when Yeats says in effect that the ancient bodily forms have been blotted out, is he not already on his way to poems and prose works concerned with eugenic reform?'
100. *Var. Poems*, p. 604.
101. Ibid., pp. 604–5. The interest Yeats had in his own ancestry is the subject of many anecdotes.
102. Ibid., pp. 598–9.
103. Ibid., pp. 626.
104. These lines probably allude to Iseult Gonne (see Torchiana, *W. B. Yeats and Georgian Ireland*, p. 353), who had in 1920 married Francis Stuart, a writer whose novels Yeats praises, but who had once 'seemed almost imbecile to his own relations', as Yeats once wrote to Olivia Shakespear (*Letters*, p. 800). In an earlier poem, Yeats had advised Iseult, 'Choose your companions from the best', and her having chosen the most important of companions with apparent heedlessness may well have embittered him, and reminded him of her mother's inexplicable preference for that 'drunken, vain-glorious lout' Major MacBride. Being of the opinion that talented women should marry talented men so as to bear talented children, Yeats of course disapproved of talented women who chose not to bear any children at all. Dorothy Wellesley records: 'Speaking to W. B. Y. of the difficulties confronting women who were creative artists, I said: "No women of genius should be expected to bear and bring up children." He, raising his hand and speaking like the prophets of old, replied: "No, we urgently need the children of women of genius!"' (*Letters on Poetry*, p. 196).
105. *Var. Poems*, p. 628.
106. When Yeats was twenty, his father painted him as King Goll (*Letters*, p. 705).
107. *Var. Poems*, p. 626.
108. Torchiana, *W. B. Yeats and Georgian Ireland*, pp. 354–6.
109. E. H. Mikhail (ed.), *W. B. Yeats: Interviews and Recollections*, II, p. 232.
110. Torchiana, *W. B. Yeats and Georgian Irelande*, pp. 357–65.
111. Mikhail, *W. B. Yeats: Interviews and Recollections*, II, p. 232.
112. Mr William Hawkes has suggested to me in conversation that the bare simplicity of 'Looked at him and married him' and the hold the phrase exercises over the Old Man may convey some of Yeats's own fascinated bewilderment at the sexual choices of the Gonne women, mother and daughter.
113. *Var. Plays*, p. 1043.
114. Ibid., p. 1047.
115. Ibid., p. 1044.

116. Ibid., p. 1045.
117. Ibid., p. 1044.
118. Ibid., p. 1049.
119. Ibid., pp. 1048–9.
120. *Var. Poems*, p. 619.
121. Ibid., p. 606.
122. Ibid., p. 605.
123. Ibid., p. 606.
124. Hone, *W. B. Years: 1865–1939*, p. 22.
125. *Var. Poems*, pp. 606–7.
126. Ibid., p. 608.
127. *Auto.*, p. 266.
128. *Var. Poems*, p. 637.
129. *Auto.*, p. 249.
130. In his *A Commentary on the Collected Poems of W. B. Yeats* (Stanford, Calif.: Stanford University Press, 1968), A. N. Jeffares writes as his only comment on this poem, 'The poem was written in a spirit of mockery' (p. 500;. Jeffares later told Augustine Martin that 'when he asked the poet's widow about the poem she replied that Yeats had given her this one cryptic comment on it' (see Augustine Martin, 'Hound Voices Were They All: an Experiment in Yeats Criticism', in A. Norman Jeffares (ed.), *Yeats, Sligo and Ireland*, Irish Literary Studies no. 6 (Gerrards Cross: Colin Smythe, 1980) p. 151.
131. *Var. Poems*, p. 621.
132. Ibid., p. 622.
133. *Auto.*, p. 395.
134. *Exp.*, p. 433.
135. *Var. Poems*, p. 611.
136. *Letters on Poetry*, p. 203.
137. *Var. Poems*, p. 638.
138. Ibid., p. 639.
139. In these lines Yeats may be remembering the old man's praise of bastards in Arland Ussher's translation of Brian Merriman's late 18th century Irish poem 'The Midnight Court': 'And better and braver in heart and head/Than the puny breed of the bridal bed.' Yeats quoted the lines in his introduction to Ussher's translation (*Exp.*, p. 285).
140. *Var. Poems*, pp. 617–18.
141. Ibid., pp. 610.
142. Ibid., p. 611.
143. Ibid., p. 625.

Notes: Conclusion

1. Yeats's copy of Thomas Common (compiler), *Nietzsche as Critic, Philosopher, Poet and Prophet*, p. 134. Yeats's copy of this book is now

held in the Special Collections department of Northwestern University Library.

2. 'The Phases of the Moon', *Var. Poems*, p. 374.
3. 'To a Friend whose Work has come to Nothing', ibid., p. 291.
4. *Exp.*, p. 325.
5. *Mythologies*, p. 325.
6. *Var. Poems*, pp. 601–2.
7. *Var. Plays*, p. 1052.
8. *Letters*, p. 886.
9. *Exp.*, p. 417.
10. *Letters*, p. 873.
11. *E.&I.*, p. 503.
12. *Letters*, p. 903.
13. 'A Player for Old Age', *Var. Poems*, p. 553.
14. *Exp.*, p. 407.
15. Thomas Parkinson, *The Later Poetry* and *W. B. Yeats, Self-Critic*, published as one volume (Berkeley, Calif. and Los Angeles: University of California Press, 1971) p. 175.
16. Stanley Sultan, *Yeats at his Last*, New Yeats Papers XI (Dublin: Dolmen Press, 1975) p. 13.
17. Denis Donoghue, *William Butler Yeats* (New York: Viking Press, 1971) p. 139.
18. *Exp.*, p. 436.

Bibliography

Adams, Michael, *Censorship: The Irish Experience* (Dublin: Sceptre Books, 1968).

Archibald, Douglas, *Yeats* (New York: Syracuse University Press, 1983).

Balzac, Honoré de, *The Touraine Edition of the Comédie humaine*, trans. Ellen Marriage, James Waring *et al.*, 32 vols (Philadelphia: Gebbie, 1899).

——, *The Works of Honoré de Balzac*, trans. Ellen Marriage, James Waring *et al.*, University Edition, 16 vols (Philadelphia: Avil Publishing, 1901).

Barnes, James Strachey, *The Universal Aspects of Fascism* (London: Williams & Northgate, 1928; 2nd edn, 1929).

Baxandall, Lee and Stefan Morawski (eds), *Karl Marx and Frederick Engels on Literature and Art: A Selection of Writings* (New York: International General, 1974).

Benson, Carl, 'Yeats and Balzac's *Louis Lambert*', *Modern Philology*, 49 (1952) 242–7.

Bloom, Harold, *The Anxiety of Influence* (London, Oxford and New York: Oxford University Press, 1973).

——, *Poetry and Repression: Revisionism from Blake to Stevens* (New Haven, Conn., and London: Yale University Press, 1976).

——, *Yeats* (New York: Oxford University Press, 1970).

Bohlmann, Otto, *Yeats and Nietzsche* (Totowa, N.J.: Barnes and Noble, 1982).

Bornstein, George, *Yeats and Shelley* (Chicago and London: University of Chicago Press, 1970).

Bowman, John, *De Valera and the Ulster Question 1917–1973* (Oxford: Clarendon Press, 1982).

Bradford, Curtis, *Yeats at Work* (Carbondale, Ill.: Southern Illinois University Press, 1965).

Brown, Malcolm, *The Politics of Irish Literature* (London: George Allen & Unwin, 1972).

Carden, Mary, 'The Few and the Many: an Examination of W. B. Yeats's Politics', *Studies*, LVIII (1969) 61.

Carpenter, Humphrey, *W. H. Auden: A Biography* (London: George Allen & Unwin, 1981).

Cattell, Raymond B., *The Fight for Our National Intelligence* (London: P. S. King, 1937).

Cohen, Joseph, 'In Memory of W. B. Yeats – and Wilfred Owen', *Journal of English and Germanic Philology*, 58 (1959) 637–49.

Common, Thomas (compiler), *Nietzsche as Critic, Philosopher, Poet and Prophet* (London: Grant Richards, 1901).

217

Craig, Cairns, *Yeats, Eliot, Pound and the Politics of Poetry: Richest to the Richest* (London and Canberra: Croom Helm, 1982).

Crawford, Virginia, 'The Rise of Fascism and what it Stands for', *Studies*, xii (1923) 539–52.

Cullingford, Elizabeth, *Yeats, Ireland and Fascism* (New York and London: New York University Press, 1981).

Davis, Herbert (ed.), *The Prose Works of Jonathan Swift*, vol. i (Oxford: Shakespeare Head Press, 1939).

Day-Lewis, Cecil, *A Hope for Poetry* (first published 1934; 8th edn, Oxford: Basil Blackwell, 1947).

Donoghue, Denis, *William Butler Yeats* (New York: Viking Press, 1971).

Ellmann, Richard (ed.), *The Artist as Critic: Critical Writings of Oscar Wilde* (New York: Random House, 1969).

——, *The Identity of Yeats* (New York: Oxford University Press, 1954).

——, *James Joyce* (New York: Oxford University Press, 1959).

——. *Yeats: The Man and the Masks* (New York: Macmillan, 1948).

Fanger, Donald, *Dostoevsky and Romantic Realism: A Study of Dostoevsky in Relation to Balzac, Dickens, and Gogol*, Harvard Studies in Comparative Literature 27 (Cambridge, Mass.: Harvard University Press, 1967).

Farag, Fahmy, *The Opposing Virtues: Two Essays*, New Yeats Papers xv (Dublin, Dolmen Press, 1978).

Finneran, Richard J., George Mills Harper and William M. Murphy (eds), *Letters to W. B. Yeats*, 2 vols (London: Macmillan, 1977).

Forster, E. M., *Two Cheers for Democracy* (London: Edward Arnold, 1951).

Freyer, Grattan, 'The Politics of W. B. Yeats', *Politics and Letters*, 1 (1947) 13–20.

Freyer, Grattan, *fils*, *W. B. Yeats and the Anti-Democratic Tradition* (Dublin: Gill & Macmillan, 1981).

Fullwood, Daphne, 'Balzac and Yeats', *Southern Review*, 5 (1969) 935–49.

Goddard, H. H., *Feeble-Mindedness: Its Causes and Consequences* (New York: Macmillan, 1914).

Gogarty, Oliver St John, *As I Was Going Down Sackville Street* (New York: Reynal & Hitchcock, 1937).

——, *Going Native* (New York: Duell, Sloan & Pearce, 1940).

Gould, Stephen J., *The Mismeasure of Man* (New York: W. W. Norton, 1981).

Green, Martin, *Children of the Sun* (New York: Basic Books, 1976).

Guyon, Bernard, *La Pensée politique et sociale de Balzac* (Paris: Arman Colin, 1967).

Haller, Mark, *Eugenics: Hereditarian Attitudes in American Thought* (New Brunswick, N.J.: Rutgers University Press, 1963).

Harper, George Mills and Walter Kelly Hood (eds), *A Critical Edition of Yeats's 'A Vision' (1925)* (London: Macmillan, 1978).

Hayes, Richard, 'W. B. Yeats, a Catholic Poet?', *Irish Monthly*, lvi (1928) 179–86.

Henn, T. R., *Last Essays* (Gerrards Cross: Colin Smythe, 1976).

——, *The Lonely Tower* (London: Methuen, 1952; 2nd edn, 1965).

Hepburn, A. C., *The Conflict of Nationality in Modern Ireland* (London: Edward Arnold, 1980).

Hogan, Robert, *The Experiments of Sean O'Casey* (New York: St Martin's Press, 1960).

Hone, Joseph, *W. B. Yeats: 1865–1939* (London: Macmillan, 1942).

——, 'Yeats as a Political Philosopher', *London Mercury*, 39 (1939) 492–6.

Hynes, Samuel, *The Auden Generation: Literature and Politics in England in the 1930s* (London: Bodley Head, 1976).

——, 'Yeats and the Poets of the Thirties', in Raymond J. Porter and James D. Brophy (eds), *Modern Irish Literature: Essays in Honour of William York Tindall* (New York: Iona College Press and Twayne Publishers, 1972) pp. 1–22.

James, Henry, *The Princess Casamassima* (New York: Charles Scribner's Sons, 1908).

James, Stanley B., 'Some Mussolini Paradoxes', *Irish Monthly*, LXI (1933) 24.

Jameson, Fredric, *The Political Unconscious: Narrative as Socially Symbolic Act* (Ithaca, N.Y.: Cornell University Press, 1981).

Jeffares, A. Norman, *A New Commentary on the Poems of W. B. Yeats* (Stanford, Calif.: Stanford University Press, 1984).

——, *W. B. Yeats: Man and Poet* (New Haven, Conn.: Yale University Press, 1949).

Joyce, James, *Finnegans Wake* (New York: Viking Press, 1939).

Kavanagh, Peter, *The Story of the Abbey Theatre: From the Origins in 1899 to the Present* (New York: Devin-Adair, 1950).

Kelley, P. J., 'Talbot, Matt', *New Catholic Encyclopedia*, 1967 edn, vol. 13, p. 919.

Kermode, Frank, *The Sense of an Ending: Studies in the Theory of Fiction* (New York: Oxford University Press, 1967).

Krause, David, *Sean O'Casey: The Man and his Work* (New York: Macmillan, rev. edn, 1975).

—— (ed.), *The Letters of Sean O'Casey*, vol. I (London: Macmillan, 1975).

Krimm, Bernard G., *W. B. Yeats and the Emergence of the Irish Free State 1918–1939: Living in the Explosion* (Troy, N.Y.: Whitson, 1981).

Laski, Harold J., *Communism* (New York: Henry Holt; London: Thornton, Butterworth, 1927).

Lewis, Wyndham, *The Revenge for Love* (first published 1937; Chicago: Henry Regenery, 1952).

Longford, Earl of and Thomas P. O'Neill, *Eamon De Valera* (London: Hutchinson, 1970).

Lukács, Georg, *Balzac et le réalisme français*, trans. Paul Laveau (Paris: François Maspero, 1967).

Lyons, F. S. L., *Ireland since the Famine* (London: Weidenfeld & Nicolson, 1971).

Lysaght, D. R. O'Connor, *The Republic of Ireland* (Cork: Mercier Press, 1970).

MacManus, Francis (ed.), *The Years of the Great Test* (Cork: Mercier Press, 1967).

MacManus, M. J., *Eamon de Valera* (Chicago: Ziff-Davis, 1946; new edition with additional matter, Dublin: Talbot Press, 1957).

'Major Cooper's Candidature', *Irish Times*, 25 August 1923, p. 7.

Manning, Maurice, *The Blueshirts* (Toronto: University of Toronto Press, 1971).

Marceau, Félicien, *Balzac et son monde* (Paris: Gallimard, 1955).

Martin, Augustine, 'Hound Voices Were They All: an Experiment in Yeats Criticism', in A. Norman Jeffares (ed.), *Yeats, Sligo and Ireland*, Irish Literary Studies no. 6 (Gerrards Cross: Colin Smyth, 1980) pp. 139–52.

Maxwell, D. E. S., 'Swift's Dark Grove: Yeats and the Anglo-Irish Tradition', in D. E. S. Maxwell and S. B. Bushrui (eds), *Centenary Essays on the Art of W. B. Yeats* (Nigeria: University of Ibadan Press, 1965) pp. 18–32.

Mendelson, Edward (ed.), *The English Auden* (London: Faber & Faber, 1977).

Mikhail, E. H. (ed.), *W. B. Yeats: Interviews and Recollections*, 2 vols (London: Macmillan, 1977).

Morris, William, *The Story of Sigurd the Volsung and the Fall of the Niblungs* (London: Longman, Green, 1898).

Murphy, Daniel J. (ed.), *Lady Gregory's Journals* (New York: Oxford University Press, 1978).

Murphy, John, A., *Ireland in the Twentieth Century*, Gill History of Ireland 11 (Dublin: Gill & Macmillan, 1975).

O'Brien, Conor Cruise, 'Passion and Cunning: an Essay on the Politics of W. B. Yeats', in A. Norman Jeffares and K. G. W. Cross (eds), *In Excited Reverie: A Centenary Tribute to William Butler Yeats 1865–1939* (New York: St Martin's Press, 1965) pp. 207–78.

——, *The Suspecting Glance* (London: Faber & Faber, 1972).

——, and Máire O'Brien, *The Story of Ireland* (New York: Viking Press, 1972).

O'Casey, Sean, *Autobiographies*, 2 vols (London: Macmillan, 1981).

——, *Collected Plays*, 4 vols (London: Macmillan, 1949–51).

O'Connell, Maurice (ed.), *The Correspondence of Daniel O'Connell*, vol. vi (Dublin: Blackwater Press, n.d.).

O'Connor, Frank, *My Father's Son* (London: Macmillan, 1968).

O'Faolain, Sean, *De Valera* (Harmondsworth: Penguin, 1939).

O'Flaherty, Liam, *The Puritan* (London: Jonathan Cape, 1932).

O'Hegarty, P. S., *A History of Ireland under the Union* (London: Methuen, 1952).

O'Herlihy, T., 'Fascist Italy', *Irish Ecclesiastical Record*, 31 (1928) 506–16.

Orwell, Sonia and Ian Angus (eds), *The Collected Essays, Journalism and Letters of George Orwell*, vols i and ii (London: Secker & Warburg, 1968).

Osborn, Frederick Henry, 'Eugenics', *Encyclopedia Britannica: Macropedia*. 1980 edn, vol. 6, p. 1023.

O'Shea, Edward, *Yeats as Editor*, New Yeats Papers xii (Dublin: Dolmen Press, 1975).

O'Sullivan, Donal, *The Irish Free State and its Senate: A Study in Contemporary Politics* (London: Faber & Faber, 1940).

Owen, Wilfred, *Collected Letters*, ed. Harold Owen and John Bell (London: Oxford University Press, 1967).

——, *The Poems of Wilfred Owen*, ed. Edmund Blunden (London: Chatto & Windus, 1931).

Parkinson, Thomas, *'The Later Poetry'* and *'W. B. Yeats, Self-Critic'* (Berkeley, Calif. and Los Angeles: University of California Press, 1971).

Peschmann, Hermann, 'Yeats and the Poetry of War', *English*, 15 (1965) 181–4.

Pound, Ezra, *Jefferson and/or Mussolini* (first published 1933; reprinted New York: Boni and Liveright, 1970).

Pritchett, V. S., *Balzac* (London: Chatto & Windus, 1973).

Robinson, Lennox (ed.), *Lady Gregory's Journals: 1916–1930* (London: Putnam, 1946).

Rossi, Mario M., *Pilgrimage in the West*, trans. J. M. Hone (Dublin: Cuala Press, 1933).

Rothenstein, William, *Since Fifty: Men and Memories, 1922–1938* (New York: Macmillan, 1940).

Savage, D. E., 'Two Prophetic Poems', *Adelphi*, 22, no. 1 (1945) 25–32.

Schiller, Ferdinand, *Eugenics and Politics* (Boston, Mass.: Houghton Mifflin, 1926).

Searle, G. R., *Eugenics and Politics in Britain 1900–1914*, Science in History no. 3 (Leyden, The Netherlands: Noordhoff International Publishing, 1976).

Silkin, Jon (ed.), *The Penguin Book of First World War Poetry* (Harmondsworth: Penguin, 1979).

Skelton, Robin (ed.), *Poetry of the Thirties* (Harmondsworth: Penguin, 1964).

Solovyof, Vladimir, *The Justification of the Good: An Essay on Moral Philosophy*, trans. Nathalie Duddington (New York: Macmillan, 1918).

Spender, Stephen, *The Destructive Element* (first published 1935; paperback edn, Philadelphia: Albert Saifer, 1953).

——, *The Thirties and After* (London: Macmillan, 1978).

——, *World Within World* (Berkeley, Calif.: University of California Press, 1966).

Stanfield, Paul Scott, 'W. B. Yeats and Politics in the 1930s' (dissertation, Northwestern University, 1984).

Stone, Lawrence, *The Family, Sex and Marriage in England 1500–1800*, abridged edn (New York: Harper Colophon Books, 1979).

Strand, Karin Margaret, 'W. B. Yeats's American Lecture Tours' (dissertation, Northwestern University, 1978).

Stuart, Francis, *The Coloured Dome* (New York: Macmillan, 1933).

Sultan, Stanley, *Yeats at his Last*, New Yeats Papers xi (Dublin: Dolmen Press, 1975).

Thatcher, David, *Nietzsche in England 1890–1914: The Growth of a Reputation* (Toronto: University of Toronto Press, 1970).

Tierney, Michael, 'Vocationalism and Parliamentary Democracy: are they Compatible?', *Irish Monthly*, lxvi (1935) 369–77.

Torchiana, Donald T., *W. B. Yeats and Georgian Ireland* (Evanston, Ill.: Northwestern University Press, 1966).

Ulam, Adam B., *Stalin: The Man and his Era* (New York: Viking Press, 1973).

Vendler, Helen Hennessy, *Yeat's Vision and the Later Plays* (Cambridge, Mass.: Harvard University Press, 1963).

Watson, George, *Politics and Literature in Modern Britain* (Totowa, N.J.: Rowman & Littlefield, 1977).

White, Terence de Vere, 'The Personality of J. B. Yeats', in Roger McHugh (ed.), *Jack B. Yeats: A Centenary Gathering*, Tower Series of Anglo-Irish Studies 3 (Dublin: Dolmen Press, 1971) pp. 22–50.

Whyte, J. H., *Church and State in Modern Ireland 1923–1970* (Dublin: Gill & Macmillan, 1971).

Wilson, F. A. C., *W. B. Yeats and Tradition* (London: Gollancz, 1958).

Wohl, Robert, *The Generation of 1914* (Cambridge, Mass.: Harvard University Press, 1979).

Woolf, S. J., 'Yeats Foresees an Ireland of Reality', *New York Times Magazine*, 13 November 1932, p. 7.

Wright, Willard Huntingdon (ed.), *The Philosophy of Nietzsche* (New York: Modern Library, n.d.).

Wurmser, André, Preface to Honoré de Balzac, *César Birotteau* (Paris: Gallimard, 1975).

Yeats, William Butler, *Autobiographies* (London: Macmillan, 1961).

——, *A Critical Edition of Yeats's A Vision (1925)*; ed. George Mills Harper and Walter Kelly Hood (London: Macmillan, 1978).

——, *Essays and Introduction* (London: Macmillan, 1961).

——, *Essays 1931–1936* (Dublin: Cuala Press, 1937).

——, *Explorations* (London: Macmillan, 1962).

——, 'A Genealogical Tree of Revolution', in A. N. Jeffares, *W. B. Yeats: Man and Poet* (New Haven, Conn.: Yale University Press, 1949) pp. 351–2.

——, *The Letters of W. B. Yeats*, ed. Allan Wade (London: Macmillan, 1955; reprinted New York: Octagon Books, 1980).

——, *Letters on Poetry from W. B. Yeats to Dorothy Wellesley* (London: Oxford University Press, 1940).

——, *Memoirs*, transcribed and edited by Denis Donoghue (London: Macmillan, 1972).

——, 'Michael Robartes: Two Occult Manuscripts', ed. Walter Kelly Hood, in George Mills Harper (ed.), *Yeats and the Occult* (Toronto: Macmillan, 1975) pp. 210–24.

——, 'Modern Ireland: an Address to American Audiences 1932–1933', ed. Curtis Bradford, *Massachusetts Review*, v (1964) 256–68.

——, *Mythologies* (London: Macmillan, 1959).

—— (ed.), *The Oxford Book of Modern Verse* (New York: Oxford University Press, 1936).

——, *The Senate Speeches of W. B. Yeats*, ed. Donald Pearce (Bloomington, Ind.: Indiana University Press, 1960).

——, *Tribute to Thomas Davis* (Oxford: Basil Blackwell for Cork University Press, 1947).

——, *Uncollected Prose by W. B. Yeats*, ed. John P. Frayne and Colton Johnson, 2 vols (New York: Columbia University Press, 1970–6).

——, *The Variorum Edition of the Plays of W. B. Yeats*, ed. Russell K.

Alspach, assisted by Catherine C. Alspach (New York: Macmillan, 1966).
——, *The Variorum Edition of the Poems of W. B. Yeats*, ed. Peter Allt and Russell K. Alspach (New York: Macmillan, 1957).
——, *A Vision* (London: Macmillan, 1956).
—— and T. Sturge Moore, *W. B. Yeats and T. Sturge Moore: Their Correspondence 1901–1937*, ed. Ursula Bridge (London: Routledge & Kegan Paul, 1953).
—— and Margot Ruddock, *Ah, Sweet Dancer. A Correspondence*, ed. Roger McHugh (New York: Macmillan, 1971).
Yerkes, Robert M., *Psychological Examining in the United States Army*, Memoirs of the National Academy of Sciences xv (Washington: Government Printing Office, 1921).

Index

Abbey Theatre, 21, 27, 84–5, 131
Anglo-Irish minority, 11–13, 14,
    30–1, 50–2
Army Comrades Association, *see*
    Blueshirts
Auden, W. H., 69, 76, 100–5
    'In Memory of W. B. Yeats', 6

Balzac, Honoré de, 1, 3, 81, 112–44
    on family, 114–22
    on history, 123–30
    as Romantic, 130–44
    La Peau de chagrin, 123–5
    'L'Ilustre Gaudissart', 127–9
    Louis Lambert, 138–9
    Sur Catherine de Médicis, 124
Behan, Brendan, *The Hostage*, 11
Berkeley, Bishop George, 17, 88
Black and Tan War, 14
Blueshirts, 21–2, 40–1, 59–75
    and Fascism, 61
Blythe, Ernest, 40, 61–3
Burke, Sir Edmund, 43

Castiglione, Baldassare, 31, 167
Cattell, Raymond B., 160–2
communism, 2, 71–4, 101–5
Coole Park, 17, 37, 41
Cooper, Major Bryan, 46
Corporate State, 61, 198 *n.*100
Cosgrave, William T., 14–16, 25
Croce, Benedetto, 71–2
Cumann na nGaedheal, 60

Davis, Thomas, 7, 27
Day-Lewis, Cecil, 76, 90, 100–5
de Valera, Eamon, 8–39, 60
    and the Abbey Theatre, 21, 33–5,
        193 *n.*102
    and censorship, 33

characterised, 10–11
and Fianna Fail, 14–16
Dowden, Edward, 5

Easter Rising (1916), 6, 32, 176–7
Eliot, T. S., 69, 99
Emmet, Robert, 31
Engels, Friedrich, 139
Eugenics, 145–83
    development and influence, 158–
        9

Flaubert, Gustave, 131
Forster, E. M., 69
Franco, Francisco, 36, 60

Gogarty, Oliver St John, 8, 16–17,
    105–8
    on de Valera, 9
    *As I Was Going Down Sackville
        Street*, 8
    Going Native, 8
Gonne, Maud, 27, 146, 174
Gregory, Lady Augusta, 3, 17–26
    passim, 45, 50, 190 *n.*48
Grenfell, Julian, 95–6
Griffith, Arthur, 30

Hayes, Dr Richard, 33
Hegel, G. F., 1, 125–7, 208 *n.*49
Hitler, Adolf, 20

Irish Academy of Letters, 9, 32–3
Irish Catholicism, 16
    and nationalism, 26
Irish Civil War, 14, 16, 18
Irish Free State, 7, 14, 68
Irish nationalism, 3, 6, 15, 19, 25–
    30, 51
Irish Republican Army(IRA), 36, 60

Joyce, James, on de Valera, 10, 18

Lane, Sir Hugh, 43–4
  and Municipal Gallery, 32

MacManus, Captain Dermot, 63–5
Macneice, Louis, 100–5
Markiewicz, Constance, 30
Marxism, 3, 71–4, 82–4
  and Balzac criticism, 113
Mendel, Gregor, 154
Morris, William, 79–81, 83, 157
Mussolini, Benito, 20, 58–9

Nietzsche, Friedrich, 85, 89, 118–
    19, 125, 129, 135, 146, 184, 201,
    n.34

O'Casey, Sean, 8, 84–90
  on de Valera, 9
  The Crimson and the TriColour, 84
  Juno and the Paycock, 11, 84
  The Plough and the Stars, 33, 84
  Shadow of the Gunman, 84
  The Silver Tassie, 84–90
O'Connell, Daniel, 17, 24, 52–3
O'Connor, Frank, 8
  The Saint and Mary Kate, 8
O'Duffy, General Eoin, 1, 25, 62–7,
    75
O'Faolain, Sean
  on de Valera, 10
O'Flaherty, Liam, 8
  Mr Gilhooley, 8
  The Informer, 11
  The Puritan, 8, 18
O'Higgins, Kevin, 14, 47, 195, n.37
O'Leary, John, 7, 18–19, 22, 47,
    191, n.50, 195 n.36
Orwell, George, 69; quoted 78
Owen, Wilfred, 90–5

Parnell, Charles Stewart, 13, 17–19,
    22, 24, 52–3
Pearse, Patrick, 18
Pound, Ezra, 99–100, 205 n.113
Purohit, Swami Shri, 1

Read, Herbert, 95–6, 105–8

Russell, George, 8, 55, 190 n.9
  on de Valera, 9

Shanks, Edward, 95–6
Shaw, George Bernard, 33, 81
  John Bull's Other Island, 19
Shawe-Taylor, John, 43–4, 46
Shelley, Percy, 4, 134–7
Sitwell, Edith, 105
Socialism, 78–111; *see also*
    Communism, Marxism
Soloviev, Vladimir, 153
Spender, Stephen, 76, 90, 100–5
Stalin, Josef, 20, 205 n.105
Stuart, Francis, 8, 214 n.104
  The Coloured Dome, 8, 18
Swift, Jonathan, 11, 17, 35, 43–6
    passim, 59, 98–9
Synge, John, 27, 28
  In the Shadow of the Glen, 27, 33,
    146
  Playboy of the Western World, 27,
    33

Turner, W. J., 105–8

Wellesley, Dorothy, 91, 105–8
Wilde, Oscar, 139

Yeats, William Butler
  on aristocracy *vs* democracy, 41–
    50
  attitude towards de Valera, 11–
    25, 36–7
  and authoritarianism, 54–5, 58–9
  on Christianity, 88–90, 93–5,
    152–3
  on family, 152–8
  and fascism, 70–7
  as Senator, 14, 47, 55–8
  and 'Stendhal's mirror', 92–3,
    130–1
  and violence, 49–50, 67–70
  and 'Vision of Evil', 81–3, 98–9,
    136–7, 142–3, 200 n.14
  Prose Writings:
  The Bounty of Sweden, 117, 154,
    156
  The Celtic Twilight, 26

Yeats, William Butler – *continued*
  Prose Writings – *continued*
  'Commentary on a Parnellite at
      Parnell's Funeral', 24–5
  'Commentary on the Three
      Songs', 22, 34, 66, 75
  'Discoveries', 135
  'A Genealogical Tree of
      Revolution', 72–4, 121–2, 155
  'A General Introduction for my
      Work', 105, 108
  'The Happiest of Poets', 79–80
  If I were Four-and-Twenty, 3, 54,
      80–1, 114, 118–20, 138, 143–
      4, 152–5
  'Introduction to *Fighting the
      Waves*', 3
  'Introduction to *The Holy
      Mountain*', 1–3, 125–7
  'Ireland, 1921–1931', 14–16
  The Irish Dramatic Movement, 34
  'J. M. Synge and the Ireland of
      his Time', 29, 32
  'Louis Lambert', 133, 142–3
  'Michael Robartes Foretells',
      128–9
  'Modern Ireland', 17–20, 23–4
  On the Boiler, 38, 77, 108, 162–9,
      186–7
  *Pages from a Diary Written in
      Nineteen Hundred and Thirty*,
      120–1
  Per Amica Silentia Lunae, 97, 133,
      185
  'The Philosophy of Shelley's
      Poetry', 135
  'The Poetry of Sir Samuel
      Ferguson', 5
  'Prometheus Unbound', 137, 143
  'A Race Philosophy', 155–6
  A Vision, 4, 48–50, 55, 72, 76–7,
      92, 94–5, 102, 123–5, 127,
      208 *n*.35
  Wheels and Butterflies, 2, 35–6, 75
  Plays:
  Calvary, 95
  Cathleen ni Houlihan, 27
  The Death of Cuchulain, 9, 186
  The Herne's Egg, 33
  The King's Threshold, 149–51
  On Baile's Strand, 147–9
  Purgatory, 9, 171, 173–4
  The Resurrection, 123
  Where There is Nothing, 146
  Poems:
  'Are You Content?', 170
  'The Ballad of Father O'Gilligan',
      26
  'The Black Tower', 37–8, 194
      n.120
  'A Bronze Head', 174
  'Byzantium', 140, 191 *n*.53
  'Church and State', 23, 70
  'Coole Park 1929', 44
  'Crazy Jane on the Mountain',
      172
  'The Curse of Cromwell', 9, 207
      n.27
  'A Dialogue of Self and Soul',
      110, 140
  'Easter 1916', 32
  'The Gyres', 25, 170
  'Hound Voice', 25, 178–80
  'In Memory of Major Robert
      Gregory', 44, 98
  'An Irish Airman Foresees his
      Death', 45, 97
  'Lapis Lazuli', 30, 108–11
  'Long-Legged Fly', 181
  'The Man and the Echo', 7
  'Meditations in Time of Civil
      War', 14, 30, 45, 49, 96, 117
  'A Model for the Laureate', 36
  The Municipal Gallery
      Revisited', 9, 30, 185–6
  'A Nativity', 182
  'News for the Delphic Oracle',
      140, 177–8
  'Nineteen Hundred and
      Nineteen', 54, 82
  'The Old Stone Cross', 170–1
  'The O'Rahilly', 9, 139
  'Parnell', 13
  'Parnell's Funeral', 9, 13, 23, 66
  'The Phases of the Moon', 97
  'Politics', 2–3, 36
  'Red Hanrahan's Song about
      Ireland', 26

Yeats, William Butler – *continued*
  Poems – *continued*
  'Roger Casement', 36
  'Sailing to Byzantium', 140
  'September 1913', 32
  'Solomon and the Witch', 97
  'The Statesman's Holiday', 36,
    172–3
  'The Statues', 2, 168, 181–2
  'Those Images', 2, 36
  'Three Marching Songs', 38
  'Three Songs to the One
    Burden', 38, 175–7
  'Three Songs to the Same Tune',
    22

  'To a Friend whose Work has
    Come to Nothing', 111
  'To Ireland in the Coming
    Times', 4
  'The Tower', 51
  'Under Ben Bulben', 25, 38, 68,
    180–1
  'Vacillation', 98, 105, 141
  The Wanderings of Oisin, 26
  'Why should not Old Men be
    Mad?', 171–2
  Edited Works:
  The Oxford Book of Modern Verse,
    3, 90–6, 99–107